TRANSLATED
Translated Language Learning

The Adventures of Pinocchio

ピノキオの冒険

Carlo Collodi
カルロ・コッローディ

English / 日本語

Copyright © 2024 Tranzlaty
All rights reserved
Published by Tranzlaty
ISBN: 978-1-83566-709-5
Le Avventure di Pinocchio. Storia di un Burattino
Original text by Carlo Callodi
First published in Italianin 1883
Illustrated By Alice Carsey
www.tranzlaty.com

The Piece of Wood that Laughed and Cried like a Child
子供のように笑い、泣いた木片

Centuries ago there lived...
何世紀も前にそこに住んでいました...
"A king!" my little readers will say immediately
「王様!」私の小さな読者はすぐに言うでしょう
No, children, you are mistaken
いいえ、子供たち、あなたは間違っています
Once upon a time there was a piece of wood
むかしむかし、木片がありました
the wood was in the shop of an old carpenter
その木は古い大工の店にありました
this old carpenter was named Master Antonio
この古い大工はマスターアントニオと名付けられました
Everybody, however, called him Master. Cherry
しかし、誰もが彼をマスターと呼んだ。桜桃
they called him Master. Cherry on account of his nose
彼らは彼をマスターと呼びました。彼の鼻のせいでチェリー
his nose was always as red and polished as a ripe cherry
彼の鼻はいつも熟した桜のように赤く磨かれていました
Master Cherry set eyes upon the piece of wood
マスターチェリーは木片に目を向けました
his face beamed with delight when he saw the log
丸太を見たとき、彼の顔は喜びで輝いていました
he rubbed his hands together with satisfaction
彼は満足そうに手をこすり合わせた
and the kind master softly spoke to himself
そして優しい主人は静かに独り言を言いました
"This wood has come to me at the right moment"
「この木はちょうどいいタイミングで私のところに来ました」
"I have been planning to make a new table"
「新しいテーブルを作る予定だったんだ」

"it is perfect for the leg of a little table"
「ちょいテーブルの脚にピッタリです」
He immediately went out to find a sharp axe
彼はすぐに鋭い斧を探しに出かけました
he was going to remove the bark of the wood first
彼は最初に木の皮を取り除くつもりでした
and then he was going to remove any rough surface
そして、彼はざらざらした表面を取り除くつもりでした
and he was just about to strike the wood with his axe
そして、彼はちょうど斧で木を打とうとしていた
but just before he struck the wood he heard something
しかし、彼が木を打つ直前に、何かが聞こえました
"Do not strike me so hard!" a small voice implored
「そんなに強く叩かないで!」小さな声が懇願した
He turned his terrified eyes all around the room
彼は怯えた目を部屋中に向けた
where could the little voice possibly have come from?
その小さな声はどこから来たのでしょうか?
he looked everywhere, but he saw nobody!
彼はどこも見ましたが、誰も見当たりませんでした。
He looked under the bench, but there was nobody
彼はベンチの下を見たが、誰もいなかった
he looked into a cupboard that was always shut
彼はいつも閉まっている食器棚を覗き込んだ
but there was nobody inside the cupboard either
しかし、食器棚の中には誰もいませんでした
he looked into a basket where he kept sawdust
彼はおがくずを保管しているバスケットを覗き込みました
there was nobody in the basket of sawdust either
おがくずの入った籠の中にも誰もいなかった
at last he even opened the door of the shop
とうとう彼は店のドアまで開けました
and he glanced up and down the empty street
そして彼は誰もいない通りを上下に見回した
But there was no one to be seen in the street either

しかし、通りにも誰も見かけませんでした
"Who, then, could it be?" he asked himself
「じゃあ、それは誰なのだろう?」と彼は自問した
at last he laughed and scratched his wig
とうとう彼は笑い、かつらを引っ掻いた
"I see how it is," he said to himself, amused
「なるほど」彼は面白がって独り言を言った
"evidently the little voice was all my imagination"
「明らかに、その小さな声は私の想像のすべてでした」
"Let us set to work again," he concluded
「また仕事に取り掛かりましょう」と彼は結論づけた
he picked up his axe again and set to work
彼は再び斧を手に取り、仕事に取り掛かった
he struck a tremendous blow to the piece of wood
彼は木片に猛烈な打撃を与えた
"Oh! oh! you have hurt me!" cried the little voice
「ああ!おや!「お前は私を傷つけた!」小さな声が叫んだ。
it was exactly the same voice as it was before
さっきと全く同じ声だった
This time Master. Cherry was petrified
今回はマスター。チェリーは石化した
His eyes popped out of his head with fright
彼の目は恐怖で頭から飛び出しました
his mouth remained open and his tongue hung out
彼の口は開いたままで、舌は垂れ下がっていました
his tongue almost came to the end of his chin
彼の舌は顎の端まで来そうになった
and he looked just like a face on a fountain
そして、彼はまるで噴水の上の顔のように見えました
Master. Cherry first had to recover from his fright
主人。チェリーはまず恐怖から立ち直らなければなりませんでした
the use of his speech returned to him
彼の言葉の使い方が彼に戻った
and he began to talk in a stutter;

そして彼はどもりながら話し始めました。
"where on earth could that little voice have come from?"
「いったい、あの小さな声はどこから来たのだろう?」
"could it be that this piece of wood has learned to cry?"
「もしかして、この木片は泣くことを学んだのだろうか?」
"I cannot believe it," he said to himself
「信じられない」と彼は独り言を言いました
"This piece of wood is nothing but a log for fuel"
「この木片は燃料の丸太に過ぎない」
"it is just like all the logs of wood I have"
「それは私が持っているすべての木の丸太のようです」
"it would only just suffice to boil a saucepan of beans"
「豆の鍋を茹でるだけで十分だろう」
"Can anyone be hidden inside this piece of wood?"
「この木片の中に誰かが隠れることができるのか?」
"If anyone is inside, so much the worse for him"
「もし誰かが中にいるとしたら、彼にとってはもっと悪い」
"I will finish him at once," he threatened the wood
「すぐにやつを殺す」と彼は森を脅した
he seized the poor piece of wood and beat it
彼は貧弱な木片をつかみ、それを叩きました
he mercilessly hit it against the walls of the room
彼は容赦なくそれを部屋の壁に叩きつけた
Then he stopped to see if he could hear the little voice
それから彼は立ち止まって、小さな声が聞こえるかどうか確かめました
He waited two minutes, nothing. Five minutes, nothing
彼は2分待ったが、何もなかった。5分、何もない
he waited another ten minutes, still nothing!
彼はさらに10分待っても、まだ何もありませんでした!
"I see how it is," he then said to himself
「なるほど」と彼は独り言を言いました
he forced himself to laugh and pushed up his wig
彼は無理に笑い、かつらを押し上げた

"evidently the little voice was all my imagination!"
「明らかに、その小さな声は私の想像のすべてでした!」

"Let us set to work again," he decided, nervously
「また仕事に取り掛かりましょう」彼は緊張しながら決心した

next he started to polish the bit of wood
次に、彼は木片を磨き始めました

but while polishing he heard the same little voice
しかし、磨いていると、同じ小さな声が聞こえました

this time the little voice was laughing uncontrollably
今度は小さな声が抑えきれずに笑っていました

"Stop! you are tickling me all over!" it said
「やめろ!あなたは私をくすぐっています!」とそれは言いました

poor Master. Cherry fell down as if struck by lightning
かわいそうなマスター。さくらんぼは雷に打たれたように落ちてきました

sometime later he opened his eyes again
しばらくして、彼は再び目を開けた

he found himself seated on the floor of his workshop
彼は自分が作業場の床に座っていることに気づきました

His face was very changed from before
彼の顔は以前とはすごく変わっていました

and even the end of his nose had changed
そして、彼の鼻の先までもが変わっていました

his nose was not its usual bright crimson colour
彼の鼻はいつもの明るい深紅色ではなかった

his nose had become icy blue from the fright
彼の鼻は恐怖で氷のように青くなっていた

Master. Cherry Gives the Wood Away
主人。チェリーは木を手放す

At that moment someone knocked at the door
その瞬間、誰かがドアをノックしました
"Come in," said the carpenter to the visitor
「入って」と大工は訪問者に言いました
he didn't have the strength to rise to his feet
立ち上がる力がなかった
A lively little old man walked into the shop
元気な小柄な老人が店に入ってきました
this lively little man was called Geppetto
この活発な小さな男はゼペットと呼ばれていました
although there was another name he was known by
彼が知られていた別の名前がありましたが
there was a group of naughty neighbourhood boys
いたずらっ子の近所の男の子のグループがいました
when they wished to anger him they called him pudding
彼らが彼を怒らせたいと思ったとき、彼らは彼をプリンと呼びました
there is a famous yellow pudding made from Indian corn
インドのトウモロコシから作られた有名なイエロープリンがあります
and Geppetto's wig looks just like this famous pudding
そして、ゼペットのかつらは、この有名なプリンにそっくりです
Geppetto was a very fiery little old man
ゼペットはとても燃えるような小さな老人でした
Woe to him who called him pudding!
彼をプリンと呼んだ彼に災いあれ!
when furious there was no holding him back
激怒したとき、彼を引き止めることはできませんでした
"Good-day, Master. Antonio," said Geppetto
「こんにちは、マスター。アントニオ」とゼペットは言った

"what are you doing there on the floor?"
「床で何をしているの?」
"I am teaching the alphabet to the ants"
「私はアリにアルファベットを教えている」
"I can't imagine what good it does to you"
「それがあなたにどんな良いことをするのか想像もつかない」
"What has brought you to me, neighbour Geppetto?"
「どうして僕のところに来たんだ、隣人のゼペット?」
"My legs have brought me here to you"
「私の足が私をここに連れて来ました」
"But let me tell you the truth, Master. Antonio"
「しかし、本当のことを言わせてください、マスター。アントニオ"
"the real reason I came is to ask a favour of you"
「私が来た本当の理由は、あなたに頼みごとをするためです」
"Here I am, ready to serve you," replied the carpenter
「ここにいます。あなたに仕える準備ができています」と大工は答えました
and he got off the floor and onto his knees
そして彼は床から降りて膝をついた
"This morning an idea came into my head"
「今朝、ある考えが頭に浮かんだ」
"Let us hear the idea that you had"
「君が持っていた考えを聞かせてください」
"I thought I would make a beautiful wooden puppet"
「綺麗な木製の人形を作ろうと思った」
"a puppet that could dance and fence"
「踊り、柵を張ることができる人形」
"a puppet that can leap like an acrobat"
「曲芸師のように跳躍できる人形」
"With this puppet I could travel about the world!"
「この人形があれば、世界中を旅できる!」
"the puppet would let me earn a piece of bread"
「人形は私に一切れのパンを稼がせるだろう」

"and the puppet would let me earn a glass of wine"
「そして、人形は私にワインを一杯稼がせるでしょう」
"What do you think of my idea, Antonio?"
「アントニオ、私の考えをどう思う?」
"Bravo, pudding!" exclaimed the little voice
「ブラボー、プリン!」小さな声が叫んだ
it was impossible to know where the voice had came from
その声がどこから来たのかを知ることは不可能でした
Geppetto didn't like hearing himself called pudding
ゼペットは自分がプリンと呼ばれるのを聞くのが好きではなかった
you can imagine he became as red as a turkey
彼が七面鳥のように赤くなったと想像できるでしょう
"Why do you insult me?" he asked his friend
「なぜ俺を侮辱するんだ?」彼は友人に尋ねた
"Who insults you?" his friend replied
「誰がお前を侮辱するんだ?」と彼の友人は答えた
"You called me pudding!" Geppetto accused him
「プリンって呼ばれたでしょ!」ゼペットは彼を非難した
"It was not I!" Antonio honestly said
「俺じゃなかった!」アントニオは正直に言った
"Do you think I called myself pudding?"
「僕が自分のことをプリンって呼んでたと思う?」
"It was you, I say!", "No!", "Yes!", "No!"
「それはあなただった、と私は言う!」、「いいえ!」、「はい!」、「いいえ!」
becoming more and more angry, they came to blows
ますます怒って、彼らは打撃を受けるようになりました
they flew at each other and bit and fought and scratched
彼らはお互いに飛びかかり、噛みつき、戦い、引っ掻き傷を負いました
as quickly as it had started the fight was over again
戦いが始まったのと同じくらい早く、戦いは再び終わった

Geppetto had the carpenter's grey wig between his teeth
ゼペットは歯の間に大工の灰色のかつらを挟んでいました
and Master. Antonio had Geppetto's yellow wig
とマスター。アントニオはゼペットの黄色いかつらを持っていました
"Give me back my wig" screamed Master. Antonio
「カツラを返して」とマスターが叫んだ。アントニオ
"and you give me back my wig" screamed Master. Cherry
「そして、カツラを返してくださる」とマスターは叫びました。桜桃
"let us be friends again" they agreed
「また友達になろう」と彼らは同意した
The two old men gave each other their wigs back
二人の老人はお互いにかつらを返しました
and the old men shook each other's hands
そして老人たちは握手を交わしました
they swore that all had been forgiven
彼らはすべてが許されたと誓った
they would remain friends to the end of their lives
彼らは人生の終わりまで友達であり続けるでしょう
"Well, then, neighbour Geppetto" said the carpenter
「じゃあ、隣人のゼペット」と大工は言った
he asked "what is the favour that you wish of me?"
彼は尋ねました「あなたが私に望む好意は何ですか?」
this would prove that peace was made
これは、和平が結ばれたことを証明するでしょう
"I want a little wood to make my puppet"
「私の人形を作るための小さな木が欲しい」
"will you give me some wood?"
「薪をくれませんか?」
Master. Antonio was delighted to get rid of the wood
主人。アントニオは木を処分して喜んでいました
he immediately went to his work bench
彼はすぐに作業台に向かった
and he brought back the piece of wood

そして彼は木片を持ち帰りました
the piece of wood that had caused him so much fear
彼をとても怖がらせた木片
he was bringing the piece of wood to his friend
彼は木片を友人のところに持って行っていました
but then the piece of wood started to shake!
しかし、その時、木片が揺れ始めました!
the piece of wood wriggled violently out of his hands
木片が彼の手から激しく蠢いた
this piece of wood knew how to make trouble!
この木片は、トラブルを起こす方法を知っていました!
with all its might it struck against poor Geppetto
全力で哀れなゼペットに打ちのめした
and it hit him right on his poor dried-up shins
そして、それは彼の哀れな乾いた脛に直撃した
you can imagine the cry that Geppetto gave
ゼペットが発した叫び声を想像できるでしょう
"is that the courteous way you make your presents?"
「それがあなたのプレゼントの作り方ですか?」
"You have almost lamed me, Master. Antonio!"
「あなたは私をほとんど足が不自由になりました、マスター。アントニオ!」
"I swear to you that it was not I!"
「誓って言うけど、それは私じゃないって!」
"Do you think I did this to myself?"
「私が自分自身にこんなことをしたと思う?」
"The wood is entirely to blame!"
「全部木のせいだ!」
"I know that it was the wood"
「木だったのは知ってる」
"but it was you that hit my legs with it!"
「でも、それで私の足を打ったのは君だったんだ!」
"I did not hit you with it!"
「お前を殴ってない!」
"Liar!" exclaimed Geppetto

「嘘つき!」とゼペットは叫んだ
"Geppetto, don't insult me or I will call you Pudding!"
「ゼペット、私を侮辱しないで、さもないとプディングって呼ばれるよ!」
"Knave!", "Pudding!", "Donkey!"
「ナベ!」、「プリン!」、「ドンキー!」
"Pudding!", "Baboon!", "Pudding!"
「プリン!」「ヒヒ!」「プリン!」
Geppetto was mad with rage all over again
ゼペットは再び怒りで狂った
he had been called been called pudding three times!
プリンって呼ばれて3回もいたんだよ!
he fell upon the carpenter and they fought desperately
彼は大工に襲いかかり、彼らは必死に戦いました
this battle lasted just as long as the first
この戦いは最初の戦いと同じくらい長く続きました
Master. Antonio had two more scratches on his nose
主人。アントニオの鼻にはさらに2つの傷がありました
his adversary had lost two buttons off his waistcoat
彼の敵は彼のチョッキから2つのボタンを失っていました
Their accounts being thus squared, they shook hands
彼らの口座はこのように二乗し、彼らは握手をしました
and they swore to remain good friends for the rest of their lives
そして、彼らは一生良い友人であり続けることを誓いました
Geppetto carried off his fine piece of wood
ゼペットは彼の素晴らしい木片を運び去りました
he thanked Master. Antonio and limped back to his house
彼はマスターに感謝した。アントニオと足を引きずりながら家に戻った

Geppetto Names his Puppet Pinocchio
ゼペットは彼の人形をピノキオと名付けます

Geppetto lived in a small ground-floor room
ゼペットは1階の小さな部屋に住んでいました
his room was only lighted from the staircase
彼の部屋は階段からだけ明かりが差し込まれていた
The furniture could not have been simpler
家具はこれ以上ないほどシンプルです
a rickety chair, a poor bed, and a broken table
ガタガタの椅子、貧弱なベッド、壊れたテーブル
At the end of the room there was a fireplace
部屋の端には暖炉がありました
but the fire was painted, and gave no fire
しかし、火は塗られていて、火は出さなかった
and by the painted fire was a painted saucepan
そして、塗装された火のそばには、塗装された鍋がありました

and the painted saucepan was boiling cheerfully
そして、塗装された鍋は元気に沸騰していました
a cloud of smoke rose exactly like real smoke
煙の雲は、本物の煙とまったく同じように立ち上っていました
Geppetto reached home and took out his tools
ゼペットは家に着き、道具を取り出しました
and he immediately set to work on the piece of wood
そして、彼はすぐに木片の作業に取り掛かりました
he was going to cut out and model his puppet
彼は自分の人形を切り取り、モデル化するつもりでした
"What name shall I give him?" he said to himself
「彼に何の名前をつけようか」と彼は独り言を言った
"I think I will call him Pinocchio"
「ピノキオと呼ぶと思う」
"It is a name that will bring him luck"
「彼に幸運を運んでくれる名前です」
"I once knew a whole family called Pinocchio"
「昔、ピノキオという家族全員を知っていた」
"There was Pinocchio the father and Pinocchio the mother"
「父のピノキオと母のピノキオがいた」
"and there were Pinocchio the children"
「そして、子供たちのピノキオがいた」
"and all of them did well in life"
「そして、彼ら全員が人生でうまくやった」
"The richest of them was a beggar"
「彼らの中で最も裕福なのは乞食だった」
he had found a good name for his puppet
彼は自分の人形にふさわしい名前を見つけたのだ
so he began to work in good earnest
そこで彼は本格的に働き始めました
he first made his hair, and then his forehead
彼は最初に髪を作り、次に額を作りました
and then he worked carefully on his eyes
そして、彼は慎重に目を鍛えました
Geppetto thought he noticed the strangest thing

ゼペットは自分が最も奇妙なことに気づいたと思った
he was sure he saw the eyes move!
彼は目が動くのを見たと確信していました!
the eyes seemed to look fixedly at him
その目は彼をじっと見つめているように見えた
Geppetto got angry from being stared at
ゼペットはじろじろ見られて怒った
the wooden eyes wouldn't let him out of their sight
木の目は彼を彼らの視界から逃がさなかった
"Wicked wooden eyes, why do you look at me?"
「邪悪な木の目、なぜ私を見るのですか?」
but the piece of wood made no answer
しかし、木片は答えを出さなかった
He then proceeded to carve the nose
その後、彼は鼻を彫り始めました
but as soon as he had made the nose it began to grow
しかし、鼻を作るとすぐにそれは成長し始めました
And the nose grew, and grew, and grew
そして、鼻は伸びて、伸びて、伸びていきました
in a few minutes it had become an immense nose
数分でそれは巨大な鼻になりました
it seemed as if it would never stop growing
それはまるで成長が止まらないかのようでした
Poor Geppetto tired himself out with cutting it off
かわいそうなゼペットはそれを切って疲れ果てました
but the more he cut, the longer the nose grew!
でも、切れば切るほど鼻が伸びていきました!
The mouth was not even completed yet
口はまだ完成すらしていなかった
but it already began to laugh and deride him
しかし、それはすでに彼を笑い、嘲笑し始めていた
"Stop laughing!" said Geppetto, provoked
「笑うのはやめろ!」ゼペットは挑発されて言った
but he might as well have spoken to the wall
しかし、彼は壁に向かって話した方がよかったかもしれない

"Stop laughing, I say!" he roared in a threatening tone
「笑うのはやめろ!」彼は脅迫的な口調で叫んだ
The mouth then ceased laughing
その後、口は笑いを止めた
but the face put out its tongue as far as it would go
しかし、顔はどこまでも舌を出しました
Geppetto did not want to spoil his handiwork
ゼペットは彼の手仕事を台無しにしたくなかった
so he pretended not to see, and continued his labours
だから彼は見て見ぬふりをして、仕事を続けました
After the mouth he fashioned the chin
口の後に彼は顎を作りました

then the throat and then the shoulders
次に喉、そして肩
then he carved the stomach and made the arms hands
それから彼は胃を彫り、腕を手のものにしました
now Geppetto worked on making hands for his puppet
今、ゼペットは彼の人形の手を作るために働いていました

and in a moment he felt his wig snatched from his head
そして一瞬で彼は自分のかつらが頭から奪われたのを感じた
He turned round, and what did he see?
彼は振り返り、何を見たのだろうか?
He saw his yellow wig in the puppet's hand
彼は人形の手に黄色いかつらを見た
"Pinocchio! Give me back my wig instantly!"
「ピノキオ!すぐにかつらを返して!」
But Pinocchio did anything but return him his wig
しかし、ピノキオは彼にかつらを返す以外に何もしませんでした
Pinocchio put the wig on his own head instead!
ピノキオは代わりに自分の頭にかつらをかぶせました!
Geppetto didn't like this insolent and derisive behaviour
ゼペットは、この横柄で嘲笑的な行動が好きではありませんでした
he felt sadder and more melancholy than he had ever felt
彼は今まで感じたことのないほど悲しく、憂鬱に感じた
turning to Pinocchio, he said "You young rascal!"
ピノキオの方を向いて、「この若き悪党め!」と彼は言った。
"I have not even completed you yet"
「まだ君を完成させてない」
"and you are already failing to respect to your father!"
「そして、あなたはすでに父親を尊敬できていません!」
"That is bad, my boy, very bad!"
「それはまずい、我が子よ、非常にまずい!」
And he dried a tear from his cheek
そして彼は頬から涙を拭った
The legs and the feet remained to be done
脚と足はまだやらなければなりませんでした
but he soon regretted giving Pinocchio feet
しかし、彼はすぐにピノキオに足を与えたことを後悔し

ました
as thanks he received a kick on the point of his nose
お礼に彼は鼻の先を蹴られた

"I deserve it!" he said to himself
「俺はそれに値する!」彼は自分に言い聞かせた

"I should have thought of it sooner!"
「もっと早く考えるべきだった!」

"Now it is too late to do anything about it!"
「もう手遅れだ!」

He then took the puppet under the arms
それから彼は人形を腕の下に連れて行きました

and he placed him on the floor to teach him to walk
そして、彼に歩くことを教えるために彼を床に置きました

Pinocchio's legs were stiff and he could not move
ピノキオの足は硬く、動けませんでした

but Geppetto led him by the hand
しかし、ゼペットは彼の手を引いて導いた

and he showed him how to put one foot before the other
そして、片方の足をもう片方の足の前に出す方法を教えました

eventually Pinocchio's legs became limber
やがてピノキオの足はしなやかになった

and soon he began to walk by himself
そしてすぐに彼は一人で歩き始めました

and he began to run about the room
そして彼は部屋の中を走り回り始めました

then he got out of the house door
それから彼は家のドアから出ました

and he jumped into the street and escaped
そして彼は通りに飛び出して逃げました

poor Geppetto rushed after him
かわいそうなゼペットが急いで追いかけた

of course he was not able to overtake him
もちろん、彼は彼を追い抜くことができませんでした

because Pinocchio leaped in front of him like a hare

ピノキオがウサギのように彼の前に飛び跳ねたからです
and he knocked his wooden feet against the pavement
そして彼は木の足を舗道にぶつけた
it made as much clatter as twenty pairs of peasants' clogs
それは農民の下駄20足ほどの音を立てました
"Stop him! stop him!" shouted Geppetto
「止めろ!止めろ!」とゼペットは叫んだ
but the people in the street stood still in astonishment
しかし、通りの人々は驚いて立ち尽くしていました
they had never seen a wooden puppet running like a horse
彼らは馬のように走る木製の人形を見たことがありませんでした
and they laughed and laughed at Geppetto's misfortune
そして、彼らはゼペットの不幸に笑い続けました
At last, as good luck would have it, a soldier arrived
ついに、幸運なことに、一人の兵士が到着しました
the soldier had heard the uproar
兵士は騒ぎを聞いていた
he imagined that a colt had escaped from his master
彼は、仔馬が主人から逃げ出したと想像した
he planted himself in the middle of the road
彼は道の真ん中に身を任せた
he waited with the determined purpose of stopping him
彼は断固として彼を止めるつもりで待った
thus he would prevent the chance of worse disasters
そうすれば、彼はより深刻な災害の可能性を防ぐことができるだろう
Pinocchio saw the soldier barricading the whole street
ピノキオは、兵士が通り全体をバリケードで囲んでいるのを見ました
so he endeavoured to take him by surprise
だから彼は彼を驚かせようと努力した
he planned to run between his legs
彼は自分の足の間を走るつもりだった
but the soldier was too clever for Pinocchio
しかし、その兵士はピノキオには賢すぎました

The soldier caught him cleverly by the nose
兵士は巧みに彼の鼻をつかんだ
and he gave Pinocchio back to Geppetto
そして彼はピノキオをゼペットに返しました
Wishing to punish him, Geppetto intended to pull his ears
彼を罰したいと願ったゼペットは、彼の耳を引っ張るつもりだった
But he could not find Pinocchio's ears!
しかし、彼はピノキオの耳を見つけることができませんでした!
And do you know the reason why?
そして、その理由を知っていますか?
he had forgotten to make him any ears
彼は耳を作るのを忘れていた
so then he took him by the collar
それで彼は彼の襟をつかんだ
"We will go home at once," he threatened him
「すぐに家に帰るよ」と彼は脅した
"as soon as we arrive we will settle our accounts"
「到着次第、清算します」
At this information Pinocchio threw himself on the ground
この情報にピノキオは地面に身を投げました
he refused to go another step
彼はもう一歩進むことを拒んだ
a crowd of inquisitive people began to assemble
好奇心旺盛な人々の群れが集まり始めました
they made a ring around them
彼らは彼らの周りに輪を作りました
Some of them said one thing, some another
彼らの中には、ある人は一つのことを言い、ある人は別のことを言いました
"Poor puppet!" said several of the onlookers
「かわいそうな人形だ!」と見物人の何人かが言いました
"he is right not to wish to return home!"
「彼が家に帰りたくないのは正しい!」

"Who knows how Geppetto will beat him!"
「ゼペットがどうやって彼を倒すかは誰にもわからない！」
"Geppetto seems a good man!"
「ゼペットはいい人だね！」
"but with boys he is a regular tyrant!"
「でも、男の子に対しては、彼は常連の暴君だよ！」
"don't leave that poor puppet in his hands"
「あの哀れな人形を彼の手に任せるな」
"he is quite capable of tearing him to pieces!"
「彼は彼をバラバラに引き裂く能力が十分にある！」
from what was said the soldier had to step in again
言われたことから、兵士は再び介入しなければならなかった
the soldier gave Pinocchio his freedom
兵士はピノキオに自由を与えました
and the soldier led Geppetto to prison
そして兵士はゼペットを刑務所に連れて行きました
The poor man was not ready to defend himself with words
哀れな男は言葉で自分を守る準備ができていませんでした
he cried like a calf "Wretched boy!"
彼は子牛のように叫んだ、「哀れな子！」
"to think how I laboured to make him a good puppet!"
「彼を良い人形にするために、私がどれほど苦労したかを考えると！」
"But all I have done serves me right!"
「でも、私がやってきたことはすべて正しいことだ！」
"I should have thought of it sooner!"
「もっと早く考えるべきだった！」

The Talking Little Cricket Scolds Pinocchio
おしゃべりなコオロギがピノキオを叱る

poor Geppetto was being taken to prison
かわいそうなゼペットは刑務所に連れて行かれていました

all of this was not his fault, of course
もちろん、これらすべてが彼のせいではありません

he had not done anything wrong at all
彼は何も悪いことをしていなかった

and that little imp Pinocchio found himself free
そして、その小さな小鬼ピノキオは自由になった

he had escaped from the clutches of the soldier
彼は兵士の手から逃れたのだ

and he ran off as fast as his legs could carry him
そして彼は自分の足が運べる限りの速さで走り去った

he wanted to reach home as quickly as possible
彼はできるだけ早く家に帰りたかった

therefore he rushed across the fields
だから彼は畑を急いで横切った

in his mad hurry he jumped over thorny hedges
彼は狂ったように急いで、とげのある生け垣を飛び越えました

and he jumped across ditches full of water
そして彼は水でいっぱいの溝を飛び越えました

Arriving at the house, he found the door ajar
家に着くと、彼はドアが半開きになっているのを見つけました

He pushed it open, went in, and fastened the latch
彼はそれを押し開けて中に入り、ラッチを締めました

he threw himself on the floor of his house
彼は家の床に身を投げた

and he gave a great sigh of satisfaction
そして彼は満足のため息をつきました

But soon he heard someone in the room
しかし、すぐに彼は部屋に誰かがいるのを聞いた

something was making a sound like "Cri-cri-cri!"

何かが「クリクリクリ!」というような音を立てていました。

"Who calls me?" said Pinocchio in a fright
「誰が私を呼ぶの?」ピノキオは怯えて言った

"It is I!" answered a voice
「私だ!」と声が答えた

Pinocchio turned round and saw a little cricket
ピノキオが振り向くと、小さなコオロギが見えました

the cricket was crawling slowly up the wall
コオロギはゆっくりと壁を這い上がっていました

"Tell me, little cricket, who may you be?"
「教えて、小さなコオロギ、君は誰になるの?」

"who I am is the talking cricket"
「私が誰であるかは話すクリケットです」

"and I have lived in this room a hundred years or more"
「そして、私はこの部屋に百年以上住んでいます」

"Now, however, this room is mine," said the puppet
「でも、この部屋は私の部屋だよ」と人形は言いました

"if you would do me the pleasure, go away at once"
「もし君が僕を喜ばせるなら、すぐに立ち去って」

"and when you're gone, please never come back"
「そして、あなたがいなくなったら、二度と戻ってこないで」

"I will not go until I have told you a great truth"
「私はあなたに大いなる真実を話すまでは行きません」

"Tell it me, then, and be quick about it"
「じゃあ、教えてくれ。早く言って」

"Woe to those boys who rebel against their parents"
「親に反抗する少年たちに災いあれ」

"and woe to boys who run away from home"
「そして家出する少年たちに災いを」

"They will never come to any good in the world"
「彼らは決して世の中に何の役にも立たない」

"and sooner or later they will repent bitterly"
「そして遅かれ早かれ、彼らは激しく悔い改めるでしょう」

"Sing all you want you little cricket"
「あなたが望むすべてを歌って、小さなコオロギ」
"and feel free to sing as long as you please"
「そして、好きなだけ歌っていただいてください」
"For me, I have made up my mind to run away"
「私としては、逃げる決心をしました」
"tomorrow at daybreak I will run away for good"
「明日の夜明けに、私は永遠に逃げます」
"if I remain I shall not escape my fate"
「もし私が留まっていたら、私は運命から逃れることはできない」
"it is the same fate as all other boys"
「それは他のすべての少年と同じ運命です」
"if I stay I shall be sent to school"
「もし私がここにいたら、私は学校に送られるでしょう」
"and I shall be made to study by love or by force"
「そして、私は愛によって、または力によって勉強させられるでしょう」
"I tell you in confidence, I have no wish to learn"
「自信を持って言っておくけど、学びたいとは思っていない」
"it is much more amusing to run after butterflies"
「蝶を追いかける方がずっと面白い」
"I prefer climbing trees with my time"
「自分の時間で木登りをするのが好きです」
"and I like taking young birds out of their nests"
「そして、私は幼鳥を巣から出すのが好きです」
"Poor little goose" interjected the talking cricket
「かわいそうな小さなガチョウ」と話すコオロギが口を挟んだ
"don't you know you will grow up a perfect donkey?"
「君が完璧なロバに育つことを知らないのか?」
"and every one will make fun of you"
「そして、誰もがあなたをからかうでしょう」
Pinocchio was not pleased with what he heard

ピノキオは彼が聞いたことに満足していませんでした
"Hold your tongue, you wicked, ill-omened croaker!"
「舌を押さえろ、邪悪で不吉なクソ野郎め!」
But the little cricket was patient and philosophical
しかし、小さなコオロギは忍耐強く、哲学的でした
he didn't become angry at this impertinence
彼はこの無礼さに腹を立てませんでした
he continued in the same tone as he had before
彼は以前と同じ口調で続けた
"perhaps you really do not wish to go to school"
「もしかしたら、本当に学校に行きたくないのかもしれない」
"so why not at least learn a trade?"
「じゃあ、せめて商売を学んでみたらどうだ?」
"a job will enable you to earn a piece of bread!"
「仕事があれば、一切れのパンを稼ぐことができる!」
"What do you want me to tell you?" replied Pinocchio
「私に何を伝えたいの?」ピノキオは答えた
he was beginning to lose patience with the little cricket
彼は小さなコオロギに我慢できなくなってきていました
"there are many trades in the world I could do"
「世界には私にできる取引がたくさんある」
"but only one calling really takes my fancy"
「でも、本当に気に入っているのは1つの電話だけです」
"And what calling is it that takes your fancy?"
「それで、あなたの空想を奪うのはどんな天職なの?」
"to eat, and to drink, and to sleep"
「食べて、飲んで、寝る」
"I am called to amuse myself all day"
「私は一日中自分自身を楽しませるように呼ばれています」
"to lead a vagabond life from morning to night"
「朝から晩まで放浪生活を送ること」
the talking little cricket had a reply for this

おしゃべりな小さなコオロギはこれに対する返事を持っていました

"most who follow that trade end in hospital or prison"
「その取引に従うほとんどの人は、病院や刑務所で終わります」

"Take care, you wicked, ill-omened croaker"
「気をつけろ、邪悪で不吉なクローカーめ」

"Woe to you if I fly into a passion!"
「もし私が情熱に飛び込んだら、お前は災いだ!」

"Poor Pinocchio I really pity you!"
「かわいそうなピノキオ、本当にかわいそうだ!」

"Why do you pity me?"
「どうして私を憐れむの?」

"I pity you because you are a puppet"
「君が人形だから可哀想だ」

"and I pity you because you have a wooden head"
「そして、君が木の頭をしているから、君をかわいそうに思う」

At these last words Pinocchio jumped up in a rage
この最後の言葉に、ピノキオは激怒して飛び上がった

he snatched a wooden hammer from the bench
彼はベンチから木製のハンマーをひったくった

and he threw the hammer at the talking cricket
そして、彼は話すコオロギにハンマーを投げつけました
Perhaps he never meant to hit him
もしかしたら、彼は彼を殴るつもりはなかったのかもしれない
but unfortunately it struck him exactly on the head
しかし、残念ながら、それは彼の頭を正確に打った
the poor Cricket had scarcely breath to cry "Cri-cri-cri!"
かわいそうなクリケットは息をするのもやっとで、「クリクリクリ!」と叫びました。
he remained dried up and flattened against the wall
彼は乾いたままで、壁に倒れ込んでいた

The Flying Egg
フライングエッグ

The night was quickly catching up with Pinocchio
その夜はすぐにピノキオに追いついてきた
he remembered that he had eaten nothing all day
彼は一日中何も食べていなかったことを思い出した
he began to feel a gnawing in his stomach
彼は胃がかじられるのを感じ始めました
the gnawing very much resembled appetite
かじりつくことは食欲に非常に似ていました
After a few minutes his appetite had become hunger
数分後、彼の食欲は空腹になっていた
and in little time his hunger became ravenous
そして、すぐに彼の飢えは貪欲になりました
Poor Pinocchio ran quickly to the fireplace
かわいそうなピノキオは急いで暖炉に駆け寄りました
the fireplace where a saucepan was boiling
鍋が沸騰していた暖炉
he was going to take off the lid
彼は蓋を外そうとしていた

then he could see what was in it
それから彼はその中に何があるかを見ることができました
but the saucepan was only painted on the wall
しかし、鍋は壁に描かれているだけでした
You can imagine his feelings when he discovered this
これを発見したときの彼の気持ちは想像に難くありません
His nose, which was already long, became even longer
すでに長かった彼の鼻はさらに長くなりました
it must have grown by at least three inches
少なくとも3インチは成長しているはずです
He then began to run about the room
それから彼は部屋の中を走り回り始めました
he searched in the drawers and every imaginable place
彼は引き出しの中や、考えられるすべての場所を探しました
he hoped to find a bit of bread or crust
彼は少しのパンや皮を見つけることを望んでいました
perhaps he could find a bone left by a dog
もしかしたら、犬が残した骨を見つけることができるかもしれない
a little moldy pudding of Indian corn
インドのトウモロコシの少しカビの生えたプリン
somewhere someone might have left a fish bone
どこかに誰かが魚の骨を残したかもしれない
even a cherry stone would be enough
さくらんぼの石でも十分でしょう
if only there was something that he could gnaw
彼がかじることができる何かがあればいいのに
But he could find nothing to get his teeth into
しかし、彼は歯を食いしばるものは何も見つけることができませんでした
And in the meanwhile his hunger grew and grew
そうこうしているうちに、彼の飢えはどんどん大きくなっていった

Poor Pinocchio had no other relief than yawning
かわいそうなピノキオは、あくびをする以外に安堵感がありませんでした

his yawns were so big his mouth almost reached his ears
彼のあくびはとても大きく、口が耳に届きそうだった

and felt as if he were going to faint
そして、彼は気を失いそうになりました

Then he began to cry desperately
それから彼は必死に泣き始めました

"The talking little cricket was right"
「おしゃべりなクリケットは正しかった」

"I did wrong to rebel against my papa"
「パパに反抗するなんて、僕は悪いことをした」

"I should not have ran away from home"
「家出すべきではなかった」

"If my papa were here I wouldn't be dying of yawning!"
「パパがここにいたら、あくびで死ぬことはなかったのに！」

"Oh! what a dreadful illness hunger is!"
「ああ！飢餓とは、何と恐ろしい病気なのでしょう！」

Just then he thought he saw something in the dust-heap
ちょうどその時、彼は埃の山に何かを見たと思った

something round and white that looked like a hen's egg
丸くて白い何か、それは鶏の卵のように見えました

he sprung up to his feet and seized hold of the egg
彼は跳び起きて卵をつかみました

It was indeed a hen's egg, as he thought
彼が思った通り、それは確かに雌鶏の卵だった

Pinocchio's joy was beyond description
ピノキオの喜びは筆舌に尽くしがたいものでした

he had to make sure that he wasn't just dreaming
彼はただ夢を見ているだけではないことを確認しなければなりませんでした

so he kept turning the egg over in his hands
だから彼は手で卵をひっくり返し続けました

he felt and kissed the egg

彼は卵を感じ、キスをした
"And now, how shall I cook it?"
「さて、どうやって作ろうか?」
"Shall I make an omelet?"
「オムレツを作ろうか?」
"it would be better to cook it in a saucer!"
「受け皿で調理した方がいいんじゃないか!」
"Or would it not be more savory to fry it?"
「それとも、揚げた方がおいしいんじゃないの?」
"Or shall I simply boil the egg?"
「それとも、ただ卵を茹でようか?」
"No, the quickest way is to cook it in a saucer"
「いや、一番手っ取り早いのはソーサーで調理することです」
"I am in such a hurry to eat it!"
「こんなに急いで食べちゃった!」
Without loss of time he got an earthenware saucer
時間を無駄にすることなく、彼は陶器の受け皿を手に入れました
he placed the saucer on a brazier full of red-hot embers
彼はその円盤を赤熱した残り火でいっぱいの火鉢の上に置いた
he didn't have any oil or butter to use
彼は使う油もバターも持っていませんでした
so he poured a little water into the saucer
そこで彼は受け皿に少量の水を注ぎました
and when the water began to smoke, crack!
そして、水が煙を出し始めたとき、割れました!
he broke the egg-shell over the saucer
彼は受け皿の上で卵の殻を割った
and he let the contents of the egg drop into the saucer
そして、彼は卵の中身をソーサーに落としました
but the egg was not full of white and yolk
しかし、卵は白身と卵黄でいっぱいではありませんでした

instead, a little chicken popped out the egg
代わりに、小さな鶏肉が卵から飛び出しました

it was a very gay and polite little chicken
それはとても陽気で礼儀正しい小さな鶏でした
the little chicken made a beautiful courtesy
小さな鶏は美しい礼儀を作った
"A thousand thanks, Master. Pinocchio"
「千の感謝です、マスター。ピノキオ」
"you have saved me the trouble of breaking the shell"
「殻を壊す手間を省いてくれた」
"Adieu, until we meet again" the chicken said
「さようなら、また会うまで」とニワトリは言った
"Keep well, and my best compliments to all at home!"
「元気で、家にいるみんなに最高の賛辞を送ります!」
the little chicken spread its little wings
小さなニワトリは小さな翼を広げました
and the little chicken darted through the open window

そして、小さな鶏は開いた窓から飛び出しました
and then the little chicken flew out of sight
そして、小さな鶏は視界から飛び出しました
The poor puppet stood as if he had been bewitched
哀れな人形は、まるで魔法にかけられたかのように立っていました
his eyes were fixed, and his mouth was open
彼の目は固定され、口は開いていました
and he still had the egg-shell in his hand
そして、彼はまだ手に卵の殻を持っていました
slowly he Recovered from his stupefaction
ゆっくりと彼は昏迷から回復しました
and then he began to cry and scream
そして、彼は泣き叫び始めました
he stamped his feet on the floor in desperation
彼は必死で床に足を踏みつけた
amidst his sobs he gathered his thoughts
すすり泣きながら、彼は考えをまとめた
"Ah, indeed, the talking little cricket was right"
「ああ、確かに、おしゃべりな小さなクリケットは正しかった」
"I should not have run away from home"
「家出をするべきではなかった」
"then I would not now be dying of hunger!"
「そうすれば、私は今、飢えで死ぬことはないでしょう!」
"and if my papa were here he would feed me"
「そして、もしパパがここにいたら、彼は私に食べさせてあげるだろう」
"Oh! what a dreadful illness hunger is!"
「ああ!飢餓とは、何と恐ろしい病気なのでしょう!」
his stomach cried out more than ever
彼の胃はこれまで以上に叫んだ
and he did not know how to quiet his hunger
そして、彼は自分の空腹を静める方法を知らなかった
he thought about leaving the house

彼は家を出ることを考えました
perhaps he could make an excursion in the neighborhood
もしかしたら、近所に遠足に出かけられるかもしれない
he hoped to find some charitable person
彼は慈善団体の人を見つけることを望んでいた
maybe they would give him a piece of bread
もしかしたら、彼らは彼に一切れのパンをくれるかもしれない

Pinocchio's Feet Burn to Cinders
ピノキオの足は燃え尽きるまで燃える

It was an especially wild and stormy night
それは特に荒れ狂った嵐の夜でした
The thunder was tremendously loud and fearful
雷鳴はものすごいほど大きく、恐ろしいものでした
the lightning was so vivid that the sky seemed on fire
稲妻は空が燃えているように思えるほど鮮やかでした
Pinocchio had a great fear of thunder
ピノキオは雷を非常に恐れていました
but hunger can be stronger than fear
しかし、飢餓は恐怖よりも強いことがあります
so he closed the door of the house
それで彼は家のドアを閉めました
and he made a desperate rush for the village
そして彼は必死に村に急いだ
he reached the village in a hundred bounds
彼は百の境界で村に到着しました
his tongue was hanging out of his mouth
彼の舌は口から垂れ下がっていました
and he was panting for breath like a dog
そして彼は犬のように息を切らしていました
But he found the village all dark and deserted
しかし、彼は村がすっかり暗く、人けのない場所である

ことに気づきました
The shops were closed and the windows were shut
店は閉まっており、窓は閉まっていました
and there was not so much as a dog in the street
そして、通りには犬ほどのものはいませんでした
It seemed like he had arrived in the land of the dead
まるで死者の国にたどり着いたかのようだった
Pinocchio was urged on by desperation and hunger
ピノキオは絶望と飢えに駆り立てられました
he took hold of the bell of a house
彼は家の鐘をつかんだ
and he began to ring the bell with all his might
そして、彼は全力で鐘を鳴らし始めました
"That will bring somebody," he said to himself
「それは誰かを連れてくるだろう」と彼は独り言を言った
And it did bring somebody!
そして、それは誰かを連れてきました!
A little old man appeared at a window
窓辺に小さな老人が現れた
the little old man still had a night-cap on his head
小柄な老人はまだ頭に寝酒をかぶっていました
he called to him angrily
彼は怒って彼に呼びかけました
"What do you want at such an hour?"
「こんな時間に何が欲しいの?」
"Would you be kind enough to give me a little bread?"
「ちょっとパンをくれませんか?」
the little old man was very obliging
小さな老人はとても親切でした
"Wait there, I will be back directly"
「そこで待ってください、直接戻ってきます」
he thought it was one of the local rascals
彼はそれが地元の悪党の一人だと思った
they amuse themselves by ringing the house-bells at night
彼らは夜に家の鐘を鳴らして楽しんでいます

After half a minute the window opened again
30分後、窓が再び開きました
the voice of the same little old man shouted to Pinocchio
ピノキオに叫んだのと同じ小さな老人の声
"Come underneath and hold out your cap"
「下に来て、帽子を差し出して」
Pinocchio pulled off his cap and held it out
ピノキオは帽子を脱いで差し出した
but Pinocchio's cap was not filled with bread or food
しかし、ピノキオの帽子にはパンや食べ物が入っていませんでした
an enormous basin of water was poured down on him
巨大な水盤が彼に降り注がれた
the water soaked him from head to foot
水は彼の頭から足までびしょ濡れになりました
as if he had been a pot of dried-up geraniums
まるで彼が干からびたゼラニウムの鍋だったかのように
He returned home like a wet chicken
彼は濡れた鶏のように家に帰りました
he was quite exhausted with fatigue and hunger
彼は疲労と空腹でかなり疲れ果てていました
he no longer had the strength to stand
彼にはもはや立つ力がなかった
so he sat down and rested his damp and muddy feet
そこで彼は座り、湿って泥だらけの足を休めました
he put his feet on a brazier full of burning embers
彼は燃えさしでいっぱいの火鉢に足を乗せた
and then he fell asleep, exhausted from the day
そして、彼は一日の疲れ果てて眠りに落ちました
we all know that Pinocchio has wooden feet
ピノキオが木製の足を持っていることは誰もが知っています
and we know what happens to wood on burning embers
そして、燃えている残り火の上の木材に何が起こるかを私たちは知っています
little by little his feet burnt away and became cinders

彼の足は少しずつ燃え尽きて燃え尽きてしまいました
Pinocchio continued to sleep and snore
ピノキオは眠り続け、いびきをかいていました
his feet might as well have belonged to someone else
彼の足はまるで他の誰かのものだったかのようだ
At last he awoke because someone was knocking at the door
とうとう彼は誰かがドアをノックしていたので目を覚ましました
"Who is there?" he asked, yawning and rubbing his eyes
「そこにいるのは誰だ?」彼はあくびをして目をこすりながら尋ねた
"It is I!" answered a voice
「私だ!」と声が答えた
And Pinocchio recognized Geppetto's voice
そしてピノキオはゼペットの声を認識しました

Geppetto Gives his own Breakfast to Pinocchio
ジェペットはピノキオに彼自身の朝食を与える

Poor Pinocchio's eyes were still half shut from sleep
かわいそうなピノキオの目はまだ半分眠りから閉ざされていました
he had not yet discovered what had happened
彼はまだ何が起こったのかを発見していなかった
his feet had were completely burnt off
彼の足は完全に焼け落ちていました
he heard the voice of his father at the door
彼はドアのところで父親の声を聞いた
and he jumped off the chair he had slept on
そして彼は寝ていた椅子から飛び降りた
he wanted to run to the door and open it
彼はドアに走って行き、それを開けたかった
but he stumbled around and fell on the floor

しかし、彼はよろめき、床に落ちました
imagine having a sack of wooden ladles
木製のお玉の袋を持っていることを想像してみてください
imagine throwing the sack off the balcony
袋をバルコニーから投げ捨てることを想像してみてください
that is was the sound of Pinocchio falling to the floor
それはピノキオが床に落ちる音でした
"Open the door!" shouted Geppetto from the street
「ドアを開けろ!」通りからゼペットが叫んだ
"Dear papa, I cannot," answered the puppet
「親愛なるパパ、できません」と人形は答えました
and he cried and rolled about on the ground
そして彼は泣き叫び、地面に転がった
"Why can't you open the door?"
「なんでドアを開けられないの?」
"Because my feet have been eaten"
「足が食べられてしまったから」
"And who has eaten your feet?"
「それで、誰があなたの足を食べたの?」
Pinocchio looked around for something to blame
ピノキオは何か責めるべきものがないか辺りを見回した
eventually he answered "the cat ate my feet"
結局、彼は「猫が私の足を食べた」と答えました
"Open the door, I tell you!" repeated Geppetto
「ドアを開けて、言ってるよ!」とゼペットは繰り返した
"If you don't open it, you shall have the cat from me!"
「開けないと、私から猫がもらうよ!」
"I cannot stand up, believe me"
「私は立ち上がることができません、私を信じてください」
"Oh, poor me!" lamented Pinocchio
「ああ、かわいそうに!」ピノキオは嘆いた

"I shall have to walk on my knees for the rest of my life!"
「私は一生、ひざまずいて歩かなければならないでしょう!」
Geppetto thought this was another one of the puppet's tricks
ゼペットは、これも人形のトリックの一つだと思った
he thought of a means of putting an end to his tricks
彼は自分の策略に終止符を打つ方法を考えた
he climbed up the wall and got in through the window
彼は壁を登り、窓から入った
He was very angry when he first saw Pinocchio
彼は初めてピノキオを見たとき、とても怒っていました
and he did nothing but scold the poor puppet
そして、彼は哀れな人形を叱るだけでした

but then he saw Pinocchio really was without feet
しかし、その後、彼はピノキオが本当に足がないことを見た

and he was quite overcome with sympathy again
そして彼は再び同情にすっかり打ちのめされました
Geppetto took his puppet in his arms
ゼペットは彼の人形を腕に抱きました
and he began to kiss and caress him
そして彼は彼にキスをし、愛撫し始めました
he said a thousand endearing things to him
彼は彼に何千もの愛らしいことを言いました
big tears ran down his rosy cheeks
彼のバラ色の頬を大粒の涙が流れ落ちた
"My little Pinocchio!" he comforted him
「私の小さなピノキオ!」彼は彼を慰めました
"how did you manage to burn your feet?"
「どうやって足を火傷したの?」
"I don't know how I did it, papa"
「どうやってやったのかわからない、パパ」
"but it has been such a dreadful night"
「でも、とても恐ろしい夜だった」
"I shall remember it as long as I live"
「生きている限り覚えておいて」
"there was thunder and lightning all night"
「一晩中雷と稲妻が鳴り響いていた」
"and I was very hungry all night"
「そして、一晩中とてもお腹が空いていました」
"and then the talking cricket scolded me"
「そして、しゃべるコオロギが私を叱った」
"the talking cricket said 'it serves you right'"
「しゃべるクリケットは『それは君に正しく役立つ』と言った」
"he said; 'you have been wicked and deserve it'"
「彼は言った。『お前は邪悪だった、それに値する』」
"and I said to him: 'Take care, little Cricket!'"
「そして私は彼に言いました。『気をつけて、小さなクリケット!』」
"and he said; 'You are a puppet'"
「そして彼は言った。『お前は操り人形だ』と」

"and he said; 'you have a wooden head'"
「そして彼は言った。『君は木の頭を持っている』」
"and I threw the handle of a hammer at him"
「そして、私は彼にハンマーの柄を投げつけた」
"and then the talking little cricket died"
「そして、おしゃべりな小さなコオロギは死んだ」
"but it was his fault that he died"
「でも、彼が死んだのは彼のせいだ」
"because I didn't wish to kill him"
「彼を殺したくなかったから」
"and I have proof that I didn't mean to"
「そして、そんなつもりはなかったという証拠がある」
"I had put an earthenware saucer on burning embers"
「燃えさしに土器の受け皿を置いた」
"but a chicken flew out of the egg"
「でも、卵から鶏が飛んでいった」
"the chicken said; 'Adieu, until we meet again'"
「鶏は言った。『さようなら、また会うまで』」
'send my compliments to all at home'
「家にいるすべての人に賛辞を送ります」
"and then I got even more hungry"
「そして、さらにお腹が空いてきました」
"then there was that little old man in a night-cap"
「それから、寝酒をかぶった小さな老人がいた」
"he opened the window up above me"
「彼は私の上の窓を開けた」
"and he told me to hold out my hat"
「そして、彼は私に帽子を差し出すように言いました」
"and he poured a basinful of water on me"
「そして彼は私に洗面器一杯の水を注いだ」
"asking for a little bread isn't a disgrace, is it?"
「パンを少し頼むのは恥ずかしいことじゃないよね?」
"and then I returned home at once"
「そして、すぐに家に帰りました」
"I was hungry and cold and tired"
「お腹が空いて寒くて疲れた」

"and I put my feet on the brazier to dry them"
「そして、火鉢に足を乗せて乾かしました」
"and then you returned in the morning"
「そして、朝になって戻ってきたんだ」
"and I found my feet were burnt off"
「そして、足が焼け焦げているのを見つけました」
"and I am still hungry"
「そしてまだお腹が空いています」
"but I no longer have any feet!"
「でも、もう足がない!」
And poor Pinocchio began to cry and roar
そしてかわいそうなピノキオは泣き叫び始めました
he cried so loudly that he was heard five miles off
彼は5マイル離れたところまで聞こえるほど大声で叫んだ
Geppetto, only understood one thing from all this
ゼペットは、これらすべてから1つのことしか理解していませんでした
he understood that the puppet was dying of hunger
彼は、人形が飢えで死にかけていることを理解した
so he drew from his pocket three pears
そこで彼はポケットから3つの梨を取り出した
and he gave the pears to Pinocchio
そして彼は梨をピノキオに与えました
"These three pears were intended for my breakfast"
「この3つの梨は私の朝食に使うつもりだった」
"but I will give you my pears willingly"
「でも、喜んで私の梨をあげるよ」
"Eat them, and I hope they will do you good"
「食べてみて、彼らが君に良いことをしてくれるといいんだけど」
Pinocchio looked at the pears distrustfully
ピノキオは不信そうに梨を見た
"but you can't expect me to eat them like that"
「でも、あんな風に食べるなんて期待できないよ」
"be kind enough to peel them for me"

「私のために皮をむくくらい親切にして」
"Peel them?" said Geppetto, astonished
「皮をむくの?」ゼペットは驚いて言った
"I didn't know you were so dainty and fastidious"
「あなたがこんなに可憐で潔癖だとは知らなかった」
"These are bad habits to have, my boy!"
「これらは悪い習慣だよ、我が子!」
"we must accustom ourselves to like and to eat everything"
「私たちは、何でも好きで食べることに慣れなければなりません」
"there is no knowing to what we may be brought"
「私たちが何をもたらすかわからない」
"There are so many chances!"
「チャンスはたくさんある!」
"You are no doubt right," interrupted Pinocchio
「君の言う通りだよ」ピノキオが口を挟んだ
"but I will never eat fruit that has not been peeled"
「でも、皮をむいていない果物は絶対に食べない」
"I cannot bear the taste of rind"
「皮の味が耐えられない」
So good Geppetto peeled the three pears
とても良いゼペットは3つの梨をむきました
and he put the pear's rinds on a corner of the table
そして、梨の皮をテーブルの隅に置いた
Pinocchio had eaten the first pear
ピノキオは最初の梨を食べました
he was about to throw away the pear's core
彼は梨の芯を捨てようとしていました
but Geppetto caught hold of his arm
しかし、ゼペットは彼の腕をつかみました
"Do not throw the core of the pear away"
「梨の芯を捨てない」
"in this world everything may be of use"
「この世界では、すべてが役に立つかもしれない」
But Pinocchio refused to see the sense in it
しかし、ピノキオはその意味を見ることを拒否しました

"I am determined I will not eat the core of the pear"
「梨の芯は食べないと決意しています」
and Pinocchio turned upon him like a viper
そしてピノキオは毒蛇のように彼に向き直った
"Who knows!" repeated Geppetto
「誰にもわからない!」とジェペットは繰り返した
"there are so many chances," he said
「チャンスはたくさんあります」と彼は言いました
and Geppetto never lost his temper even once
そして、ゼペットは一度たりとも冷静さを失わなかった
And so the three pear cores were not thrown out
そして、3つの梨の芯は捨てられませんでした
they were placed on the corner of the table with the rinds
それらは皮と一緒にテーブルの隅に置かれました
after his small feast Pinocchio yawned tremendously
彼の小さなごちそうの後、ピノキオは途方もなくあくびをしました
and he spoke again in a fretful tone
そして彼は再び苛立った口調で話した
"I am as hungry as ever!"
「相変わらずお腹が空いています!」
"But, my boy, I have nothing more to give you!"
「でも、息子よ、これ以上あげるものはないよ!」
"You have nothing? Really? Nothing?"
「何もないの?ほんとですか。何もないの?」
"I have only the rind and the cores of the pears"
「梨の皮と芯しかない」
"One must have patience!" said Pinocchio
「忍耐力が必要だ!」とピノキオは言った
"if there is nothing else I will eat the pear's rind"
「他に何もないなら、梨の皮を食べます」
And he began to chew the rind of the pear
そして、彼は梨の皮を噛み始めました
At first he made a wry face
最初、彼は苦笑いを浮かべた
but then, one after the other, he quickly ate them

しかし、その後、彼は次々とそれらをすぐに食べました
and after the pear's rinds he even ate the cores
そして、梨の皮をむいた後、彼は芯さえ食べました
when he had eaten everything he rubbed his belly
全部食べ終えると、彼は腹をさすった
"Ah! now I feel comfortable again"
「あぁ!今ではまた快適に感じています」
"Now you see I was right," smiled Gepetto
「今、私が正しかったことがわかるでしょう」とジェペットは微笑んだ
"it's not good to accustom ourselves to our tastes"
「自分の好みに慣れるのは良くない」
"We can never know, my dear boy, what may happen to us"
「親愛なる息子よ、私たちに何が起こるかは決してわかりません」
"There are so many chances!"
「チャンスはたくさんある!」

Geppetto Makes Pinocchio New Feet
Geppettoはピノキオの新しい足を作る

the puppet had satisfied his hunger
人形は彼の空腹を満たした
but he began to cry and grumble again
しかし、彼は再び泣き始め、不平を言い始めました
he remembered he wanted a pair of new feet
彼は新しい足が欲しかったことを思い出しました
But Geppetto punished him for his naughtiness
しかし、ゼペットは彼のいたずらを罰しました
he allowed him to cry and to despair a little
彼は彼に泣き叫び、少し絶望することを許しました
Pinocchio had to accept his fate for half the day
ピノキオは半日、自分の運命を受け入れなければなりませんでした

at the end of the day he said to him:
一日の終わりに、彼は彼に言いました。
"Why should I make you new feet?"
「なぜ新しい足を作らなきゃいけないの?」
"To enable you to escape again from home?"
「再び家から逃げ出すことができるように?」
Pinocchio sobbed at his situation
ピノキオは自分の状況にすすり泣いた
"I promise you that for the future I will be good"
「これからも僕は元気になると約束する」
but Geppetto knew Pinocchio's tricks by now
しかし、ゼペットはもうピノキオのトリックを知っていました
"All boys who want something say the same thing"
「何かを欲しがる男の子はみんな同じことを言う」
"I promise you that I will go to school"
「学校に行く約束をする」
"and I will study and bring home a good report"
「そして、私は勉強して良いレポートを家に持ち帰ります」
"All boys who want something repeat the same story"
「何かを欲しがる男の子はみんな同じ話を繰り返す」
"But I am not like other boys!" Pinocchio objected
「でも、僕は他の男の子とは違うんだ!」ピノキオは異議を唱えた
"I am better than all of them," he added
「私は彼ら全員よりも優れている」と彼は付け加えた
"and I always speak the truth," he lied
「そして、私はいつも真実を話す」と彼は嘘をついた
"I promise you, papa, that I will learn a trade"
「パパ、約束するよ、僕は商売を学ぶって」
"I promise that I will be the consolation of your old age"
「私があなたの老後の慰めになることを約束します」
Geppetto's eyes filled with tears on hearing this
それを聞いて涙を浮かべたゼペットの目
his heart was sad at seeing his son like this

彼の心は息子のこのような姿を見て悲しかった
Pinocchio was in such a pitiable state
ピノキオはこんなに哀れな状態だった
He did not say another word to Pinocchio
彼はピノキオに一言も言わなかった
he got his tools and two small pieces of seasoned wood
彼は道具と2つの小さな木片を手に入れました
he set to work with great diligence
彼は非常に勤勉に仕事に取り掛かりました
In less than an hour the feet were finished
1時間も経たないうちに、足元は完成しました
They might have been modelled by an artist of genius
彼らは天才的な芸術家によってモデルにされたかもしれません
Geppetto then spoke to the puppet
その後、ゼペットは人形に話しかけました
"Shut your eyes and go to sleep!"
「目を閉じて眠りなさい!」
And Pinocchio shut his eyes and pretended to sleep
そしてピノキオは目を閉じて寝たふりをしました
Geppetto got an egg-shell and melted some glue in it
ゼペットは卵の殻を手に入れ、その中の接着剤を溶かしました
and he fastened Pinocchio's feet in their place
そして彼はピノキオの足をその場所に固定しました
it was masterfully done by Geppetto
それはGeppettoによって見事に行われました
not a trace could be seen of where the feet were joined
足が接合された場所の痕跡は見当たりませんでした
Pinocchio soon realized that he had feet again
ピノキオはすぐに、自分が再び足を持っていることに気づきました
and then he jumped down from the table
そして、彼はテーブルから飛び降りた
he jumped around the room with energy and joy
彼はエネルギーと喜びで部屋中を飛び跳ねました

he danced as if he had gone mad with his delight
彼は喜びで気が狂ったかのように踊った
"thank you for all you have done for me"
「あなたが私のためにしてくれたすべてのことに感謝します」
"I will go to school at once," Pinocchio promised
「すぐに学校に行きます」とピノキオは約束しました
"but to go to school I shall need some clothes"
「でも、学校に行くには服が必要だよ」
by now you know that Geppetto was a poor man
もうお分かりでしょうが、ゼペットは貧しい人でした
he had not so much as a penny in his pocket
彼のポケットには一銭も入っていなかった
so he made him a little dress of flowered paper
それで彼は彼に花のついた紙の小さなドレスを作りました
a pair of shoes from the bark of a tree
木の皮から出た一足の靴
and he made a hat out of the bread
そして、そのパンで帽子を作った

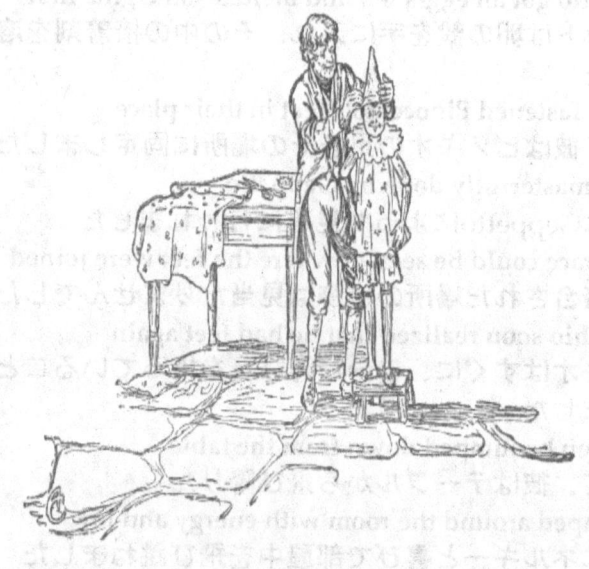

Pinocchio ran to look at himself in a crock of water
ピノキオは走って水の入った壺の中の自分を見つめました
he was ever so pleased with his appearance
彼は自分の姿にとても満足していました
and he strutted about the room like a peacock
そして、孔雀のように部屋の中を闊歩した
"I look quite like a gentleman!"
「なかなか紳士っぽい!」
"Yes, indeed," answered Geppetto
「ええ、確かに」とゼペットは答えた
"it is not fine clothes that make the gentleman"
「紳士らしくするのは上質な服ではない」
"rather, it is clean clothes that make a gentleman"
「むしろ、紳士らしくするのは清潔な服装」
"By the way," added the puppet
「ところで」と人形は付け加えました
"to go to school there's still something I need"
「学校に行くために、まだ何かが必要だ」
"I am still without the best thing"
「私はまだ最高のものがない」
"it is the most important thing for a school boy"
「男子生徒にとって最も重要なこと」
"And what is it?" asked Geppetto
「それで、それは何なの?」とゼペットは尋ねた
"I have no spelling-book"
「綴り方の本がない」
"You are right" realized Geppetto
「君の言う通りだ」とジェペットは悟った
"but what shall we do to get one?"
「でも、どうすれば手に入れることができるの?」
Pinocchio comforted Geppetto, "It is quite easy"
ピノキオはゼペットを慰め、「それはかなり簡単です」
"all we have to do is go to the bookseller's"
「私たちがしなければならないのは、書店に行くことだ

けです」
"all I have to do is buy from them"
「私がしなければならないのは、彼らから買うことだけだ」
"but how do we buy it without money?"
「でも、お金なしでどうやって買うの?」
"I have got no money," said Pinocchio
「お金がないんだ」とピノキオは言った
"Neither have I," added the good old man, very sadly
「私も」と、善良な老人は非常に悲しそうに付け加えました
although he was a very merry boy, Pinocchio became sad
とても陽気な男の子だったのに、ピノキオは悲しくなってしまいました
poverty, when it is real, is understood by everybody
貧困は、それが現実であるとき、誰もが理解します
"Well, patience!" exclaimed Geppetto, rising to his feet
「まあ、忍耐だ!」とゼペットは叫び、立ち上がった
and he put on his old corduroy jacket
そして彼は古いコーデュロイのジャケットを着ました
and he ran out of the house into the snow
そして彼は家を飛び出し、雪の中へ走り出しました
He returned back to the house soon after
彼はすぐに家に戻りました
in his hand he held a spelling-book for Pinocchio
彼の手にはピノキオの綴り方の本を持っていました
but the old jacket he had left with was gone
しかし、彼が残していた古いジャケットはなくなっていました
The poor man was in his shirt-sleeves
哀れな男はシャツの袖を着ていました
and outdoors it was cold and snowing
そして屋外は寒くて雪が降っていました
"And your jacket, papa?" asked Pinocchio
「それで、パパ、あなたのジャケットは?」ピノキオが尋ねた

"I have sold it," confirmed old Geppetto
「売ったよ」と老ゼペットは確認した
"Why did you sell it?" asked Pinocchio
「どうして売ったの?」とピノキオは尋ねた
"Because I found my jacket was too hot"
「ジャケットが熱すぎるとわかったから」
Pinocchio understood this answer in an instant
ピノキオはこの答えを一瞬で理解しました
Pinocchio was unable to restrain the impulse of his heart
ピノキオは心臓の衝動を抑えることができませんでした
Because Pinocchio did have a good heart after all
なぜなら、ピノキオは結局、善良な心を持っていたからです
he sprang up and threw his arms around Geppetto's neck
彼は跳び上がり、ゼペットの首に腕を回した
and he kissed him again and again a thousand times
そして彼は彼に何度も何度も千回キスをしました

Pinocchio Goes to See a Puppet Show
ピノキオは人形劇を見に行く

eventually it stopped snowing outside
結局、外の雪は止みました
and Pinocchio set out to go to school
そしてピノキオは学校に行くために出発しました
and he had his fine spelling-book under his arm
そして、彼は立派なスペリングブックを小脇に抱えていました
he walked along with a thousand ideas in his head
彼は頭の中で千のアイデアを持って歩いていました
his little brain thought of all the possibilities
彼の小さな脳は、すべての可能性を考えていた
and he built a thousand castles in the air
そして、空中に千の城を建てた

each castle was more beautiful than the other
それぞれの城は他の城よりも美しかったです
And, talking to himself, he said;
そして、独り言を言いながら、彼は言った。
"Today at school I will learn to read at once"
「今日は学校ですぐに読むことを学びます」
"then tomorrow I will begin to write"
「じゃあ、明日から書き始めるよ」
"and the day after tomorrow I will learn the numbers"
「そして明後日には数字を覚える」
"all of these things will prove very useful"
「これらすべてが非常に役立つことが証明されます」
"and then I will earn a great deal of money"
「そうすれば、私はたくさんのお金を稼ぐでしょう」
"I already know what I will do with the first money"
「最初のお金で何をするかはもうわかっています」
"I will immediately buy a beautiful new cloth coat"
「すぐに綺麗な新しい布製コートを買います」
"my papa will not have to be cold anymore"
「パパはもう寒くなくていいよ」
"But what am I saying?" he realized
「でも、何を言っているんだ?」彼は気づいた
"It shall be all made of gold and silver"
「すべて金と銀でできている」
"and it shall have diamond buttons"
「そして、それはひし形のボタンを持つべき」
"That poor man really deserves it"
「あの可哀想な男は本当にそれに値する」
"he bought me books and is having me taught"
「彼は私に本を買って、教えてもらっています」
"and to do so he has remained in a shirt"
「そして、そのために彼はシャツを着たままだった」
"he has done all this for me in such cold weather"
「彼はこんなに寒い時期に、私のためにこれだけのことをしてくれた」
"only papas are capable of such sacrifices!"

「こんな犠牲を払うことができるのはパパだけだ!」
he said all this to himself with great emotion
彼はこれらすべてを大きな感情で自分自身に言い聞かせました
but in the distance he thought he heard music
しかし、遠くで音楽が聞こえたと思った
it sounded like pipes and the beating of a big drum
それはパイプと大きな太鼓の叩き声のように聞こえました
He stopped and listened to hear what it could be
彼は立ち止まり、それが何であるかを聞くために耳を傾けました
The sounds came from the end of a street
その音は通りの端から聞こえてきた
and the street led to a little village on the seashore
そして、通りは海岸の小さな村に通じていました
"What can that music be?" he wondered
「あの音楽は何だろう?」と彼は疑問に思いました
"What a pity that I have to go to school"
「学校に行かなければならないなんて、なんて残念なの」
"if only I didn't have to go to school..."
「学校に行かなくて済んだら...」
And he remained irresolute
そして彼は毅然とした態度を崩さなかった
It was, however, necessary to come to a decision
しかし、決断を下す必要があった
"Should I go to school?" he asked himself
「学校に行くべきだろうか?」と彼は自問した
"or should I go after the music?"
「それとも、音楽を追いかけるべきか?」
"Today I will go and hear the music" he decided
「今日、音楽を聴きに行く」と彼は決めた
"and tomorrow I will go to school"
「そして明日は学校に行く」
the young scapegrace of a boy had decided

少年の若きスケープグレースは決めた
and he shrugged his shoulders at his choice
そして彼は自分の選択に肩をすくめた
The more he ran the nearer came the sounds of the music
走れば走るほど、音楽の音が近づいてきました
and the beating of the big drum became louder and louder
そして、大きな太鼓の鼓動はますます大きくなりました
At last he found himself in the middle of a town square
とうとう彼は町の広場の真ん中にいることに気づきました
the square was quite full of people
広場はかなり人でいっぱいでした
all the people were all crowded round a building
すべての人々が建物の周りに集まっていました
and the building was made of wood and canvas
そして建物は木とキャンバスでできていました
and the building was painted a thousand colours
そして、建物は千色に塗られました
"What is that building?" asked Pinocchio
「あの建物は何だ?」とピノキオは尋ねた
and he turned to a little boy
そして彼は小さな男の子に向き直りました
"Read the placard," the boy told him
「プラカードを読んでみて」と少年は彼に言った
"it is all written there," he added
「それはすべてそこに書かれています」と彼は付け加えました
"read it and and then you will know"
「読んでみればわかる」
"I would read it willingly," said Pinocchio
「私は喜んでそれを読みます」とピノキオは言いました
"but it so happens that today I don't know how to read"
「でも、たまたま今日は読み方がわからないんだ」
"Bravo, blockhead! Then I will read it to you"
「ブラボー、ブロックヘッド!それから私があなたにそれを読みます」

"you see those words as red as fire?"
「その言葉が火のように赤いのが見えるか?」
"The Great Puppet Theatre," he read to him
「大人形劇」と彼は彼に読み聞かせました
"Has the play already begun?"
「もう芝居は始まってるの?」
"It is beginning now," confirmed the boy
「今、始まっているよ」と少年は確認した
"How much does it cost to go in?"
「入るのにいくらかかるの?」
"A dime is what it costs you"
「10セント硬貨はそれがあなたにかかるものです」
Pinocchio was in a fever of curiosity
ピノキオは好奇心にあふれていました
full of excitement he lost all control of himself
興奮でいっぱいの彼は、自分自身のコントロールをすべて失った
and Pinocchio lost all sense of shame
そしてピノキオはすべての恥ずかしさを失った
"Would you lend me a dime until tomorrow?"
「明日まで一銭貸してもらえませんか?」
"I would lend it to you willingly," said the boy
「喜んで貸してあげるよ」と少年は言いました
"but unfortunately today I cannot give it to you"
「でも残念ながら、今日は君にあげることができない」
Pinocchio had another idea to get the money
ピノキオは、お金を得るための別のアイデアを持っていました
"I will sell you my jacket for a dime"
「私のジャケットを10セント硬貨で売る」
"but your jacket is made of flowered paper"
「でも、あなたのジャケットは花の咲く紙でできています」
"what use could I have for such a jacket?"
「こんなジャケットに何の役に立つの?」
"imagine it rained and the jacket got wet"

「雨が降ってジャケットが濡れたと想像してみて」
"it would be impossible to get it off my back"
「背中から外すのは無理だろう」
"Will you buy my shoes?" tried Pinocchio
「私の靴を買ってくれる?」とピノキオは試した
"They would only be of use to light the fire"
「火をつけるのにしか役に立たないだろう」
"How much will you give me for my cap?"
「帽子代いくらくれるの?」
"That would be a wonderful acquisition indeed!"
「それは本当に素晴らしい買収になるでしょう!」
"A cap made of bread crumb!" joked the boy
「パンくずでできた帽子だ!」と少年は冗談を言いました
"There would be a risk of the mice coming to eat it"
「ネズミが食べに来るリスクがある」
"they might eat it whilst it was still on my head!"
「まだ頭に乗ったまま食べられちゃうかもしれない!」
Pinocchio was on thorns about his predicament
ピノキオは彼の苦境について悩んでいました
He was on the point of making another offer
彼は別のオファーを出すところだった
but he had not the courage to ask him
しかし、彼に尋ねる勇気はなかった
He hesitated, felt irresolute and remorseful
彼は躊躇し、毅然とした態度を崩し、後悔していると感じました
At last he raised the courage to ask
とうとう彼は勇気を出して尋ねた
"Will you give me a dime for this new spelling-book?"
「この新しい綴り方の本に10セント硬貨をくれませんか?」
but the boy declined this offer too
しかし、少年はこの申し出も断りました
"I am a boy and I don't buy from boys"

「私は男の子で、男の子からは買わない」
a hawker of old clothes had overheard them
古着の行商人がそれを耳にしていた
"I will buy the spelling-book for a dime"
「綴り方の本を10セント硬貨で買います」
And the book was sold there and then
そして、その本はそこで売られました
poor Geppetto had remained at home trembling with cold
かわいそうなゼペットは、寒さに震えながら家に残っていました
in order that his son could have a spelling-book
彼の息子が綴りの本を持つことができるように

The Puppets Recognize their Brother Pinocchio
人形たちは兄のピノキオを認識する

Pinocchio was in the little puppet theatre
ピノキオは小さな人形劇にいました
an incident occurred that almost produced a revolution
革命を起こすほどの事件が起こりました
The curtain had gone up and the play had already begun
幕が上がり、すでに芝居が始まっていました
Harlequin and Punch were quarrelling with each other
ハーレクインとパンチは喧嘩していた
every moment they were threatening to come to blows
一瞬一瞬、彼らは殴り合いになりそうだった
All at once Harlequin stopped and turned to the public
ハーレクインは突然立ち止まり、大衆の方を向いた
he pointed with his hand to someone far down in the pit
彼は手で穴のはるか下の誰かを指差した
and he exclaimed in a dramatic tone
そして彼は劇的な口調で叫んだ
"Gods of the firmament!"
「大空の神々!」

"Do I dream or am I awake?"
「私は夢を見ているのか、それとも起きているのか?」
"But, surely that is Pinocchio!"
「でも、きっとピノキオだよ!」
"It is indeed Pinocchio!" cried Punch
「ほんとにピノキオだ!」パンチが叫んだ
And Rose peeped out from behind the scenes
そして、舞台裏から覗いたローズ
"It is indeed himself!" screamed Rose
「本当に彼自身だ!」ローズは叫んだ
and all the puppets shouted in chorus
そして、すべての人形が合唱しました
"It is Pinocchio! it is Pinocchio!"
「ピノキオだよ!ピノキオだ!」
and they leapt from all sides onto the stage
そして、彼らは四方八方から舞台に飛び降りました
"It is Pinocchio!" all the puppets exclaimed
「ピノキオだ!」と人形全員が叫びました
"It is our brother Pinocchio!"
「私たちの兄弟、ピノキオです!」
"Long live Pinocchio!" they cheered together
「ピノキオ万歳!」と彼らは一緒に歓声を上げました
"Pinocchio, come up here to me," cried Harlequin
「ピノキオ、こっちに来て」とハーレクインが叫びました
"throw yourself into the arms of your wooden brothers!"
「木造の兄弟たちの腕の中に身を投げ出せ!」
Pinocchio couldn't decline this affectionate invitation
ピノキオは、この愛情のこもった招待を断ることができませんでした
he leaped from the end of the pit into the reserved seats
彼はピットの端から指定席に飛び込んだ
another leap landed him on the head of the drummer
別の跳躍で彼はドラマーの頭に着地した
and he then sprang upon the stage

そして彼は舞台に飛び上がった
The embraces and the friendly pinches
抱擁と友好的なピンチ
and the demonstrations of warm brotherly affection
そして、温かい兄弟愛の表現
Pinocchio reception from the puppets was beyond description
人形からのピノキオの反応は筆舌に尽くしがたいものでした
The sight was doubtless a moving one
その光景は間違いなく感動的なものでした
but the public in the pit had become impatient
しかし、ピットの中の大衆は焦りを感じていました
they began to shout, "we came to watch a play"
彼らは「私たちは演劇を見に来た」と叫び始めました
"go on with the play!" they demanded
「遊びを続けろ!」と彼らは要求した
but the puppets didn't continue the recital
しかし、人形たちはリサイタルを続けませんでした
the puppets doubled their noise and outcries
人形たちは彼らの騒音と叫び声を倍増させました
they put Pinocchio on their shoulders
彼らはピノキオを肩に乗せました
and they carried him in triumph before the footlights
そして、彼らはフットライトの前で彼を勝利のうちに運びました
At that moment the ringmaster came out
その時、首謀者が出てきた
He was a big and ugly man
彼は大きくて醜い男だった
the sight of him was enough to frighten anyone
彼の姿は、誰もが怖がるほどでした
His beard was as black as ink and long
彼のあごひげはインクのように黒く、長くて長かった
and his beard reached from his chin to the ground
そして彼の髭は顎から地面まで伸びていた

and he trod upon his beard when he walked
そして、歩くときには髭を踏んだ
His mouth was as big as an oven
彼の口はオーブンのように大きかった
and his eyes were like two lanterns of burning red glass
そして彼の目は燃える赤いガラスの2つのランタンのようでした
He carried a large whip of twisted snakes and foxes' tails
彼はねじれた蛇とキツネの尻尾の大きな鞭を持っていました
and he cracked his whip constantly
そして彼は絶えず鞭を鳴らしました
At his unexpected appearance there was a profound silence
彼の予期せぬ出現には、深い沈黙が流れた
no one dared to even breathe
誰も息をする勇気さえありませんでした
A fly could have been heard in the stillness
静寂の中でハエの声が聞こえたかもしれません
The poor puppets of both sexes trembled like leaves
男女の哀れな人形は葉のように震えました
"have you come to raise a disturbance in my theatre?"
「私の劇場に騒ぎを起こしに来たのですか？」
he had the gruff voice of a goblin
彼はゴブリンのようなぶっきらぼうな声をしていた
a goblin suffering from a severe cold
ひどい風邪に苦しむゴブリン
"Believe me, honoured sir, it it not my fault!"
「私を信じてください、名誉ある旦那様、それは私のせいではありません！」
"That is enough from you!" he blared
「お前からもう十分だ！」彼は唸った
"Tonight we will settle our accounts"
「今夜、私たちは会計を精算します」
soon the play was over and the guests left
すぐに劇は終わり、ゲストは去りました
the ringmaster went into the kitchen

首謀者は台所に入った
a fine sheep was being prepared for his supper
彼の夕食には立派な羊が用意されていました
it was turning slowly on the fire
火の上でゆっくりと回転していました
there was not enough wood to finish roasting the lamb
子羊のローストを終えるのに十分な木材がありませんでした
so he called for Harlequin and Punch
そこで彼はハーレクインとパンチを呼びました
"Bring that puppet here," he ordered them
「あの人形をここに持ってこい」と彼は彼らに命じた
"you will find him hanging on a nail"
「彼が釘にぶら下がっているのを見つけるでしょう」
"It seems to me that he is made of very dry wood"
「彼は非常に乾燥した木でできているように私には思えます」
"I am sure he would make a beautiful blaze"
「きっと綺麗な炎をつくるよ」
At first Harlequin and Punch hesitated
最初、ハーレクインとパンチは躊躇した
but they were appalled by a severe glance from their master
しかし、彼らは主人からの厳しい視線に愕然としました
and they had no choice but to obey his wishes
そして、彼らは彼の願いに従うしかありませんでした
In a short time they returned to the kitchen
すぐに彼らは台所に戻りました
this time they were carrying poor Pinocchio
今回は、彼らはかわいそうなピノキオを運んでいました
he was wriggling like an eel out of water
彼は水から出たウナギのように身をよじっていました
and he was screaming desperately
そして彼は必死に叫んでいました
"Papa! papa! save me! I will not die!"
「パパ!パパ!助けてください!私は死なない!」

The Fire-Eater Sneezes and Pardons Pinocchio
火を食べる人はくしゃみをし、ピノキオを許す

The ringmaster looked like a wicked man
首謀者は邪悪な男のように見えました
and he was known by all as Fire-eater
そして彼は皆から火を食べる者として知られていました
his black beard covered his chest and legs
彼の黒いあごひげが彼の胸と脚を覆っていました
it was like he was wearing an apron
まるでエプロンを着ているかのようだった
and this made him look especially wicked
そして、これが彼を特に邪悪に見せました
On the whole, however, he did not have a bad heart
しかし、全体としては、彼は悪い心を持っていませんでした
he saw poor Pinocchio brought before him
彼は哀れなピノキオが彼の前に連れてこられるのを見ました
he saw the puppet struggling and screaming
彼は人形がもがき、叫んでいるのを見ました
"I will not die, I will not die!"
「私は死なない、私は死なない!」
and he was quite moved by what he saw
そして、彼は見たものにかなり感動しました
he felt very sorry for the helpless puppet
彼は無力な人形をとても気の毒に思いました
he tried to hold his sympathies within himself
彼は自分の中に同情を抱こうとした
but after a little they all came out
しかし、少しすると、彼らはすべて出てきました
he could contain his sympathy no longer
彼はもはや同情を抑えることができなかった
and he let out an enormous violent sneeze

そして彼は激しいくしゃみをした
up until that moment Harlequin had been worried
その瞬間まで、ハーレクインは心配していた
he had been bowing down like a weeping willow
彼はしだれ柳のようにお辞儀をしていた
but when he heard the sneeze he became cheerful
しかし、くしゃみを聞いたとき、彼は元気になりました
he leaned towards Pinocchio and whispered;
彼はピノキオの方に身を乗り出してささやいた。
"Good news, brother, the ringmaster has sneezed"
「朗報だよ、兄さん、リングマスターがくしゃみをしたよ」
"that is a sign that he pities you"
「それは彼があなたを憐れんでいるしるしです」
"and if he pities you, then you are saved"
「そして、彼があなたを憐れむなら、あなたは救われます」
most men weep when they feel compassion
ほとんどの男性は、同情を感じると泣きます
or at least they pretend to dry their eyes
または、少なくとも彼らは目を乾かすふりをします
Fire-Eater, however, had a different habit
しかし、ファイヤーイーターには別の習慣がありました
when moved by emotion his nose would tickle him
感情に動かされると、彼の鼻は彼をくすぐったいでしょう
the ringmaster didn't stop acting the ruffian
首謀者は悪党の演技を止めなかった
"are you quite done with all your crying?"
「泣きっぱなしゃ終わったの?」
"my stomach hurts from your lamentations"
「あなたの嘆きで胃が痛い」
"I feel a spasm that almost..."
「痙攣しそうになる...」
and the ringmaster let out another loud sneeze
そして、首謀者は再び大きなくしゃみをした

"Bless you!" said Pinocchio, quite cheerfully
「おめでとうございます!」ピノキオは上機嫌で言った
"Thank you! And your papa and your mamma?"
「ありがとう!そして、あなたのパパとあなたのママは?」
"are they still alive?" asked Fire-Eater
「彼らはまだ生きているのか?」とファイヤーイーターは尋ねた
"My papa is still alive and well," said Pinocchio
「私のパパはまだ生きていて元気です」とピノキオは言いました
"but my mamma I have never known," he added
「でも、ママは知らないんだ」と彼は付け加えた
"good thing I did not have you thrown on the fire"
「火に投げ込まれなくてよかった」
"your father would have lost all who he still had"
「お前の父さんは、まだ持っていたものをすべて失っていただろう」
"Poor old man! I pity him!"
「かわいそうなおじいさん!彼を哀れに思います!」
"Etchoo! etchoo! etchoo!" Fire-eater sneezed
「エッチョー!エッチュー!エッチョー!」火を食べる人がくしゃみをした
and he sneezed again three times
そして彼は再び3回くしゃみをしました
"Bless you," said Pinocchio each time
「おめでとうございます」とピノキオは毎回言いました
"Thank you! Some compassion is due to me"
「ありがとう!いくらかの思いやりは私によるものです」
"as you can see I have no more wood"
「ご覧の通り、私にはもう木がありません」
"so I will struggle to finish roasting my mutton"
「だから、マトンの焙煎を終えるのに苦労するでしょう」

"you would have been of great use to me!"
「君は僕にとって大いに役立っただろう!」
"However, I have had pity on you"
「しかし、私はあなたを憐れんでいました」
"so I must have patience with you"
「だから、君には忍耐が必要だ」
"Instead of you I will burn another puppet"
「お前の代わりに、もう一人の人形を燃やしてやる」
At this call two wooden gendarmes immediately appeared
この呼びかけで、二人の木造憲兵がすぐに現れた
They were very long and very thin puppets
彼らはとても長くて、とても細い人形でした
and they had wonky hats on their heads
そして、彼らの頭には風変わりな帽子がかぶっていました
and they held unsheathed swords in their hands
そして、彼らは鞘を抜いた剣を手に持っていた
The ringmaster said to them in a hoarse voice:
首謀者はかすれた声で彼らに言った。
"Take Harlequin and bind him securely"
「ハーレクインを取って、しっかりと縛って」
"and then throw him on the fire to burn"
「そして、彼を火に投げて燃やす」
"I am determined that my mutton shall be well roasted"
「私は、私の羊肉をよく焼くことを決意しています」
imagine how poor Harlequin must have felt!
ハーレクインがどんなにかわいそうに感じたか想像してみてください。
His terror was so great that his legs bent under him
彼の恐怖はあまりにも大きかったので、彼の足は彼の下で曲がった
and he fell with his face on the ground
そして、彼は顔を地面につけて倒れた
Pinocchio was agonized by what he was seeing
ピノキオは自分が見ているものに苦しんでいました
he threw himself at the ringmaster's feet

彼はリングマスターの足元に身を投げ出した
he bathed his long beard with his tears
彼は長い髭を涙で濡らした
and he tried to beg for Harlequin's life
そして彼はハーレクインの命乞いを試みた
"Have pity, Sir Fire-Eater!" Pinocchio begged
「同情してください、火喰い卿!」ピノキオは懇願した
"Here there are no sirs," the ringmaster answered severely
「ここにはサーはいません」と首謀者は厳しく答えた
"Have pity, Sir Knight!" Pinocchio tried
「同情してください、騎士様!」ピノキオが試してみた
"Here there are no knights!" the ringmaster answered
「ここには騎士はいない!」首謀者が答えた
"Have pity, Commander!" Pinocchio tried
「同情してください、司令官!」ピノキオが試してみた
"Here there are no commanders!"
「ここには司令官はいない!」
"Have pity, Excellence!" Pinocchio pleaded
「同情せよ、エクセレンス!」ピノキオは嘆願した
Fire-eater quite liked what he had just heard
火を食べる人は、今聞いたことをとても気に入った
Excellence was something he did aspire to
卓越性は彼が目指していたものでした
and the ringmaster began to smile again
そして、首謀者は再び微笑み始めました
and he became at once kinder and more tractable
そして彼はすぐに親切になり、扱いやすくなりました
Turning to Pinocchio, he asked:
ピノキオの方を向いて、彼は尋ねた。
"Well, what do you want from me?"
「さて、私に何を望んでいるの?」
"I implore you to pardon poor Harlequin"
「可哀想なハーレクインを許してください」
"For him there can be no pardon"
「彼にとって許しはあり得ない」
"I have spared you, if you remember"

「覚えているなら、私は君を救った」
"so he must be put on the fire"
「だから彼は火にかけられなければならない」
"I am determined that my mutton shall be well roasted"
「私は、私の羊肉をよく焼くことを決意しています」
Pinocchio stood up proudly to the ringmaster
ピノキオは誇らしげに立ち上がった
and he threw away his cap of bread crumb
そして、パンくずの帽子を投げ捨てました
"In that case I know my duty"
「その場合、私は自分の義務を知っています」
"Come on, gendarmes!" he called the soldiers
「来い、憲兵!」彼は兵士たちを呼んだ
"Bind me and throw me amongst the flames"
「私を縛り、炎の中に投げ捨ててください」
"it would not be just for Harlequin to die for me!"
「ハーレクインが私のために死ぬだけじゃない!」
"he has been a true friend to me"
「彼は私にとって真の友人でした」
Pinocchio had spoken in a loud, heroic voice
ピノキオは大声で英雄的な声で話していた
and his heroic actions made all the puppets cry
そして彼の英雄的な行動はすべての人形を泣かせました
Even though the gendarmes were made of wood
憲兵は木でできていたにもかかわらず
they wept like two newly born lambs
彼らは生まれたばかりの二匹の子羊のように泣きました
Fire-eater at first remained as hard and unmoved as ice
火を食べる者は最初、氷のように硬く、動かなかった
but little by little he began to melt and sneeze
しかし、少しずつ溶けてくしゃみをし始めました
he sneezed again four or five times
彼はまた4、5回くしゃみをしました
and he opened his arms affectionately
そして彼は愛情を込めて両手を広げた
"You are a good and brave boy!" he praised Pinocchio

「君は善良で勇敢な少年だ!」彼はピノキオを称賛した
"Come here and give me a kiss"
「こっちに来て、キスして」
Pinocchio ran to the ringmaster at once
ピノキオはすぐに首謀者のところに走った
he climbed up the ringmaster's beard like a squirrel
彼はリスのように首謀者の髭を登った
and he deposited a hearty kiss on the point of his nose
そして、彼は鼻の先に心のこもったキスをしました
"Then the pardon is granted?" asked poor Harlequin
「じゃあ、恩赦は与えられたの?」とかわいそうなハーレクインが尋ねた
in a faint voice that was scarcely audible
ほとんど聞き取れないほどのかすかな声で
"The pardon is granted!" answered Fire-Eater
「恩赦が与えられた!」と火喰いは答えました
he then added, sighing and shaking his head:
そして、ため息をついて首を振りながら付け加えた。
"I must have patience with my puppets!"
「私は自分の人形に忍耐しなければならない!」
"Tonight I shall have to eat the mutton half raw;"
「今夜は羊肉を半分生で食べなきゃだめだよ」
"but another time, woe to him who displeases me!"
「しかし、また別の機会に、私を不快にさせる者には災いが降りかかる!」
At the news of the pardon the puppets all ran to the stage
恩赦の知らせに、人形たちは皆、舞台に駆け寄りました
they lit all the lamps and chandeliers of the show
彼らはショーのすべてのランプとシャンデリアを照らしました
it was as if there was a full-dress performance
まるで正装のパフォーマンスがあるかのようでした
they began to leap and to dance merrily
彼らは跳躍し、陽気に踊り始めました
when dawn had come they were still dancing
夜が明けても、彼らはまだ踊っていました

Pinocchio Receives Five Gold Pieces
ピノキオは5つの金貨を受け取ります

The following day Fire-eater called Pinocchio over
次の日、火を食べる者がピノキオを呼んだ
"What is your father's name?" he asked Pinocchio
「お父さんの名前は?」彼はピノキオに尋ねた
"My father is called Geppetto," Pinocchio answered
「私の父はゼペットと呼ばれています」とピノキオは答えました
"And what trade does he follow?" asked Fire-eater
「それで、彼はどんな取引をしているの?」と火喰いは尋ねた
"He has no trade, he is a beggar"
「彼には商売がない、彼は乞食だ」
"Does he earn much?" asked Fire-eater
「彼はたくさん稼いでいるの?」と火を食べる人は尋ねた
"No, he has never a penny in his pocket"

"いいえ、彼はポケットに一銭も持っていません」
"once he bought me a spelling-book"
「一度、彼は私に綴りの本を買ってくれた」
"but he had to sell the only jacket he had"
「でも、彼は持っていた唯一のジャケットを売らなければならなかった」
"Poor devil! I feel almost sorry for him!"
「かわいそうな悪魔!彼を気の毒に思います!」
"Here are five gold pieces for him"
「これが彼のための5つの金貨です」
"Go at once and take the gold to him"
「さっさと行って、金を彼のところに持って行って」
Pinocchio was overjoyed by the present
ピノキオはプレゼントに大喜びしました
he thanked the ringmaster a thousand times
彼はリングマスターに千回も感謝した
He embraced all the puppets of the company
彼は会社のすべての人形を受け入れました
he even embraced the troop of gendarmes
彼は憲兵隊さえ抱きしめました
and then he set out to return straight home
そして、彼はまっすぐ家に帰ろうとしました
But Pinocchio didn't get very far
しかし、ピノキオはそれほど遠くまでは行きませんでした
on the road he met a Fox with a lame foot
道で彼は足が不自由なキツネに出会いました
and he met a Cat blind in both eyes
そして、彼は両目に猫の盲目を見ました
they were going along helping each other
彼らは互いに助け合いながら進んでいました
they were good companions in their misfortune
彼らは不幸な中でも良き仲間だった
The Fox, who was lame, walked leaning on the Cat
足が不自由なキツネは、猫にもたれかかって歩いていました

and the Cat, who was blind, was guided by the Fox
そして、盲目の猫はキツネに導かれました
the Fox greeted Pinocchio very politely
キツネはピノキオにとても丁寧に挨拶しました
"Good-day, Pinocchio," said the Fox
「こんにちは、ピノキオ」とキツネは言いました
"How do you come to know my name?" asked the puppet
「どうやって私の名前を知ったの?」と人形は尋ねました
"I know your father well," said the fox
「お父さんのことはよく知ってるよ」とキツネは言いました
"Where did you see him?" asked Pinocchio
「彼をどこで見かけたの?」ピノキオが尋ねた
"I saw him yesterday, at the door of his house"
「昨日、彼の家の玄関で彼を見た」
"And what was he doing?" asked Pinocchio
「それで、彼は何をしていたの?」ピノキオは尋ねた
"He was in his shirt and shivering with cold"
「彼はシャツを着て、寒さで震えていました」
"Poor papa! But his suffering is over now"
「かわいそうなパパ!しかし、彼の苦しみはもう終わった」
"in the future he shall shiver no more!"
「将来、彼はもう震えなくなるだろう!」
"Why will he shiver no more?" asked the fox
「どうしてもう震えないの?」とキツネは尋ねました。
"Because I have become a gentleman" replied Pinocchio
「だって、僕は紳士になったんだ」とピノキオは答えた
"A gentleman—you!" said the Fox
「紳士だな、お前だ!」と狐は言った
and he began to laugh rudely and scornfully
そして彼は無礼で軽蔑的に笑い始めました
The Cat also began to laugh with the fox
猫もキツネと一緒に笑い始めました
but she did better at concealing her laughter

しかし、彼女は笑いを隠すのが上手でした
and she combed her whiskers with her forepaws
そして彼女は前足でひげをとかしました
"There is little to laugh at," cried Pinocchio angrily
「笑うことはほとんどない」とピノキオは怒って叫んだ
"I am really sorry to make your mouth water"
「お口の中を水にして本当にごめんなさい」
"if you know anything then you know what these are"
「何か知っているなら、それが何であるかを知っている」
"you can see that they are five pieces of gold"
「金貨5枚であることがわかる」
And he pulled out the money that Fire-eater had given him
そして、彼は火喰いが彼にくれたお金を引き出しました
for a moment the fox and the cat did a strange thing
一瞬、キツネと猫は奇妙なことをしました
the jingling of the money really got their attention
お金のジャラジャラという音が本当に彼らの注意を引きました
the Fox stretched out the paw that seemed crippled
キツネは不自由そうな前足を伸ばした
and the Cat opened wide her two eyes
そして猫は彼女の両目を大きく見開いた
her eyes looked like two green lanterns
彼女の目は2つの緑の提灯のように見えました

it is true that she shut her eyes again
彼女が再び目を閉じたのは事実です
she was so quick that Pinocchio didn't notice
彼女はピノキオが気づかなかったほど素早かった
the Fox was very curious about what he had seen
キツネは自分が見たものにとても興味津々でした
"what are you going to do with all that money?"
「そのお金で何をするつもりですか？」
Pinocchio was all too proud to tell them his plans
ピノキオは誇らしげに自分の計画を彼らに話すことができませんでした
"First of all, I intend to buy a new jacket for my papa"
「まずはパパのために新しいジャケットを買うつもりです」
"the jacket will be made of gold and silver"
「ジャケットはゴールドとシルバーで作られます」
"and the coat will come with diamond buttons"
「そしてコートにはダイヤのボタンが付きます」
"and then I will buy a spelling-book for myself"
「それから、自分用の綴り方の本を買うよ」

"You will buy a spelling book for yourself?"
「自分でスペリングブックを買うの?」
"Yes indeed, for I wish to study in earnest"
「はい、もちろんです。本格的に勉強したいです」
"Look at me!" said the Fox
「俺を見て!」とキツネは言いました
"Through my foolish passion for study I have lost a leg"
「愚かな勉強への情熱により、私は片足を失った」
"Look at me!" said the Cat
「俺を見て!」と猫は言いました
"Through my foolish passion for study I have lost my eyes"
「愚かな勉強への情熱によって、私は目を失ってしまった」
At that moment a white Blackbird began his usual song
その瞬間、白いクロウタドリがいつもの歌を始めました
"Pinocchio, don't listen to the advice of bad companions"
「ピノキオ、悪い仲間の忠告に耳を傾けるな」
"if you listen to their advice you will repent it!"
「彼らの忠告に耳を傾ければ、あなたはそれを悔い改めるでしょう!」
Poor Blackbird! If only he had not spoken!
かわいそうなクロウタドリ!彼が話さなかったら!
The Cat, with a great leap, sprang upon him
猫は大きく跳躍して彼に飛びかかりました
she didn't even give him time to say "Oh!"
彼女は彼に「ああ!」と言う時間さえ与えませんでした。
she ate him in one mouthful, feathers and all
彼女は彼を一口で食べ、羽毛も何もかも食べました
Having eaten him, she cleaned her mouth
彼を食べた後、彼女は口をきれいにしました
and then she shut her eyes again
そして彼女は再び目を閉じました
and she feigned blindness just as before
そして彼女は以前と同じように盲目を装った
"Poor Blackbird!" said Pinocchio to the Cat

「かわいそうなクロウタドリ!」ピノキオは猫に言いました
"why did you treat him so badly?"
「どうしてあんなにひどい扱いをしたの?」
"I did it to give him a lesson"
「彼に教訓を与えるためにやったんだ」
"He will learn not to meddle in other people's affairs"
「彼は他人の事柄に干渉しないことを学ぶでしょう」
by now they had gone almost half-way home
その頃には、彼らは家に帰る道のほぼ半分を過ぎていました
the Fox, halted suddenly, and spoke to the puppet
キツネは突然立ち止まり、人形に話しかけました
"Would you like to double your money?"
「お金を2倍にしますか?」
"In what way could I double my money?"
「どうすればお金を倍増できるの?」
"Would you like to multiply your five miserable coins?"
「あなたの5枚の惨めなコインを掛けますか?」
"I would like that very much! but how?"
「それはとても嬉しいです!でも、どうやって?」
"The way to do it is easy enough"
「やり方は簡単だよ」
"Instead of returning home you must go with us"
「家に帰る代わりに、私たちと一緒に行かなければなりません」
"And where do you wish to take me?"
「それで、私をどこに連れて行きたいの?」
"We will take you to the land of the Owls"
「お前をフクロウの国へ連れて行く」
Pinocchio reflected a moment to think
ピノキオは考える瞬間を振り返った
and then he said resolutely "No, I will not go"
そして、彼は断固として「いいえ、行きません」と言いました

"I am already close to the house"
「もう家の近くにいるよ」
"and I will return home to my papa"
「そして、私はパパの家に帰ります」
"he has been waiting for me in the cold"
「彼は寒い中、僕を待っていた」
"all day yesterday I did not come back to him"
「昨日一日中、彼のところに戻らなかった」
"Who can tell how many times he sighed!"
「彼が何回ため息をついたか、誰にもわからない!」
"I have indeed been a bad son"
「私は本当に悪い息子だった」
"and the talking little cricket was right"
「そして、おしゃべりなクリケットは正しかった」
"Disobedient boys never come to any good"
「反抗的な男の子は決して良いことには来ない」
"what the talking little cricket said is true"
「おしゃべりな小さなクリケットが言ったことは本当だ」
"many misfortunes have happened to me"
「私にはたくさんの不幸が起こりました」
"Even yesterday in fire-eater's house I took a risk"
「昨日も火喰いの家で危険を冒した」
"Oh! it makes me shudder to think of it!"
「ああ!考えるとゾッとします!」
"Well, then," said the Fox, "you've decided to go home?"
「じゃあ、家に帰ることにしたのか?」とキツネは言いました。
"Go, then, and so much the worse for you"
「じゃあ、行け。お前にとってはもっと悪いことだ」
"So much the worse for you!" repeated the Cat
「おまえにとってはもっとひどいことだ!」と猫は繰り返しました
"Think well of it, Pinocchio," they advised him
「よく考えろ、ピノキオ」と彼らは彼に忠告した
"because you are giving a kick to fortune"

「お前が運勢に蹴りを入れているから」
"a kick to fortune!" repeated the Cat
「幸運への蹴りだ!」と猫は繰り返しました
"all it would have taken would have been a day"
「1日で済むだけだった」
"by tomorrow your five coins could have multiplied"
「明日までに、あなたの5枚のコインは倍増していたかもしれません」
"your five coins could have become two thousand"
「お前の5枚の硬貨は2000枚になれたかもしれない」
"Two thousand sovereigns!" repeated the Cat
「二千人のソブリン!」と猫は繰り返しました
"But how is it possible?" asked Pinocchio
「でも、どうしてそんなことが可能なの?」とピノキオは尋ねた
and he remained with his mouth open from astonishment
そして彼は驚きから口を開けたままでした
"I will explain it to you at once," said the Fox
「すぐに説明しよう」とキツネは言いました
"in the land of the Owls there is a sacred field"
「フクロウの国には神聖なフィールドがあります」
"everybody calls it the field of miracles"
「誰もがそれを奇跡のフィールドと呼んでいます」
"In this field you must dig a little hole"
「この畑では、小さな穴を掘らなければなりません」
"and you must put a gold coin into the hole"
「そして、穴に金貨を入れなければなりません」
"then you cover up the hole with a little earth"
「それから、穴を小さな土で覆います」
"you must get water from the fountain nearby"
「近くの噴水から水を汲まなければなりません」
"you must water they hole with two pails of water"
「あなたは彼らが2つの水のバケツで穴を開けることをしなければなりません」
"then sprinkle the hole with two pinches of salt"

"次に、穴に2つのつまみの塩を振りかけます"
"and when night comes you can go quietly to bed"
「そして夜になったら静かに寝ることができる」
"during the night the miracle will happen"
「夜の間に奇跡が起こる」
"the gold pieces you planted will grow and flower"
「あなたが植えた金のかけらは成長して花を咲かせます」
"and what do you think you will find in the morning?"
「それで、朝には何が見つかると思う?」
"You will find a beautiful tree where you planted it"
「植えた場所には美しい木が見つかります」
"they tree will be laden with gold coins"
「彼らの木には金貨が積まれる」
Pinocchio grew more and more bewildered
ピノキオはますます戸惑いながら成長していきました
"let's suppose I bury my five coins in that field"
「そのフィールドに5枚のコインを埋めるとしよう」
"how many coins might I find the following morning?"
「翌朝、何枚のコインが見つかるだろう?」
"That is an exceedingly easy calculation," replied the Fox
「それは非常に簡単な計算だよ」とキツネは答えました
"a calculation you can make with your hands"
「手で計算できる」
"Every coin will give you an increase of five-hundred"
「すべてのコインはあなたに500の増加を与えます」
"multiply five hundred by five and you have your answer"
「500に5を掛ければ、答えが出る」
"you will find two-thousand-five-hundred shining gold pieces"
「あなたは2500の輝く金貨を見つけるでしょう」
"Oh! how delightful!" cried Pinocchio, dancing for joy
「ああ!なんて楽しいんだろう!」とピノキオは叫び、喜びのあまり踊りました
"I will keep two thousand for myself"

「私は自分のために2000を取っておきます」
"and the other five hundred I will give you two"
「そして残りの500ドルを2つあげるよ」
"A present to us?" cried the Fox with indignation
「プレゼントか?」キツネは憤慨して叫びました
and he almost appeared offended at the offer
そして、彼はその申し出にほとんど気分を害しているように見えた
"What are you dreaming of?" asked the Fox
「何を夢見ているの?」と狐は尋ねました。
"What are you dreaming of?" repeated the Cat
「何を夢見ているの?」と猫は繰り返しました
"We do not work to accumulate interest"
「利息を溜めるために働いているのではない」
"we work solely to enrich others"
「私たちは、他者を豊かにするためだけに働きます」
"to enrich others!" repeated the Cat
「他人を豊かにするために!」と猫は繰り返しました
"What good people!" thought Pinocchio to himself
「なんて良い人たちなんだ!」とピノキオは心の中で思いました
and he forgot all about his papa and the new jacket
そして、彼はパパと新しいジャケットのことをすっかり忘れてしまいました
and he forgot about the spelling-book
そして彼は綴り方の本を忘れてしまいました
and he forgot all of his good resolutions
そして、彼は自分の良い決意をすべて忘れてしまった
"Let us be off at once" he suggested
「すぐに出発しましょう」と彼は提案しました
"I will go with you two to the field of Owls"
「お前たち二人と一緒にフクロウの畑へ行くよ」

The Inn of the Red Craw-Fish
レッドザリガニの宿

They walked, and walked, and walked
彼らは歩いて、歩いて、歩いて
all tired out, they finally arrived at an inn
疲れ果てて、ようやく宿屋にたどり着きました
The Inn of The Red Craw-Fish
レッドザリガニの宿
"Let us stop here a little," said the Fox
「ここで少しやめましょう」とキツネは言いました
"we should have something to eat," he added
「何か食べるものがあるべきだ」と彼は付け加えた
"we need to rest ourselves for an hour or two"
「1時間か2時間休む必要がある」
"and then we will start again at midnight"
「そして、真夜中に再び出発します」
"we'll arrive at the Field of Miracles in the morning"
「朝、奇跡のフィールドに到着します」
Pinocchio was also tired from all the walking
ピノキオも歩くたびに疲れていました
so he was easily convinced to go into the inn
だから彼は簡単に宿に入るように説得されました
all three of them sat down at a table
3人ともテーブルに座った
but none of them really had any appetite
しかし、彼らの誰も本当に食欲がありませんでした

The Cat was suffering from indigestion
猫は消化不良に苦しんでいました
and she was feeling seriously indisposed
そして彼女は真剣に落ち着かなかった
she could only eat thirty-five fish with tomato sauce
彼女はトマトソースで35匹の魚しか食べられませんでした
and she had just four portions of noodles with Parmesan
そして、彼女はパルメザンチーズの麺を4人前しか持っていませんでした
but she thought the noodles weres not seasoned enough
しかし、彼女は麺が十分に味付けされていないと思った
so she asked three times for the butter and grated cheese!
それで彼女はバターと粉チーズを3回頼みました！
The Fox could also have gone without eating
キツネは食べずに行くこともできました
but his doctor had ordered him a strict diet
しかし、彼の医者は彼に厳格な食事療法を命じました

so he was forced to content himself simply with a hare
だから彼はただウサギで満足することを余儀なくされた
the hare was dressed with a sweet and sour sauce
うさぎは甘酸っぱいソースをまとっていました
it was garnished lightly with fat chickens
太った鶏が軽く添えられていました
then he ordered a dish of partridges and rabbits
それから彼はヤマウズラとウサギの料理を注文しました
and he also ate some frogs, lizards and other delicacies
そして、彼はまた、いくつかのカエル、トカゲ、その他の珍味を食べました
he really could not eat anything else
彼は本当に他に何も食べることができませんでした
He cared very little for food, he said
彼は食べ物にはほとんど関心がなかった、と彼は言った
and he said he struggled to put it to his lips
そして、彼はそれを唇に当てるのに苦労したと言った
The one who ate the least was Pinocchio
一番食べなかったのはピノキオでした
He asked for some walnuts and a hunch of bread
彼はクルミとパンを頼んだ
and he left everything on his plate
そして、彼はすべてを皿に残しました
The poor boy's thoughts were not with the food
かわいそうな少年の考えは食べ物にはありませんでした
he continually fixed his thoughts on the Field of Miracles
彼は絶えず自分の考えを奇跡の分野に固定しました
When they had supped, the Fox spoke to the host
彼らが食事を終えると、キツネはホストに話しかけました
"Give us two good rooms, dear inn-keeper"
「いい部屋を二つください、親愛なる宿屋の主人様」
"please provide us one room for Mr. Pinocchio"
「ピノキオさんのために一部屋提供してください」
"and I will share the other room with my companion"
「そして、もう一つは仲間とシェアします」

"We will snatch a little sleep before we leave"
「出発する前に少し寝ます」
"Remember, however, that we wish to leave at midnight"
「ただし、深夜に出発したいことを忘れないでください」
"so please call us, to continue our journey"
「だから、私たちの旅を続けるために、私たちに電話してください」
"Yes, gentlemen," answered the host
「はい、紳士諸君」と司会者は答えた
and he winked at the Fox and the Cat
そして彼はキツネと猫にウィンクしました
it was as if he said "I know what you are up to"
それはまるで彼が「君が何をしようとしているのか知っている」と言ったかのようでした
the wink seemed to say, "we understand one another!"
ウィンクは「私たちはお互いを理解している!」と言っているように見えました。
Pinocchio was very tired from the day
ピノキオはその日からとても疲れていました
he fell asleep as soon as he got into his bed
彼はベッドに入るとすぐに眠りに落ちました
and as soon as he started sleeping he started to dream
そして、眠り始めるとすぐに夢を見始めました
he dreamed that he was in the middle of a field
彼は自分が野原の真ん中にいる夢を見ました
the field was full of shrubs as far as the eye could see
見渡す限り、畑は低木でいっぱいでした
the shrubs were covered with clusters of gold coins
低木は金貨の塊で覆われていました
the gold coins swung in the wind and rattled
金貨が風に揺れてガタガタと音を立てた
and they made a sound like, "tzinn, tzinn, tzinn"
そして、彼らは「ツィン、ツィン、ツィン」のような音を出した
they sounded as if they were speaking to Pinocchio

まるでピノキオに話しかけているように聞こえた
"Let who whoever wants to come and take us"
「誰でも来て、私たちを連れて行ってみてください」
Pinocchio was just about to stretch out his hand
ピノキオはちょうど手を伸ばそうとしていた
he was going to pick handfuls of those beautiful gold pieces
彼はその美しい金貨を一握り選ぶつもりでした
and he almost was able to put them in his pocket
そして、彼はほとんどそれらをポケットに入れることができました
but he was suddenly awakened by three knocks on the door
しかし、彼は突然、ドアを3回ノックして目が覚めました
It was the host who had come to wake him up
彼を起こすために来たのはホストでした
"I have come to let you know it's midnight"
「真夜中であることをお知らせしに来ました」
"Are my companions ready?" asked the puppet
「仲間たちは準備ができているか?」と人形は尋ねました
"Ready! Why, they left two hours ago"
「準備ができました!なぜ、彼らは2時間前に出発したのですか」
"Why were they in such a hurry?"
「なんでそんなに急いでいたの?」
"Because the Cat had received a message"
「猫が伝言を受け取っていたから」
"she got news that her eldest kitten was ill"
「彼女は一番上の子猫が病気になったという知らせを受けました」
"Did they pay for the supper?"
「彼らは夕食の代金を払ったの?」
"What are you thinking of?"
「何を考えてるの?」
"They are too well educated to dream of insulting you"

「彼らはあなたを侮辱する夢を見るにはあまりにも教育を受けすぎています」
"a gentleman like you would not let his friends pay"
「君みたいな紳士なら、友達に払わせないだろう」
"What a pity!" thought Pinocchio
「なんて残念なことだろう!」とピノキオは思いました
"such an insult would have given me much pleasure!"
「そんな侮辱は私に大きな喜びを与えたでしょう!」
"And where did my friends say they would wait for me?"
「そして、私の友人たちはどこで私を待つと言ったの?」
"At the Field of Miracles, tomorrow morning at daybreak"
「奇跡のフィールドで、明日の朝の夜明け」
Pinocchio paid a coin for the supper of his companions
ピノキオは仲間の夕食にコインを支払いました
and then he left for the field of Miracles
そして、彼は奇跡の分野へと旅立ちました
Outside the inn it was almost pitch black
宿の外はほとんど真っ暗でした
Pinocchio could only make progress by groping his way
ピノキオは手探りで進むしかありませんでした
it was impossible to see his hand's in front of him
彼の手が彼の前にあるのを見ることは不可能でした
Some night-birds flew across the road
夜の鳥が何羽か道を飛んでいった
they brushed Pinocchio's nose with their wings
彼らは翼でピノキオの鼻を撫でました
it caused him a terrible fright
それは彼にひどい恐怖を引き起こしました
springing back, he shouted: "who goes there?"
彼は跳ね返って叫んだ、「誰がそこに行くの?」
and the echo in the hills repeated in the distance
そして遠くで繰り返される丘の反響
"Who goes there?" - "Who goes there?" - "Who goes there?"
「誰がそこに行くの?」- 「誰が行くの?」-

「誰がそこに行くの?」
on the trunk of the tree he saw a little light
彼は木の幹に小さな光を見ました
it was a little insect he saw shining dimly
彼がぼんやりと光っているのを見たのは小さな虫だった
like a night-light in a lamp of transparent china
透明な陶磁器のランプの常夜灯のように
"Who are you?" asked Pinocchio
「あなたは誰ですか?」ピノキオは尋ねました
the insect answered in a low voice;
昆虫は低い声で答えた。
"I am the ghost of the talking little cricket"
「私はしゃべる小さなコオロギの幽霊です」
the voice was fainter than can be described
その声は言葉では言い表せないほど弱かった
the voice seemed to come from the other world
その声はあの世から来たようだった
"What do you want with me?" said the puppet
「私に何が欲しいの?」と人形は言いました
"I want to give you some advice"
「アドバイスをしたい」
"Go back and take the four coins that you have left"
「戻って、残った4枚のコインを持って行って」
"take your coins to your poor father"
「貧しいお父さんに小銭を持って行って」
"he is weeping and in despair at home"
「彼は家で泣き、絶望している」
"because you have not returned to him"
「あなたが彼の元に戻っていないから」
but Pinocchio had already thought of this
しかし、ピノキオはすでにこのことを考えていました
"By tomorrow my papa will be a gentleman"
「明日までには、パパは紳士になっているよ」
"these four coins will become two thousand"
「この4枚の硬貨が二千枚になる」
"Don't trust those who promise to make you rich in a day"

「一日で金持ちになると約束する人を信用するな」
"Usually they are either mad or rogues!"
「たいてい、彼らは狂っているか、ならず者だ!」
"Give ear to me, and go back, my boy"
「俺に耳を傾けて、戻ってこい、我が息子よ」
"On the contrary, I am determined to go on"
「それどころか、私は続けることを決意しています」
"The hour is late!" said the cricket
「時間が遅い!」とコオロギは言いました
"I am determined to go on"
「私は続ける決意です」
"The night is dark!" said the cricket
「夜は暗い!」とコオロギは言いました
"I am determined to go on"
「私は続ける決意です」
"The road is dangerous!" said the cricket
「道が危ない!」とクリケットは言った
"I am determined to go on"
「私は続ける決意です」
"boys are bent on following their wishes"
「男の子は自分の願いに従うことに固執しています」
"but remember, sooner or later they repent it"
「しかし、遅かれ早かれ彼らはそれを悔い改めることを忘れないでください」
"Always the same stories. Good-night, little cricket"
「いつも同じ話です。おやすみなさい、小さなコオロギ」
The Cricket wished Pinocchio a good night too
クリケットもピノキオに良い夜を願った
"may Heaven preserve you from dangers and assassins"
「天があなたを危険や暗殺者から守ってくださいますように」
then the talking little cricket vanished suddenly
それから、しゃべる小さなコオロギは突然消えました
like a light that has been blown out
吹き飛ばされた光のように

and the road became darker than ever
そして道はこれまで以上に暗くなりました

Pinocchio Falls into the Hands of the Assassins
ピノキオは暗殺者の手に落ちる

Pinocchio resumed his journey and spoke to himself
ピノキオは旅を再開し、独り言を言いました

"how unfortunate we poor boys are"
「私たち可哀想な少年たちは、なんと不幸なことでしょう」

"Everybody scolds us and gives us good advice"
「みんなに叱られて、いいアドバイスをくれる」

"but I don't choose to listen to that tiresome little cricket"
「でも、あのうんざりするような小さなコオロギを聴くことは選ばない」

"who knows how many misfortunes are to happen to me!"
「私にどれだけの不幸が起こるか、誰にもわからない!」

"I haven't even met any assassins yet!"
「まだ暗殺者にも出会ったことない!」

"That is, however, of little consequence"
「しかし、それはほとんど重要ではありません」

"for I don't believe in assassins"
「私は暗殺者を信じていないから」

"I have never believed in assassins"
「暗殺者なんて信じたことない」

"I think that assassins have been invented purposely"
「暗殺者は意図的に発明されたのだと思います」

"papas use them to frighten little boys"
「パパは小さな男の子を怖がらせるためにそれらを使う」

"and then little boys are scared of going out at night"
「そして、小さな男の子は夜に外出するのが怖いです」

"Anyway, let's suppose I was to come across assassins"
「とにかく、私が暗殺者に出くわすことになったとしよう」
"do you imagine they would frighten me?"
「彼らが私を怖がらせると思う?」
"they would not frighten me in the least"
「彼らは少しも私を怖がらせないだろう」
"I will go to meet them and call to them"
「私は彼らに会いに行き、彼らを呼びます」
'Gentlemen assassins, what do you want with me?'
「紳士の暗殺者たちよ、私をどうしたいの?」
'Remember that with me there is no joking'
「私と一緒にいると冗談は言わないことを忘れないでください」
'Therefore, go about your business and be quiet!'
「だから、静かにして、自分の仕事に取り掛かってください!」
"At this speech they would run away like the wind"
「この演説で、彼らは風のように逃げるだろう」
"it could be that they are badly educated assassins"
「彼らは教育が不十分な暗殺者かもしれない」
"then the assassins might not run away"
「それなら、暗殺者たちは逃げないかもしれない」
"but even that isn't a great problem"
「でも、それも大した問題じゃない」
"then I would just run away myself"
「それなら、自分で逃げるだけだ」
"and that would be the end of that"
「そして、それで終わりです」
But Pinocchio had no time to finish his reasoning
しかし、ピノキオには彼の推論を終える時間がありませんでした
he thought that he heard a slight rustle of leaves
彼は葉のわずかなざわめきを聞いたと思った
He turned to look where the noise had come from
彼は振り返って、音がどこから来たのかを見ました

and he saw in the gloom two evil-looking black figures
そして彼は暗闇の中で、邪悪そうな黒い人影を二人見た
they were completely enveloped in charcoal sacks
彼らは完全に炭の袋に包まれていました
They were running after him on their tiptoes
彼らはつま先立ちで彼を追いかけていました
and they were making great leaps like two phantoms
そして、彼らは二つの幻影のように大きな飛躍を遂げていました
"Here they are in reality!" he said to himself
「これが現実だ!」彼は独り言を言いました
he didn't have anywhere to hide his gold pieces
彼は金貨を隠す場所がありませんでした
so he put them in his mouth, under his tongue
それで彼はそれらを口の中、舌の下に入れました
Then he turned his attention to escaping
それから彼は逃げることに注意を向けました
But he did not manage to get very far
しかし、彼はあまり遠くまで行くことができませんでした
he felt himself seized by the arm
彼は自分が腕をつかまれているのを感じた

and he heard two horrid voices threatening him
そして、彼を脅かす二つの恐ろしい声を聞いた
"Your money or your life!" they threatened
「お前の金か、お前の命か!」と彼らは脅迫した
Pinocchio was not able to answer in words
ピノキオは言葉で答えることができませんでした
because he had put his money in his mouth
彼は自分のお金を口に入れたからです
so he made a thousand low bows
それで彼は低い弓を千本立てました
and he offered a thousand pantomimes
そして彼は千のパントマイムを提供しました
He tried to make the two figures understand
彼は二人の人物に理解させようとした
he was just a poor puppet without any money
彼はお金のないただの貧しい人形でした
he had not as much as a nickel in his pocket
ポケットにはニッケル一個も入っていなかった
but the two robbers were not convinced
しかし、二人の強盗は納得しませんでした
"Less nonsense and out with the money!"
「ナンセンスを減らして、お金を持って出かける!」
And the puppet made a gesture with his hands
そして人形は手でジェスチャーをしました
he pretended to turn his pockets inside out
彼はポケットを裏返しにするふりをした
Of course Pinocchio didn't have any pockets
もちろんピノキオにはポケットがありませんでした
but he was trying to signify, "I have no money"
しかし、彼は「私にはお金がない」と示そうとしていました
slowly the robbers were losing their patience
強盗たちは徐々に我慢できなくなっていきました
"Deliver up your money or you are dead," said the taller one
「お金を返さなければ、お前は死ぬ」と背の高い方が言った

"Dead!" repeated the smaller one
「死んだ!」小さい方が繰り返しました
"And then we will also kill your father!"
「そして、お前の父さんも殺すぞ!」
"Also your father!" repeated the smaller one again
「お父さんも!」小さい方がまた繰り返した
"No, no, no, not my poor papa!" cried Pinocchio in despair
「いやいや、かわいそうなパパじゃない!」ピノキオは絶望して叫んだ
and as he said it the coins clinked in his mouth
そして彼がそう言ったとき、硬貨が彼の口の中でカチカチと音を立てた
"Ah! you rascal!" realized the robbers
「あぁ!「この悪党め!」強盗たちは悟った
"you have hidden your money under your tongue!"
「お前は舌の下に金を隠した!」
"Spit it out at once!" he ordered him
「すぐに吐き出せ!」と彼は命じた
"spit it out," repeated the smaller one
「吐き出して」と小さい方が繰り返した
Pinocchio was obstinate to their commands
ピノキオは彼らの命令に頑固でした
"Ah! you pretend to be deaf, do you?"
「あぁ!耳が聞こえないふりをしているのね?」
"leave it to us to find a means"
「手段を見つけるのは私たちに任せてください」
"we will find a way to make you give up your money"
「私たちはあなたにお金をあきらめさせる方法を見つけます」
"We will find a way," repeated the smaller one
「道を見つけるよ」と小さい方が繰り返した
And one of them seized the puppet by his nose
そして、そのうちの一人が人形の鼻をつかみました
and the other took him by the chin
そしてもう一人は彼の顎をつかんだ

and they began to pull brutally
そして、彼らは残酷に引っ張り始めました
one pulled up and the other pulled down
1つは引き上げられ、もう1つは引き下げられました
they tried to force him to open his mouth
彼らは彼に口を開けさせようとした
But it was all to no purpose
しかし、それはすべて無駄でした
Pinocchio's mouth seemed to be nailed together
ピノキオの口は釘付けにされているようだった
Then the shorter assassin drew out an ugly knife
それから背の低い暗殺者は醜いナイフを抜いた
and he tried to put it between his lips
そして彼はそれを唇の間に入れようとしました
But Pinocchio, as quick as lightning, caught his hand
しかし、ピノキオは稲妻のように素早く彼の手をつかんだ
and he bit him with his teeth
そして彼は歯で彼を噛んだ
and with one bite he bit the hand clean off
そして一口で彼は手をきれいに噛みちぎりました
but it wasn't a hand that he spat out
しかし、彼が吐き出したのは手ではなかった
it was hairier than a hand, and had claws
それは手よりも毛が生えていて、爪がついていました
imagine Pinocchio's astonishment when saw a cat's paw
猫の足を見たときのピノキオの驚きを想像してみてください
or at least that's what he thought he saw
少なくとも、彼はそれを見たと思っていた
Pinocchio was encouraged by this first victory
ピノキオはこの初勝利に勇気づけられました
now he used his fingernails to break free
今、彼は爪を使って自由になりました
he succeeded in liberating himself from his assailants
彼は攻撃者から自分自身を解放することに成功しました

he jumped over the hedge by the roadside
彼は道端の生け垣を飛び越えた
and began to run across the fields
そして、フィールドを横切って走り始めました
The assassins ran after him like two dogs chasing a hare
暗殺者たちは、ウサギを追いかける二匹の犬のように彼を追いかけました
and the one who had lost a paw ran on one leg
そして、片足を失った人は片足で走りました
and no one ever knew how he managed it
そして、彼がそれをどのように管理したかは誰も知りませんでした
After a race of some miles Pinocchio could run no more
何マイルかのレースの後、ピノキオはもう走ることができなくなりました
he thought his situation was lost
彼は自分の状況が失われたと思った
he climbed the trunk of a very high pine tree
彼は非常に高い松の木の幹に登った
and he seated himself in the topmost branches
そして、一番上の枝に座った
The assassins attempted to climb after him
暗殺者たちは彼の後を追おうとした
when they reached half-way up the tree they slid down again
木の半分まで上がったとき、彼らは再び滑り降りました
and they arrived on the ground with their skin grazed
そして、彼らは皮膚をかすめた状態で地面に到着しました
But they didn't give up so easily
しかし、彼らはそう簡単には諦めませんでした
they piled up some dry wood beneath the pine
彼らは松の下に乾いた木を積み上げました
and then they set fire to the wood
そして、彼らは薪に火をつけた
very quickly the pine began to burn higher

あっという間に松は燃え上がり始めました
like a candle blown by the wind
風に吹かれたろうそくのように
Pinocchio saw the flames rising higher and higher
ピノキオは炎がどんどん高くなっていくのを見た
he did not wish to end his life like a roasted pigeon
彼は鳩の丸焼きのように自分の人生を終わらせたくなかった
so he made a stupendous leap from the top of the tree
それで彼は木のてっぺんから驚くような跳躍をしました
and he ran across the fields and vineyards
そして、彼は畑やぶどう畑を横切って走りました
The assassins followed him again
暗殺者たちは再び彼を追いかけた
and they kept behind him without giving up
そして、彼らは諦めずに彼の後ろにいた
The day began to break and they were still pursuing him
夜が明け始め、彼らはまだ彼を追いかけていた
Suddenly Pinocchio found his way barred by a ditch
突然、ピノキオは溝に阻まれて道を見つけました
it was full of stagnant water the colour of coffee
それはコーヒーの色をした淀んだ水でいっぱいでした
What was our Pinocchio to do now?
私たちのピノキオは今何をすべきだったのでしょうか?
"One! two! three!" cried the puppet
「1つ!2!「三人だ!」と人形は叫びました。
making a rush, he sprang to the other side
急いで、彼は反対側に跳びました
The assassins also tried to jump over the ditch
暗殺者たちも溝を飛び越えようとした
but they had not measured the distance
しかし、彼らは距離を測定していませんでした
splish splash! they fell into the middle of the ditch
スプラッシュ!彼らは溝の真ん中に落ちました

Pinocchio heard the plunge and the splashing
ピノキオは急降下と水しぶきを聞いた
"A fine bath to you, gentleman assassins"
「君に上質な風呂を」紳士の暗殺者たちよ
And he felt convinced that they were drowned
そして彼は彼らが溺れたと確信した
but it's good that Pinocchio did look behind him
しかし、ピノキオが彼の後ろを見たのは良いことです
because his two assassins had not drowned
彼の二人の暗殺者が溺れていなかったからだ
the two assassins had got out the water again
二人の暗殺者は再び水から出てきた
and they were both still running after him
そして、彼らはまだ彼を追いかけていました
they were still enveloped in their sacks
彼らはまだ袋に包まれていました
and the water was dripping from them
そして、水が滴り落ちていました
as if they had been two hollow baskets
まるで2つの中空のバスケットだったかのように

The Assassins Hang Pinocchio to the Big Oak Tree
暗殺者はピノキオを大きな樫の木に吊るす

At this sight, the puppet's courage failed him
この光景に、人形の勇気は彼を失望させました
he was on the point of throwing himself on the ground
彼は地面に身を投げ出す寸前だった
and he wanted to give himself over for lost
そして彼は失われた自分を捧げたかったのです
he turned his eyes in every direction
彼はあらゆる方向に目を向けた
he saw a small house as white as snow
彼は雪のように白い小さな家を見ました
"If only I had breath to reach that house"
「あの家にたどり着く息さえあれば」
"perhaps then I might be saved"
「そうすれば、僕は救われるかもしれない」
without delaying an instant he recommenced running
一瞬たりとも遅れることなく、彼は走りを再開した
poor little Pinocchio was running for his life
かわいそうな小さなピノキオは彼の命のために走っていました
he ran through the wood with the assassins after him
彼は暗殺者たちを追いかけながら森の中を走り抜けた
there was a desperate race of nearly two hours
2時間近い必死のレースが繰り広げられました
and finally he arrived quite breathless at the door
そしてついに彼は息を切らしてドアに到着しました
he desperately knocked on the door of the house
彼は必死に家のドアをノックしました
but no one answered Pinocchio's knock
しかし、誰もピノキオのノックに答えませんでした
He knocked at the door again with great violence
彼は再び激しい暴力でドアをノックした
because he heard the sound of steps approaching him

彼は彼に近づいてくる足音を聞いたからです
and he heard the the heavy panting of his persecutors
そして、迫害者たちの激しい息遣いを聞いた
there was the same silence as before
以前と同じ静寂が流れていた
he saw that knocking was useless
彼はノックしても無駄だとわかった
so he began in desperation to kick and pommel the door
だから彼は必死になってドアを蹴ったり、柄掌をあけたりし始めた
The window next to the door then opened
ドアの隣の窓が開いた
and a beautiful Child appeared at the window
そして窓のところに美しい子供が現れました
the beautiful child had blue hair
美しい子供は青い髪をしていました
and her face was as white as a waxen image
そして彼女の顔は蝋人形のように白かった
her eyes were closed as if she was asleep
彼女の目は眠っているかのように閉じられていました
and her hands were crossed on her breast
そして彼女の手は彼女の胸の上で交差していました
Without moving her lips in the least, she spoke
彼女は少しも唇を動かさずに話した
"In this house there is no one, they are all dead"
「この家には誰もいない、みんな死んでいる」
and her voice seemed to come from the other world
そして彼女の声はあの世から来たようだった
but Pinocchio shouted and cried and implored
しかし、ピノキオは叫び、泣き、懇願しました
"Then at least open the door for me"
「じゃあ、せめて私のためにドアを開けて」
"I am also dead," said the waxen image
「私も死んだ」と蝋人形は言った
"Then what are you doing there at the window?"
「じゃあ、窓辺で何をしているの?」

"I am waiting to be taken away"
「連れ去られるのを待っています」
Having said this she immediately disappeared
そう言って、彼女はすぐに姿を消しました
and the window was closed again without the slightest noise
そして、窓は少しの音もなく再び閉められました
"Oh! beautiful Child with blue hair," cried Pinocchio"
「ああ!青い髪の美しい子供」とピノキオは叫んだ。
"open the door, for pity's sake!"
「ドアを開けて、哀れみのために!」
"Have compassion on a poor boy pursued..."
「哀れな少年に同情を抱く...」
But he could not finish the sentence
しかし、彼は文章を終えることができなかった
because he felt himself seized by the collar
なぜなら、彼は自分が襟をつかまれているのを感じたからだ
the same two horrible voices said to him threateningly:
同じ二つの恐ろしい声が彼に脅迫的に言った。
"You shall not escape from us again!"
「お前はもう二度と我々から逃げるな!」
"You shall not escape," panted the little assassin
「逃げるな」と小さな暗殺者は息を切らした
The puppet saw death was staring him in the face
人形は死が彼の顔を見つめているのを見ました
he was taken with a violent fit of trembling
彼は激しく震えながら連れて行かれた
the joints of his wooden legs began to creak
彼の木製の脚の関節がきしみ始めました
and the coins hidden under his tongue began to clink
そして、彼の舌の下に隠された硬貨がカチカチと音を立て始めました
"will you open your mouth—yes or no?" demanded the assassins
「口を開けますか——はい、それともいいえですか?」と暗殺者たちは尋ねた

"Ah! no answer? Leave it to us"
「あぁ!答えがありませんか?お任せください」
"this time we will force you to open it!"
「今度は無理やり開けさせてやる!」
"we will force you," repeated the second assassin
「お前たちを強制する」と二人目の暗殺者が繰り返した
And they drew out two long, horrid knives
そして、彼らは長くて恐ろしいナイフを二本取り出しました
and the knifes were as sharp as razors
そしてナイフはカミソリのように鋭かった
they attempted to stab him twice
彼らは彼を二度刺そうと試みた
but the puppet was lucky in one regard
しかし、人形はある点で幸運でした
he had been made from very hard wood
彼は非常に硬い木で作られていました
the knives broke into a thousand pieces
ナイフは千個に砕け散った
and the assassins were left with just the handles
そして、暗殺者にはハンドルだけが残されました
for a moment they could only stare at each other
一瞬、彼らはただ見つめ合うことしかできませんでした
"I see what we must do," said one of them
「やるべきことはわかる」と彼らの一人が言った
"He must be hung! Let us hang him!"
「彼は絞首刑に違いない!彼を絞首刑にしよう!」
"Let us hang him!" repeated the other
「彼を絞首刑にしよう!」もう一人が繰り返した
Without loss of time they tied his arms behind him
時間を無駄にすることなく、彼らは彼の腕を後ろで縛った
and they passed a running noose round his throat
そして、彼らは彼の喉の周りに走る縄を通しました
and they hung him to the branch of the Big Oak
そして彼らは彼をビッグオークの枝に吊るしました

They then sat down on the grass watching Pinocchio
その後、彼らは芝生に座ってピノキオを見ました
and they waited for his struggle to end
そして、彼らは彼の闘争が終わるのを待った
but three hours had already passed
しかし、すでに3時間が経過していました
the puppet's eyes were still open
人形の目はまだ開いていました
his mouth was closed just as before
彼の口は以前と同じように閉じられていました
and he was kicking more than ever
そして、彼はこれまで以上に蹴っていました
they had finally lost their patience with him
彼らはついに彼に対する忍耐力を失った
they turned to Pinocchio and spoke in a bantering tone
彼らはピノキオの方を向いて、冗談めかした口調で話しました
"Good-bye Pinocchio, see you again tomorrow"
「さようならピノキオ、また明日ね」
"hopefully you'll be kind enough to be dead"
「うまくいけば、君は死んでもいいほど親切になるだろう」
"and hopefully you will have your mouth wide open"
「そして、うまくいけば、あなたは口を大きく開けているでしょう」
And they walked off in a different direction
そして、彼らは別の方向に歩き去りました
In the meantime a northerly wind began to blow and roar
そうこうしているうちに、北風が吹き始め、轟音を立て始めた
and the wind beat the poor puppet from side to side
そして風が哀れな人形を左右に打ち負かしました

the wind made him swing about violently
風が彼を激しく揺らした
like the clatter of a bell ringing for a wedding
結婚式のために鳴る鐘の音のように
And the swinging gave him atrocious spasms
そして、その揺れは彼にひどい痙攣を引き起こした
and the noose became tighter and tighter around his throat
そして、縄は彼の喉の周りでますますきつくなりました
and finally it took away his breath
そしてついにそれは彼の息を奪った
Little by little his eyes began to grow dim
少しずつ彼の目が暗くなり始めた
he felt that death was near
彼は死が近いと感じた

but Pinocchio never gave up hope
しかし、ピノキオは決して希望を捨てませんでした
"perhaps some charitable person will come to my assistance"
「もしかしたら、慈善団体の人が助けに来るかもしれない」
But he waited and waited and waited
しかし、彼は待って待って待っていた
and in the end no one came, absolutely no one
そして結局、誰も来ませんでした、絶対に誰も来ませんでした
then he remembered his poor father
その時、彼は哀れな父のことを思い出した
thinking he was dying, he stammered out
自分が死ぬと思った彼は、どもりながら声を出した
"Oh, papa! papa! if only you were here!"
「ああ、パパ!パパ!あなたがここにいてくれたらいいのに!」
His breath failed him and he could say no more
息が詰まり、それ以上何も言えなくなった
He shut his eyes and opened his mouth
彼は目を閉じ、口を開いた
and he stretched out his arms and legs
そして彼は手足を伸ばしました
he gave one final long shudder
彼は最後にもう一度長い震えをした
and then he hung stiff and insensible
そして、彼は硬直して無感覚にぶら下がった

The Beautiful Child Rescues the Puppet
美しい子供が人形を救出する

poor Pinocchio was still suspended from the Big Oak tree
かわいそうなピノキオはまだビッグオークの木から吊るされていました

but apparently Pinocchio was more dead than alive
しかし、どうやらピノキオは生きているよりも死んでいたようです

the beautiful Child with blue hair came to the window again
青い髪の美しい子供が再び窓にやって来ました

she saw the unhappy puppet hanging by his throat
彼女は不幸な人形が彼の喉元にぶら下がっているのを見た

she saw him dancing up and down in the gusts of the wind
彼女は彼が突風の中で上下に踊っているのを見た

and she was moved by compassion for him
そして彼女は彼への同情に動かされました

the beautiful child struck her hands together
美しい子供は彼女の手を合わせました

and she gave three little claps
そして彼女は小さな拍手を三回しました

there came a sound of wings flying rapidly
翼が速く飛ぶ音がしました

a large Falcon flew on to the window-sill
大きなファルコンが窓枠に飛んできた

"What are your orders, gracious Fairy?" he asked
「お前の命令は何か、慈悲深い妖精?」彼は尋ねた
and he inclined his beak in sign of reverence
そして彼は敬意の印としてくちばしを傾けた
"Do you see that puppet dangling from the Big Oak tree?"
「あの人形がビッグオークの木からぶら下がっているのが見えるか?」
"I see him," confirmed the falcon
「見えるよ」と鷹は確認しました
"Fly over to him at once," she ordered him
「すぐに彼のところに飛んで行きなさい」と彼女は彼に命じた
"use your strong beak to break the knot"
「強いくちばしを使って結び目を壊す」
"lay him gently on the grass at the foot of the tree"
「彼を木の根元の草の上にそっと寝かせて」
The Falcon flew away to carry out his orders
ファルコン号は彼の命令を実行するために飛び去った

and after two minutes he returned to the child
そして2分後、彼は子供のところに戻りました
"I have done as you commanded"
「私はあなたの命じられたとおりにしました」
"And how did you find him?"
「それで、どうやって彼を見つけたの?」
"when I first saw him he appeared dead"
「初めて彼を見たとき、彼は死んでいるように見えた」
"but he couldn't really have been entirely dead"
「しかし、彼は本当に完全に死んでいたわけではなかった」
"I loosened the noose around his throat"
「彼の喉の周りの縄を緩めた」
"and then he gave soft a sigh"
「そして、彼は静かにため息をついた」
"he muttered to me in a faint voice"
「彼はかすかな声で私につぶやいた」
"'Now I feel better!' he said"
「『今、気分が良くなったよ!』と彼は言った」
The Fairy then struck her hands together twice
それから妖精は彼女の手を二度叩きました
as soon as she did this a magnificent Poodle appeared
彼女がこれを行うとすぐに、立派なプードルが現れました
the poodle walked upright on his hind legs
プードルは後ろ足で直立して歩きました
it was exactly as if he had been a man
それはまるで彼が男だったかのようでした
He was in the full-dress livery of a coachman
彼は御者のフルドレスの服を着ていました
On his head he had a three-cornered cap braided with gold
彼の頭には、金で編まれた三角の帽子をかぶっていました
his curly white wig came down on to his shoulders
彼の巻き毛の白いかつらが肩まで落ちていました
he had a chocolate-collared waistcoat with diamond buttons

彼はダイヤモンドのボタンが付いたチョコレートカラーのチョッキを着ていました

and he had two large pockets to contain bones
そして、骨を入れるための大きなポケットが2つありました

the bones that his mistress gave him at dinner
彼の愛人が夕食時に彼にくれた骨

he also had a pair of short crimson velvet breeches
彼はまた、短い真紅のベルベットのズボンを持っていました

and he wore some silk stockings
そして彼はいくつかの絹のストッキングを履いていました

and he wore smart Italian leather shoes
そして彼はスマートなイタリアンレザーシューズを履いていました

hanging behind him was a species of umbrella case
彼の後ろにぶら下がっていたのは、傘ケースの一種でした

the umbrella case was made of blue satin
アンブレラケースはブルーサテン製

he put his tail into it when the weather was rainy
彼は天気が雨のときに尻尾を入れました

"Be quick, Medoro, like a good dog!"
「早くしろ、メドロ。いい犬みたいに!」

and the fairy gave her poodle the commands
そして妖精は彼女のプードルに命令を与えました

"get the most beautiful carriage harnessed"
「最も美しい馬車をハーネスでつなぐ」

"and have the carriage waiting in my coach-house"
「そして、馬車は私の馬車小屋で待っています」

"and go along the road to the forest"
「そして道を進んで森へ」

"When you come to the Big Oak tree you will find a poor puppet"
「ビッグオークの木に来ると、かわいそうな人形が見つ

"he will be stretched on the grass half dead"
「彼は草の上に伸びて半分死んでしまいます」
"you will have to pick him up gently"
「彼を優しく抱き上げてあげてください」
"lay him flat on the cushions of the carriage"
「彼を馬車のクッションに平らに寝かせて」
"when you have done this bring him here to me"
「それが終わったら、彼をここに連れてきてください」
"Do you understand?" she asked one last time
「わかるの?」彼女は最後にもう一度尋ねた
The Poodle showed that he had understood
プードルは彼が理解していることを示しました
he shook the case of blue satin three or four times
彼はブルーサテンのケースを3、4回振った
and then he ran off like a race-horse
そして、彼は競走馬のように走り去った
soon a beautiful carriage came out of the coach-house
すぐに美しい馬車が馬車小屋から出てきました
The cushions were stuffed with canary feathers
クッションにはカナリアの羽が詰められていました
the carriage was lined on the inside with whipped cream
馬車の内側にはホイップクリームが敷かれていました
and custard and vanilla wafers made the seating
そして、カスタードとバニラのウエハースが座席を作りました
The little carriage was drawn by a hundred white mice
小さな馬車は百匹の白いネズミに引かれていました
and the Poodle was seated on the coach-box
そしてプードルはコーチボックスに座っていました
he cracked his whip from side to side
彼は鞭を左右に鳴らした
like a driver when he is afraid that he is behind time
彼が時間に遅れているのではないかと恐れているドライバーのように
less than a quarter of an hour passed

15分も経たないうちに
and the carriage returned to the house
そして馬車は家に戻りました
The Fairy was waiting at the door of the house
妖精は家の戸口で待っていました
she took the poor puppet in her arms
彼女は哀れな人形を腕に抱きました
and she carried him into a little room
そして彼女は彼を小さな部屋に運びました
the room was wainscoted with mother-of-pearl
部屋はマザーオブパールの羽目板で覆われていました
she called for the most famous doctors in the neighbourhood
彼女は近所で最も有名な医者を呼びました
They came immediately, one after the other
彼らはすぐに、次々とやって来ました
a Crow, an Owl, and a talking little cricket
カラス、フクロウ、そしてしゃべる小さなコオロギ
"I wish to know something from you, gentlemen," said the Fairy
「紳士諸君、君たちから何か知りたいことがあるんだ」と妖精は言った
"is this unfortunate puppet alive or dead?"
「この不幸な人形は生きているのか、それとも死んでいるのか?」
the Crow started by feeling Pinocchio's pulse
カラスはピノキオの鼓動を感じることから始まりました
he then felt his nose and his little toe
それから彼は鼻と小指を感じました
he carefully made his diagnosis of the puppet
彼は慎重に人形の診断を下しました
and then he solemnly pronounced the following words:
そして、彼は厳粛に次の言葉を発音しました。
"To my belief the puppet is already dead"
「私の考えでは、人形はすでに死んでいる」
"but there is always the chance he's still alive"
「でも、彼がまだ生きている可能性は常にある」

"I regret," said the Owl, "to contradict the Crow"
「カラスに反論して、後悔している」とフクロウは言いました
"my illustrious friend and colleague"
「私の輝かしい友人であり同僚」
"in my opinion the puppet is still alive"
「私の意見では、人形はまだ生きています」
"but there's always a chance he's already dead"
「でも、彼がすでに死んでいる可能性は常にある」
lastly the Fairy asked the talking little Cricket
最後に、妖精はおしゃべりな小さなコオロギに尋ねました
"And you, have you nothing to say?"
「それで、君は何も言うことがないのか?」
"doctors are not always called upon to speak"
「医師はいつも話すように求められているわけではありません」
"sometimes the wisest thing is to be silent"
「時には沈黙することが最も賢明なことである」
"but let me tell you what I know"
「でも、私が知っていることを話させてください」
"that puppet has a face that is not new to me"
「あの人形の顔は、僕にとっては目新しいものではない」
"I have known him for some time!"
「彼とは以前から知ってるよ!」
Pinocchio had lain immovable up to that moment
ピノキオはその瞬間まで動かずに横たわっていました
he was just like a real piece of wood
彼はまるで本物の木片のようでした
but then he was seized with a fit of convulsive trembling
しかし、その後、彼は痙攣的な震えに襲われた
and the whole bed shook from his shaking
そして彼の揺れでベッド全体が揺れました
the talking little Cricket continued talking
しゃべる小さなクリケットは話し続けた

"That puppet there is a confirmed rogue"
「あそこの操り人形は確認されたならず者だ」
Pinocchio opened his eyes, but shut them again immediately
ピノキオは目を開けたが、すぐにまた閉じた
"He is a good for nothing ragamuffin vagabond"
「彼は何の役にも立たないラガマフィンの放浪者だ」
Pinocchio hid his face beneath the clothes
ピノキオは服の下に顔を隠した
"That puppet there is a disobedient son"
「あそこの人形は反抗的な息子だ」
"he will make his poor father die of a broken heart!"
「彼は哀れな父を失恋で死なせるだろう!」
At that instant everyone could hear something
その瞬間、誰もが何かを聞くことができました
suffocated sound of sobs and crying was heard
息が詰まったようなすすり泣きの声が聞こえた
the doctors raised the sheets a little
医者はシーツを少し上げました
Imagine their astonishment when they saw Pinocchio
彼らがピノキオを見たときの彼らの驚きを想像してみてください
the crow was the first to give his medical opinion
カラスが最初に彼の医学的意見を述べました
"When a dead person cries he's on the road to recovery"
「死者が泣くとき、彼は回復への道を歩んでいる」
but the owl was of a different medical opinion
しかし、フクロウは異なる医学的意見を持っていました
"I grieve to contradict my illustrious friend"
「私の輝かしい友人と矛盾することを悲しんでいます」
"when the dead person cries it means he's is sorry to die"
「死んだ人が泣くとき、それは彼が死ぬことを悔やんでいることを意味します」

Pinocchio Refuses to Take his Medicine
ピノキオは彼の薬を飲むことを拒否します

The doctors had done all that they could
医師たちはできる限りのことをしました
so they left Pinocchio with the fairy
それで彼らは妖精と一緒にピノキオを去りました
the Fairy touched Pinocchio's forehead
妖精はピノキオの額に触れた
she could tell that he had a high fever
彼は高熱を出しているのがわかった
the Fairy knew exactly what to give Pinocchio
妖精はピノキオに何を与えるべきかを正確に知っていました
she dissolved a white powder in some water
彼女は白い粉を水に溶かしました
and she offered Pinocchio the tumbler of water
そして彼女はピノキオに水のタンブラーを提供しました
and she reassured him that everything would fine
そして彼女は彼を安心させました、すべてがうまくいくと
"Drink it and in a few days you will be cured"
「飲めば数日で治るよ」
Pinocchio looked at the tumbler of medicine
ピノキオは薬のタンブラーを見た
and he made a wry face at the medicine
そして彼は薬に苦笑いを浮かべた
"Is it sweet or bitter?" he asked plaintively
「甘いのか、苦いのか?」彼は悲しげに尋ねた
"It is bitter, but it will do you good"
「苦いけど、いいことするよ」
"If it is bitter, I will not drink it"
「苦いなら飲まない」
"Listen to me," said the Fairy, "drink it"
「聞いてくれ」と妖精は言いました。

"I don't like anything bitter," he objected
「苦いものは好きじゃない」と彼は反論した
"I will give you a lump of sugar"
「砂糖の塊をあげる」
"it will take away the bitter taste"
「苦味がなくなる」
"but first you have to drink your medicine"
「でも、まずは薬を飲まなきゃ」
"Where is the lump of sugar?" asked Pinocchio
「砂糖の塊はどこにあるの?」とピノキオは尋ねた。
"Here is the lump of sugar," said the Fairy
「これが砂糖の塊です」と妖精は言いました
and she took out a piece from a gold sugar-basin
そして、彼女は金の砂糖盆地から一切れ取り出しました
"please give me the lump of sugar first"
「まず砂糖の塊をください」
"and then I will drink that bad bitter water"
「そして、その悪い苦い水を飲む」
"Do you promise me?" she asked Pinocchio
「約束してくれるの?」彼女はピノキオに尋ねた
"Yes, I promise," answered Pinocchio
「はい、約束します」とピノキオは答えました
so the Fairy gave Pinocchio the piece of sugar
それで妖精はピノキオに砂糖をあげました
and Pinocchio crunched up the sugar and swallowed it
そしてピノキオは砂糖をカリカリにして飲み込みました
he licked his lips and enjoyed the taste
彼は唇を舐め、その味を楽しみました
"It would be a fine thing if sugar were medicine!"
「砂糖が薬だったらいいのに!」
"then I would take medicine every day"
「それから毎日薬を飲む」
the Fairy had not forgotten Pinocchio's promise
妖精はピノキオの約束を忘れていませんでした
"keep your promise and drink this medicine"
「約束を守ってこの薬を飲んで」

"it will restore you back to health"
「それはあなたを健康に戻します」
Pinocchio took the tumbler unwillingly
ピノキオは不本意ながらタンブラーを手に取った
he put the point of his nose to the tumbler
彼は鼻の先をタンブラーに当てた
and he lowered the tumbler to his lips
そして彼はタンブラーを唇に下げた
and then again he put his nose to it
そしてまた、彼はそれに鼻を当てた
and at last he said, "It is too bitter!"
そしてついに彼は言いました、「それはあまりにも苦いです!」。
"I cannot drink anything so bitter"
「こんなに苦いものは飲めない」
"you don't know yet if you can't," said the Fairy
「できないかどうか、まだわからないよ」と妖精は言いました
"you have not even tasted it yet"
「まだ味わったことすらない」
"I can imagine how it's going to taste!"
「どんな味になるか想像がつく!」
"I know it from the smell," objected Pinocchio
「匂いからわかるよ」とピノキオは反論した
"first I want another lump of sugar please"
「まず、砂糖の塊がもう一つ欲しいです」
"and then I promise that will drink it!"
「そして、それを飲むことを約束します!」
The Fairy had all the patience of a good mamma
妖精は良いママの忍耐力をすべて持っていました
and she put another lump of sugar in his mouth
そして彼女は彼の口に別の砂糖の塊を入れました
and again, she presented the tumbler to him
そして再び、彼女はタンブラーを彼に差し出しました
"I still cannot drink it!" said the puppet
「まだ飲めない!」と人形は言いました

and Pinocchio made a thousand grimaced faces
そしてピノキオは千のしかめっ面をした
"Why can't you drink it?" asked the fairy
「どうして飲めないの?」と妖精は尋ねました
"Because that pillow on my feet bothers me"
「足元の枕が気になるから」
The Fairy removed the pillow from his feet
妖精は彼の足から枕を取り除いた
Pinocchio excused himself again
ピノキオは再び自分に言い訳をした
"I've tried my best but it doesn't help me"
「頑張ったけど、役に立たない」
"Even without the pillow I cannot drink it"
「枕がないのに飲めない」
"What is the matter now?" asked the fairy
「どうしたの?」と妖精は尋ねました
"The door of the room is half open"
「部屋のドアは半開です」
"it bothers me when doors are half open"
「ドアが半分開いていると気になる」
The Fairy went and closed the door for Pinocchio
妖精はピノキオのためにドアを閉めに行きました
but this didn't help, and he burst into tears
しかし、これでは役に立たず、彼は泣き出しました
"I will not drink that bitter water—no, no, no!"
「あの苦い水は飲まない——いや、いや、いや!」
"My boy, you will repent it if you don't"
「私の息子よ、そうしないとあなたはそれを後悔するでしょう」
"I don't care if I will repent it," he replied
「悔い改めるかどうかは気にしない」と彼は答えた
"Your illness is serious," warned the Fairy
「あなたの病気は深刻です」と妖精は警告しました
"I don't care if my illness is serious"
「病気が深刻でも構わない」
"The fever will carry you into the other world"

「熱が君をあの世に連れて行く」
"then let the fever carry me into the other world"
「じゃあ、熱に任せてあの世に行かせて」
"Are you not afraid of death?"
「死を恐れないのか?」
"I am not in the least afraid of death!"
「私は死を少しも恐れていません!」
"I would rather die than drink bitter medicine"
「苦い薬を飲むくらいなら死んだ方がまし」
At that moment the door of the room flew open
その瞬間、部屋のドアが飛んで開いた
four rabbits as black as ink entered the room
インクのように黒いウサギが4匹部屋に入ってきた
on their shoulders they carried a little bier
彼らは肩に小さなビールを運んでいました

"What do you want with me?" cried Pinocchio
「私に何が欲しいの?」ピノキオは叫んだ
and he sat up in bed in a great fright
そして彼はひどく怯えてベッドに座り込んだ
"We have come to take you," said the biggest rabbit
「お前を連れて行きに来たんだ」と一番大きなウサギが言いました
"you cannot take me yet; I am not dead"
「まだ私を連れて行くことはできません。私は死んでいません」
"where are you planning to take me to?"
「私をどこに連れて行くつもりなの?」
"No, you are not dead yet," confirmed the rabbit
「いや、まだ死んでないよ」とウサギは確認した
"but you have only a few minutes left to live"
「でも、君の人生はあと数分しかない」
"because you refused the bitter medicine"
「苦い薬を拒んだから」
"the bitter medicine would have cured your fever"
「苦い薬を飲めば熱が治っただろう」
"Oh, Fairy, Fairy!" the puppet began to scream
「ああ、妖精、妖精!」人形は叫び始めました
"give me the tumbler at once," he begged
「すぐにタンブラーをください」と彼は懇願した
"be quick, for pity's sake, I do not want die"
「早く、哀れみのために、私は死にたくない」
"no, I will not die today"
「いや、今日は死なない」
Pinocchio took the tumbler with both hands
ピノキオは両手でタンブラーを取りました

- 115 -

and he emptied the water one one big gulp
そして彼は水を一口飲み干しました
"We must have patience!" said the rabbits
「我慢しなきゃ！」とウサギたちは言いました
"this time we have made our journey in vain"
「今回は旅が無駄になってしまいました」
they took the little bier on their shoulders again
彼らは再び小さなビールを肩に乗せました
and they left the room back to where they came from
そして、彼らは部屋を出て元の場所に戻りました
and they grumbled and murmured between their teeth
そして彼らは歯の間で不平を言い、つぶやきました
Pinocchio's recovery did not take long at all
ピノキオの回復は、まったく長くはかかりませんでした
a few minutes later he jumped down from the bed
数分後、彼はベッドから飛び降りた
wooden puppets have a special privilege
木製の人形には特別な特権があります
they seldom get seriously ill like us

彼らは私たちのように重篤な病気になることはめったにありません
and they are lucky to be cured very quickly
そして、彼らは非常に早く治るのが幸運です
"has my medicine done you good?" asked the fairy
「私の薬はあなたに良い影響を与えましたか?」と妖精は尋ねました
"your medicine has done me more than good"
「あなたの薬は私に良い以上のことをしました」
"your medicine has saved my life"
「あなたの薬が私の命を救ってくれました」
"why didn't you take your medicine sooner?"
「なんでもっと早く薬を飲まなかったの?」
"Well, Fairy, we boys are all like that!"
「まあ、妖精、私たち男の子はみんなそうだよ!」
"We are more afraid of medicine than of the illness"
「私たちは病気よりも薬を恐れている」
"Disgraceful!" cried the fairy in indignation
「恥ずかしい!」妖精は憤慨して叫びました
"Boys ought to know the power of medicine"
「男の子は薬の力を知るべき」
"a good remedy may save them from a serious illness"
「良い治療法は彼らを深刻な病気から救うかもしれません」
"and perhaps it even saves you from death"
「そして、もしかしたら死から救ってくれるかもしれない」
"next time I shall not require so much persuasion"
「次回はそんなに説得する必要はないよ」
"I shall remember those black rabbits"
「あの黒ウサギたちを思い出す」
"and I shall remember the bier on their shoulders"
「そして、私は彼らの肩の上の棺を覚えているでしょう」
"and then I shall immediately take the tumbler"
「そして、すぐにタンブラーを取ります」

"and I will drink all the medicine in one go!"
「そして、一度にすべての薬を飲みます!」
The Fairy was happy with Pinocchio's words
妖精はピノキオの言葉に満足しました
"Now, come here to me and sit on my lap"
「さあ、私のところに来て、私の膝の上に座ってください」
"and tell me all about the assassins"
「そして、暗殺者についてすべて教えて」
"how did you end up hanging from the big Oak tree?"
「どうして大きなオークの木にぶら下がることになったの?」
And Pinocchio ordered all the events that happened
そしてピノキオは、起こったすべての出来事を命じました
"You see, there was a ringmaster; Fire-eater"
「ほら、リングマスターがいたんだよ。火を食べる人」
"Fire-eater gave me some gold pieces"
「火喰いが金貨をくれた」
"he told me to take the gold to my father"
「彼は私に金を父に持って行くように言いました」
"but I didn't take the gold straight to my father"
「でも、私は金を直接父に持っていかなかった」
"on the way home I met a Fox and a Cat"
「家に帰る途中でキツネと猫に会った」
"they made me an offer I couldn't refuse"
「彼らは私に断ることのできない申し出をしました」
'Would you like those pieces of gold to multiply?'
「その金貨を倍増させたいですか?」
"'Come with us and,' they said"
「『私たちと一緒に来て』と彼らは言いました」
'we will take you to the Field of Miracles'
「私たちはあなたを奇跡のフィールドに連れて行きます」
"and I said, 'Let's go to the Field of Miracles'"
「そして私は言いました。『奇跡のフィールドへ行こう

』と」
"And they said, 'Let us stop at this inn'"
「そして、彼らは『この宿に立ち寄ろう』と言いました」

"and we stopped at the Red Craw-Fish in"
「そして、レッド・クロウフィッシュ・インで止まった」

"all of us went to sleep after our food"
「私たち全員が食事の後に眠りにつきました」

"when I awoke they were no longer there"
「目が覚めたとき、彼らはもういませんでした」

"because they had to leave before me"
「彼らは私より先に去らなければならなかったから」

"Then I began to travel by night"
「それから夜に旅行を始めました」

"you cannot imagine how dark it was"
「どれだけ暗かったか想像もつかない」

"that's when I met the two assassins"
「その時、二人の暗殺者に出会った」

"and they were wearing charcoal sacks"
「そして、彼らは炭の袋を着ていました」

"they said to me: 'Out with your money'"
「彼らは私に言いました。『あなたのお金を持って出て行け』」

"and I said to them, 'I have no money'"
「そして私は彼らに言った、『私にはお金がない』」

"because I had hidden the four gold pieces"
「金貨4枚を隠していたから」

"I had put the money in my mouth"
「お金を口に入れちゃった」

"one tried to put his hand in my mouth"
「一人が私の口に手を入れようとした」

"and I bit his hand off and spat it out"
「そして私は彼の手を噛みちぎり、吐き出しました」

"but instead of a hand it was a cat's paw"
「でも、手の代わりに猫の足だった」

"and then the assassins ran after me"
「そして、暗殺者たちは私を追いかけた」
"and I ran and ran as fast as I could"
「そして、私は走って、できるだけ速く走りました」
"but in the end they caught me anyway"
「でも結局、彼らは僕を捕まえたんだ」
"and they tied a noose around my neck"
「そして、彼らは私の首に縄を巻きつけた」
"and they hung me from the Big Oak tree"
「そして、彼らは私をビッグオークの木から吊るしました」
"they waited for me to stop moving"
「彼らは私が動きを止めるのを待っていました」
"but I never stopped moving at all"
「でも、全然動きを止めなかった」
"and then they called up to me"
「そして、彼らは私に電話をかけてきた」
'Tomorrow we shall return here'
「明日、ここに戻るよ」
'then you will be dead with your mouth open'
「それなら、口を開けたまま死んでしまうよ」
'and we will have the gold under your tongue'
「そして、私たちはあなたの舌の下に金を手に入れるでしょう」
the Fairy was interested in the story
妖精はその話に興味を持っていました
"And where have you put the pieces of gold now?"
「それで、金貨は今どこに置いたの?」
"I have lost them!" said Pinocchio, dishonestly
「私は彼らを失った!」ピノキオは不誠実に言った
he had the pieces of gold in his pocket
彼はポケットに金貨を持っていました
as you know Pinocchio already had a long nose
ご存知のように、ピノキオはすでに長い鼻を持っていました
but lying made his nose grow even longer

しかし、嘘をつくと彼の鼻はさらに長くなりました
and his nose grew another two inches
そして彼の鼻はさらに2インチ伸びた
"And where did you lose the gold?"
「それで、金はどこで失ったの?」
"I lost it in the woods," he lied again
「森でなくしたんだ」と彼はまた嘘をついた
and his nose also grew at his second lie
そして、彼の鼻も二度目の嘘で成長しました
"worry not about the gold," said the fairy
「金のことは心配しないで」と妖精は言いました
"we will go to the woods and find your gold"
「森に行って、お前の金を見つけよう」
"all that is lost in those woods is always found"
「あの森で失われたものはすべていつも見つかります」
Pinocchio got quite confused about his situation
ピノキオは自分の状況についてかなり混乱しました
"Ah! now I remember all about it," he replied
「あぁ!今、私はそれについてすべて覚えています」と彼は答えました
"I didn't lose the four gold pieces at all"
「金貨4枚は全然なくちゃいなかった」
"I just swallowed your medicine, didn't I?"
「さっき君の薬を飲み込んでしまったよね?」
"I swallowed the coins with the medicine"
「薬で硬貨を飲み込んでしまった」
at this daring lie his nose grew even longer
この大胆な嘘で、彼の鼻はさらに長くなりました
now Pinocchio could not move in any direction
今やピノキオはどの方向にも動けなくなった
he tried to turn to his left side
彼は左側を向こうとしました
but his nose struck the bed and window-panes
しかし、彼の鼻はベッドと窓ガラスにぶつかった
he tried to turn to the right side
彼は右側を曲がろうとした

but now his nose struck against the walls
しかし今、彼の鼻は壁にぶつかった
and he could not raise his head either
そして、彼も顔を上げることができなかった
because his nose was long and pointy
彼の鼻は長くて尖っていたから
and his nose could have poke the Fairy in the eye
そして彼の鼻は妖精の目を突くことができたでしょう
the Fairy looked at him and laughed
妖精は彼を見て笑った
Pinocchio was very confused about his situation
ピノキオは自分の状況に非常に混乱していました
he did not know why his nose had grown
彼はなぜ自分の鼻が成長したのかわからなかった
"What are you laughing at?" asked the puppet
「何を笑っているの?」と人形は尋ねました
"I am laughing at the lies you've told me"
「君がついた嘘に笑っている」
"how can you know that I have told lies?"
「私が嘘をついたことをどうして知ることができるの?」
"Lies, my dear boy, are found out immediately"
「嘘は、私の愛する少年、すぐに見つかる」
"in this world there are two sorts of lies"
「この世には二種類の嘘がある」
"There are lies that have short legs"
「足が短い嘘がある」
"and there are lies that have long noses"
「そして、鼻の長い嘘がある」
"Your lie is one of those that has a long nose"
「あなたの嘘は鼻が長い人の一人です」
Pinocchio did not know where to hide himself
ピノキオはどこに身を隠すべきかわからなかった
he was ashamed of his lies being discovered
彼は自分の嘘が発覚したことを恥じていました
he tried to run out of the room

彼は部屋から走り出そうとした
but he did not succeed at escaping
しかし、彼は逃げることに成功しませんでした
his nose had gotten too long to escape
彼の鼻は逃げるには長すぎた
and he could no longer pass through the door
そして彼はもはやドアを通り抜けることができませんでした

Pinocchio Meets the Fox and the Cat Again
ピノキオは再びキツネと猫に会います

the Fairy understood the importance of the lesson
妖精はレッスンの重要性を理解しました
she let the puppet to cry for a good half-hour
彼女は人形に30分も泣かせました
his nose could no longer pass through the door
彼の鼻はもはやドアを通り抜けることができなかった
telling lies is the worst thing a boy can do
嘘をつくことは、男の子ができる最悪のことです
and she wanted him to learn from his mistakes
そして、彼は自分の過ちから学ぶことを望んでいました
but she could not bear to see him weeping
しかし、彼が泣いているのを見るのは耐えられなかった
she felt full of compassion for the puppet
彼女は人形に同情の念でいっぱいでした
so she clapped her hands together again
だから彼女は再び手を叩いた
a thousand large Woodpeckers flew in from the window
窓から1000匹の大きなキツツキが飛んできました
The woodpeckers immediately perched on Pinocchio's nose
キツツキはすぐにピノキオの鼻に止まりました
and they began to peck at his nose with great zeal
そして、彼らは非常に熱心に彼の鼻をつつき始めました

you can imagine the speed of a thousand woodpeckers
千匹のキツツキの速さを想像できるよ
within no time at all Pinocchio's nose was normal
あっという間にピノキオの鼻は正常になりました
of course you remember he always had a big nose
もちろん、彼がいつも大きな鼻を持っていたことを覚えています
"What a good Fairy you are," said the puppet
「お前はなんていい妖精なんだろう」と人形は言いました
and Pinocchio dried his tearful eyes
そしてピノキオは涙を流した目を乾かしました
"and how much I love you!" he added
「そして、どれだけ君を愛しているか!」と彼は付け加えた
"I love you also," answered the Fairy
「私もあなたを愛しています」と妖精は答えました
"if you remain with me you shall be my little brother"
「もし君が僕と一緒にいたら、君は僕の弟になるよ」
"and I will be your good little sister"
「そして、私はあなたの良い妹になります」
"I would like to remain very much," said Pinocchio
「私はとても残っていたい」とピノキオは言った
"but I have to go back to my poor papa"
「でも、かわいそうなパパのところに戻らなきゃ」
"I have thought of everything," said the fairy
「私はすべて考えました」と妖精は言いました
"I have already let your father know"
「もうお父さんに知らせてるよ」
"and he will come here tonight"
「そして彼は今夜ここに来るでしょう」
"Really?" shouted Pinocchio, jumping for joy
「本当ですか?」ピノキオは喜びに飛び跳ねながら叫びました
"Then, little Fairy, I have a wish"
「じゃあ、小さな妖精、願い事があるんだ」

"I would very much like to go and meet him"
「彼に会いに行きたいです」
"I want to give a kiss to that poor old man"
「あの可哀想なおじさんにキスをしたい」
"he has suffered so much on my account"
「彼は私のせいでとても苦しんでいます」
"Go, but be careful not to lose your way"
「行くけど、道に迷わないように気をつけて」
"Take the road that goes through the woods"
「森の中を通る道を進む」
"I am sure that you will meet him there"
「きっとそこで彼に会うでしょう」
Pinocchio set out to go through the woods
ピノキオは森の中を進むために出発しました
once in the woods he began to run like a kid
森に入ると、彼は子供のように走り始めました
But then he had reached a certain spot in the woods
しかし、その時、彼は森のある場所にたどり着いていた
he was almost in front of the Big Oak tree
彼はほとんどビッグオークの木の前にいました
he thought he heard people amongst the bushes
茂みの中に人の声が聞こえると思った
In fact, two persons came out on to the road
実際、2人の人が道路に出てきました
Can you guess who they were?
彼らが誰だったかわかりますか?
they were his two travelling companions
彼らは彼の二人の旅の仲間でした
in front of him was the Fox and the Cat
彼の前にはキツネと猫がいました
his companions who had taken him to the inn
彼を宿に連れて行った仲間たち

"Why, here is our dear Pinocchio!" cried the Fox
「なんで、ここに私たちの愛するピノキオがいるんだ！」とキツネは叫びました

and he kissed and embraced his old friend
そして彼は旧友にキスをし、抱きしめた

"How came you to be here?" asked the fox
「どうしてここに来たの？」とキツネは尋ねました

"How come you to be here?" repeated the Cat
「どうしてここにいるの？」と猫は繰り返しました

"It is a long story," answered the puppet
「それは長い話だよ」と人形は答えました

"I will tell you the story when I have time"
「時間があるときにお話をします」

"but I must tell you what happened to me"
「でも、僕に何が起こったのか話さなきゃ」

"do you know that the other night I met with assassins?"
「この前の夜、私が暗殺者と出会ったことを知ってる？」

"Assassins! Oh, poor Pinocchio!" worried the Fox
「暗殺者たち!ああ、かわいそうなピノキオ!」とキツネは心配しました
"And what did they want?" he asked
「それで、彼らは何を望んでいたのですか?」彼は尋ねました
"They wanted to rob me of my gold pieces"
「彼らは私の金貨を奪いたかった」
"Villains!" said the Fox
「悪党め!」とキツネは言いました
"Infamous villains!" repeated the Cat
「悪名高い悪党ども!」と猫は繰り返しました
"But I ran away from them," continued the puppet
「でも、私は彼らから逃げた」と人形は続けた
"they did their best to catch me"
「彼らは私を捕まえるために最善を尽くしました」
"and after a long chase they did catch me"
「そして長い追跡の末、彼らは私を捕まえました」
"they hung me from a branch of that oak tree"
「あの樫の木の枝に吊るされたんだ」
And Pinocchio pointed to the Big Oak tree
そしてピノキオはビッグオークの木を指差しました
the Fox was appalled by what he had heard
キツネは聞いたことに愕然としました
"Is it possible to hear of anything more dreadful?"
「もっと恐ろしいことを聞くことができるの?」
"In what a world we are condemned to live!"
「私たちは何という世界に住むことを強いられているのでしょう!」
"Where can respectable people like us find a safe refuge?"
「私たちのような立派な人間は、どこで安全な避難所を見つけることができるのだろう?」
the conversation went on this way for some time
会話はしばらくの間このように続きました
in this time Pinocchio observed something about the Cat

この時、ピノキオは猫について何かを観察しました
the Cat was lame of her front right leg
猫は彼女の右前足が不自由でした
in fact, she had lost her paw and all its claws
実際、彼女は前足とそのすべての爪を失っていました
Pinocchio wanted to know what had happened
ピノキオは何が起こったのか知りたがっていました
"What have you done with your paw?"
「前足で何をしたの?」
The Cat tried to answer, but became confused
猫は答えようとしましたが、混乱してしまいました
the Fox jumped in to explain what had happened
フォックスは何が起こったのかを説明するために飛び込みました
"you must know that my friend is too modest"
「私の友達が謙虚すぎることを知っていなければならない」
"her modesty is why she doesn't usually speak"
「彼女の謙虚さが、彼女が普段話さない理由です」
"so let me tell the story for her"
「だから、彼女のために話をさせてください」
"an hour ago we met an old wolf on the road"
「1時間前、道で年老いたオオカミに会った」
"he was almost fainting from want of food"
「彼は食べ物が欲しくて気を失いそうだった」
"and he asked alms of us"
「そして彼は私たちに施しを求めました」
"we had not so much as a fish-bone to give him"
「彼にあげる魚の骨ほどのものはなかった」
"but what did my friend do?"
「でも、友達は何をしたの?」
"well, she really has the heart of a César"
「まあ、彼女は本当にセザールの心を持っている」
"She bit off one of her fore paws"
「彼女は前足の1つを噛みちぎった」
"and the threw her paw to the poor beast"

「そして、その前足を哀れな獣に投げつけた」
"so that he might appease his hunger"
「彼が空腹を癒すために」
And the Fox was brought to tears by his story
そして、キツネは彼の話に涙を流しました
Pinocchio was also touched by the story
ピノキオもその話に感動しました
approaching the Cat, he whispered into her ear
猫に近づくと、彼は彼女の耳元でささやいた
"If all cats resembled you, how fortunate the mice would be!"
「もしすべての猫が君に似ていたら、ネズミはどんなに幸運だろう!」
"And now, what are you doing here?" asked the Fox
「それで、ここで何をしているの?」とキツネは尋ねました
"I am waiting for my papa," answered the puppet
「パパを待っています」と人形は答えました
"I am expecting him to arrive at any moment now"
「彼が今にも到着することを期待しています」
"And what about your pieces of gold?"
「それで、君の金貨はどうなの?」
"I have got them in my pocket," confirmed Pinocchio
「ポケットに入れてあるよ」とピノキオは確認した
although he had to explain that he had spent one coin
彼は1枚のコインを使ったことを説明しなければなりませんでした
the cost of their meal had come to one piece of gold
彼らの食事代は金貨一枚に膨れ上がった
but he told them not to worry about that
しかし、彼は彼らにそれについて心配しないように言いました
but the Fox and the Cat did worry about it
しかし、キツネと猫はそれを心配していました
"Why do you not listen to our advice?"
「なぜ私たちのアドバイスを聞かないのですか?」

"by tomorrow you could have one or two thousand!"
「明日までには、1000人か2000人になるかもしれない！」
"Why don't you bury them in the Field of Miracles?"
「なぜ奇跡のフィールドに埋めないのですか？」
"Today it is impossible," objected Pinocchio
「今日では不可能です」とピノキオは反論しました
"but don't worry, I will go another day"
「でも心配しないで、また別の日に行くから」
"Another day it will be too late!" said the Fox
「また別の日では手遅れになるぞ！」とキツネは言いました
"Why would it be too late?" asked Pinocchio
「なぜ手遅れになるのですか？」とピノキオは尋ねました
"Because the field has been bought by a gentleman"
「紳士に畑を買ってしまったから」
"after tomorrow no one will be allowed to bury money there"
「明日以降、誰もそこにお金を埋めることを許されません」
"How far off is the Field of Miracles?"
「奇跡の場はどれくらい離れていますか？」
"It is less than two miles from here"
「ここから2マイルも離れていない」
"Will you come with us?" asked the Fox
「一緒に来てくれるか？」とキツネは尋ねました
"In half an hour we can be there"
「30分で到着できます」
"You can bury your money straight away"
「すぐにお金を埋められる」
"and in a few minutes you will collect two thousand coins"
「そして数分であなたは2000枚のコインを集めるでしょう」
"and this evening you will return with your pockets full"

「そして今夜、あなたはポケットをいっぱいにして戻ってきます」
"Will you come with us?" the Fox asked again
「一緒に来てくれるか?」とキツネは再び尋ねました
Pinocchio thought of the good Fairy
ピノキオは善良な妖精を思い浮かべました
and Pinocchio thought of old Geppetto
そしてピノキオは古いゼペットを思い浮かべました
and he remembered the warnings of the talking little cricket
そして彼は、しゃべる小さなコオロギの警告を思い出しました
and he hesitated a little before answering
そして彼は答える前に少し躊躇した
by now you know what kind of boy Pinocchio is
もう、ピノキオがどんな男の子かはお分かりでしょう
Pinocchio is one of those boys without much sense
ピノキオは、あまりセンスのない少年の一人です
he ended by giving his head a little shake
彼は少し首を振って終わりました
and then he told the Fox and the Cat his plans
そして、彼はキツネと猫に自分の計画を話しました
"Let us go: I will come with you"
「行こう。私も一緒に行く」
and they went to the field of miracles
そして、彼らは奇跡の野に行きました
they walked for half a day and reached a town
彼らは半日歩いて町に着きました
the town was the Trap for Blockheads
町はブロックヘッドの罠でした
Pinocchio noticed something interesting about this town
ピノキオは、この町について何か面白いことに気づきました
everywhere where you looked there were dogs
どこを見ても犬がいました
all the dogs were yawning from hunger
すべての犬が空腹であくびをしていました

and he saw shorn sheep trembling with cold
そして、刈り取られた羊が寒さに震えているのを見た
even the cockerels were begging for Indian corn
おんどりでさえ、インドのトウモロコシを物乞いしていました
there were large butterflies that could no longer fly
もう飛べない大きな蝶がいました
because they had sold their beautiful coloured wings
なぜなら、彼らは美しい色の翼を売ったからです
there were peacocks that were ashamed to be seen
見られるのが恥ずかしかった孔雀がいました
because they had sold their beautiful coloured tails
なぜなら、彼らは美しい色の尻尾を売っていたからです
and pheasants went scratching about in a subdued fashion
そしてキジは控えめに引っ掻き回しました
they were mourning for their gold and silver feathers
彼らは金と銀の羽を嘆いていました
most were beggars and shamefaced creatures
ほとんどが物乞いで恥ずかしい生き物でした
but among them some lordly carriage passed
しかし、その中には立派な馬車が通っていました
the carriages contained a Fox, or a thieving Magpie
馬車にはキツネ、または泥棒のカササギが乗っていました
or the carriage seated some other ravenous bird of prey
あるいは、馬車が他の貪欲な猛禽類を座らせていた
"And where is the Field of Miracles?" asked Pinocchio
「それで、奇跡の場はどこにあるの?」ピノキオが尋ねた
"It is here, not two steps from us"
「ここにある、私たちから2歩も離れていない」
They crossed the town and and went over a wall
彼らは町を渡り、壁を越えた
and then they came to a solitary field
そして、彼らは孤独な野原に来ました
"Here we are," said the Fox to the puppet

「着いたぞ」とキツネは人形に言いました
"Now stoop down and dig with your hands a little hole"
「さあ、身をかがめて手で小さな穴を掘ってください」
"and put your gold pieces into the hole"
「そして、金貨を穴に入れて」
Pinocchio obeyed what the fox had told him
ピノキオはキツネの言うことに従った
He dug a hole and put into it the four gold pieces
彼は穴を掘り、そこに4枚の金貨を入れました
and then he filled up the hole with a little earth
そして、彼は穴を小さな土で埋めました
"Now, then," said the Fox, "go to that canal close to us"
「さあ、じゃあ」とキツネは言いました、「私たちの近くの運河に行ってみて」
"fetch a bucket of water from the canal"
「運河からバケツ一杯の水を汲んで」
"water the ground where you have sowed the gold"
「金を蒔いた地面に水をまく」
Pinocchio went to the canal without a bucket
ピノキオはバケツなしで運河に行きました
as he had no bucket, he took off one of his old shoes
バケツがなかったので、彼は古い靴を脱ぎました
and he filled his shoe with water
そして、彼は靴に水を入れました
and then he watered the ground over the hole
そして、彼は穴の上の地面に水をやった
He then asked, "Is there anything else to be done?
そして、「他にやるべきことはありますか？
"you need not do anything else," answered the Fox
「他に何もする必要はないよ」とキツネは答えました
"there is no need for us to stay here"
「私たちがここにいる必要はありません」
"you can return in about twenty minutes"
「20分ほどでお戻りいただけます」
"and then you will find a shrub in the ground"
「そして、地面に低木を見つけるでしょう」

"the tree's branches will be loaded with money"
「木の枝にはお金が積まれる」
The poor puppet was beside himself with joy
哀れな人形は喜びで自分のそばにいました
he thanked the Fox and the Cat a thousand times
彼はキツネと猫に千回も感謝しました
and he promised them many beautiful presents
そして、彼は彼らにたくさんの美しいプレゼントを約束しました
"We wish for no presents," answered the two rascals
「プレゼントは欲しくないよ」と二人の悪党は答えました
"It is enough for us to have taught you how to enrich yourself"
「私たちがあなたに自分を豊かにする方法を教えただけで十分です」
"there is nothing worse than seeing others do hard work"
「他人が一生懸命働いているのを見ることほど悪いことはありません」
"and we are as happy as people out for a holiday"
「そして、私たちは休暇に出かける人々と同じくらい幸せです」
Thus saying, they took leave of Pinocchio
こう言って、彼らはピノキオを去った
and they wished him a good harvest
そして、彼らは彼に豊作を願った
and then they went about their business
そして、彼らは自分たちの仕事に取り掛かった

Pinocchio is Robbed of his Money
ピノキオは彼のお金を奪われています

The puppet returned to the town
人形は町に戻りました
and he began to count the minutes one by one
そして、彼は分を一つ一つ数え始めました
and soon he thought he had counted long enough
そしてすぐに、彼は十分に長く数えたと思った
so he took the road leading to the Field of Miracles
そこで彼は奇跡の分野に通じる道を進みました
And he walked along with hurried steps
そして、彼は急いで歩いた
and his heart beat fast with great excitement
そして彼の心臓は大きな興奮で速く鼓動しました
like a drawing-room clock going very well
まるで応接室の時計がとてもうまくいっているように
Meanwhile he was thinking to himself:
その間、彼は心の中で考えていました。
"what if I don't find a thousand gold pieces?"
「金貨が千枚も見つからなかったらどうしますか?」
"what if I find two thousand gold pieces instead?"
「もし私が代わりに2000枚の金貨を見つけたらどうしますか?」
"but what if I don't find two thousand gold pieces?"
「でも、金貨が二千枚見つからなかったらどうするの?」
"what if I find five thousand gold pieces!"
「もし金貨が5000枚見つかったらどうしよう!」
"what if I find a hundred thousand gold pieces??"
「もし10万枚の金貨を見つけたらどうするの??」
"Oh! what a fine gentleman I should then become!"
「ああ!それなら、私は何と立派な紳士になれるのでしょう!」
"I could live in a beautiful palace"

「美しい宮殿に住むことができた」
"and I would have a thousand little wooden horses"
「そして、私は千頭の小さな木馬を持つでしょう」
"a cellar full of currant wine and sweet syrups"
「スグリワインと甘いシロップがいっぱいのセラー」
"and a library quite full of candies and tarts"
「そして、キャンディーやタルトでいっぱいの図書館」
"and I would have plum-cakes and macaroons"
「そして、プラムケーキとマカロンを食べるだろう」
"and I would have biscuits with cream"
「そして、私はクリームとビスケットを食べるでしょう」

he walked along building castles in the sky
彼は空に城を建てながら歩きました
and he build many of these castles in the sky
そして、彼はこれらの城の多くを空に建てました
and eventually he arrived at the edge of the field
そしてついに彼はフィールドの端に到着しました
and he stopped to look about for a tree
そして彼は立ち止まって木を探しました
there were other trees in the field
野原には他にも木がありました
but they had been there when he had left
しかし、彼が去ったとき、彼らはそこにいた
and he saw no money tree in all the field
そして、彼はすべての畑に金のなる樹を見つけませんでした
He walked along the field another hundred steps
彼はさらに百歩の草原を歩いた
but he couldn't find the tree he was looking for
しかし、探していた木を見つけることができませんでした
he then entered into the field
その後、彼は現場に入りました
and he went up to the little hole
そして彼は小さな穴に上がった

the hole where he had buried his coins
彼が硬貨を埋めた穴
and he looked at the hole very carefully
そして、彼は穴を非常に注意深く見ました
but there was definitely no tree growing there
しかし、そこには絶対に木は生えていませんでした
He then became very thoughtful
その後、彼は非常に思慮深くなりました
and he forget the rules of society
そして彼は社会のルールを忘れます
and he didn't care for good manners for a moment
そして、彼は一瞬たりともマナーを気にしませんでした
he took his hands out of his pocket
彼はポケットから手を出した
and he gave his head a long scratch
そして彼は頭を長く引っ掻いた
At that moment he heard an explosion of laughter
その瞬間、彼は爆笑の爆発を聞いた
someone close by was laughing himself silly
近くにいた誰かが自分をバカに笑っていました
he looked up one of the nearby trees
彼は近くの木の一つを見上げた
he saw a large Parrot perched on a branch
彼は大きなオウムが枝にとまっているのを見ました
the parrot brushed the few feathers he had left
オウムは彼が残した数枚の羽を撫でた
Pinocchio asked the parrot in an angry voice;
ピノキオは怒った声でオウムに尋ねました。
"Why are you here laughing so loud?"
「なんでこんなに大声で笑ってるの?」
"I am laughing because in brushing my feathers"
「羽を磨くのに笑っているから」
"I was just brushing a little under my wings"
「翼の下を少し磨いていただけだった」
"and while brushing my feathers I tickled myself"
「そして、羽をブラッシングしながら自分をくすぐりま

した」
The puppet did not answer the parrot
人形はオウムに答えませんでした
but instead Pinocchio went to the canal
しかし、ピノキオは運河に行きました
he filled his old shoe full of water again
彼は古い靴を再び水でいっぱいにしました
and he proceeded to water the hole once more
そして彼はもう一度穴に水をやり始めました
While he was busy doing this he heard more laughter
彼がこれをするのに忙しい間、彼はさらに笑い声を聞きました
the laughter was even more impertinent than before
笑い声は以前よりもさらに無礼でした
it rang out in the silence of that solitary place
それはその孤独な場所の静寂の中で鳴り響いた
Pinocchio shouted out even angrier than before
ピノキオはさっきよりもさらに怒って叫んだ
"Once for all, may I know what you are laughing at?"
「きっぱりと、君が何を笑っているのか教えてもいいですか?」
"I am laughing at simpletons," answered the parrot
「私は単純なものを笑っています」とオウムは答えました
"simpletons who believe in foolish things
「愚かなことを信じる愚かな人
"the foolish things that people tell them"
「人々が彼らに言う愚かなこと」
"I laugh at those who let themselves be fooled"
「自分を騙す者を笑う」
"fooled by those more cunning than they are"
「自分よりも狡猾な者たちに騙される」
"Are you perhaps speaking of me?"
「もしかして、私のことを言っているの?」
"Yes, I am speaking of you, poor Pinocchio"
「はい、私はあなたのことを言っています、かわいそう

なピノキオ」
"you have believed a very foolish thing"
「あなたはとても愚かなことを信じていました」
"you believed that money can be grown in fields"
「あなたはお金は畑で育てることができると信じていました」
"you thought money can be grown like beans"
「お金は豆のように育てられると思っていたんじゃないか」
"I also believed it once," admitted the parrot
「私も一度は信じました」とオウムは認めました
"and today I am suffering for having believed it"
「そして今日、私はそれを信じていたために苦しんでいます」
"but I have learned my lesson from that trick"
「でも、あのトリックから教訓を学んだんだ」
"I turned my efforts to honest work"
「正直な仕事に力を注ぎました」
"and I have put a few pennies together"
「そして、私は数ペニーをまとめました」
"it is necessary to know how to earn your pennies"
「それはあなたのペニーを稼ぐ方法を知る必要があります」
"you have to earn them either with your hands"
「あなたはあなたの手でそれらを獲得する必要があります」
"or you have to earn them with your brains"
「それとも、頭で稼ぐしかない」
"I don't understand you," said the puppet
「おまえのことが理解できない」と人形は言いました
and he was already trembling with fear
そして彼はすでに恐怖に震えていました
"Have patience!" rejoined the parrot
「我慢しろ!」とオウムは再び加わりました
"I will explain myself better, if you let me"
「もし許してもらえば、もっとよく説明してあげるよ」

"there is something that you must know"
「知っておかなければならないことがある」
"something happened while you were in the town"
「君が町にいる間に何かあった」
"the Fox and the Cat returned to the field"
「キツネと猫は畑に戻った」
"they took the money you had buried"
「彼らはあなたが埋めたお金を持っていった」
"and then they fled from the scene of the crime"
「そして、彼らは犯行現場から逃げた」
"And now he that catches them will be clever"
「そして今、彼らを捕まえる者は賢くなる」
Pinocchio remained with his mouth open
ピノキオは口を開けたままだった
and he chose not to believe the Parrot's words
そして彼はオウムの言葉を信じないことを選びました
he began with his hands to dig up the earth
彼は自分の手で土を掘り始めました
And he dug deep into the ground
そして、彼は地面を深く掘りました
a rick of straw could have stood in the hole
穴には一本の藁が立っていたかもしれない
but the money was no longer there
しかし、お金はもうそこにありませんでした
He rushed back to the town in a state of desperation
彼は絶望的な状態で町に急いで戻った
and he went at once to the Courts of Justice
そして彼はすぐに裁判所に行きました
and he spoke directly with the judge
そして彼は裁判官と直接話しました
he denounced the two knaves who had robbed him
彼は自分を奪った二人のナイフを非難した
The judge was a big ape of the gorilla tribe
裁判官はゴリラ族の大きな類人猿でした
an old ape respectable because of his white beard
白いあごひげを生やした立派な老猿

and he was respectable for other reasons
そして、彼は他の理由で立派でした
because he had gold spectacles on his nose
なぜなら、彼は鼻に金の眼鏡をつけていたからです
although, his spectacles were without glass
しかし、彼の眼鏡にはガラスがありませんでした
but he was always obliged to wear them
しかし、彼は常にそれらを着用する義務がありました
on account of an inflammation of the eyes
目の炎症のため

Pinocchio told him all about the crime
ピノキオは彼に犯罪についてすべて話しました
the crime of which he had been the victim of
彼が犠牲者となった犯罪
He gave him the names and the surnames

彼は彼に名前と姓を与えました
and he gave all the details of the rascals
そして、彼は悪党たちの詳細をすべて話しました
and he ended by demanding to have justice
そして彼は正義を要求することで終わりました
The judge listened with great benignity
裁判官は大いに温和に耳を傾けた
he took a lively interest in the story
彼はその話に活発な興味を持っていました
he was much touched and moved by what he heard
彼は聞いたものに大いに感動し、感動しました
finally the puppet had nothing further to say
とうとう人形はそれ以上何も言わなくなりました
and then the gorilla rang a bell
そして、ゴリラがベルを鳴らしました
two mastiffs appeared at the door
ドアに現れたのは2匹のマスティフ
the dogs were dressed as gendarmes
犬たちは憲兵の格好をしていました
The judge then pointed to Pinocchio
その後、裁判官はピノキオを指差した
"That poor devil has been robbed"
「あの可哀想な悪魔が奪われた」
"rascals took four gold pieces from him"
「悪党どもが彼から金貨を四枚奪った」
"take him away to prison immediately," he ordered
「すぐに彼を刑務所に連れて行け」と彼は命じた
The puppet was petrified on hearing this
人形はこれを聞いて石化しました
it was not at all the judgement he had expected
それは彼が期待していた判断では全くありませんでした
and he tried to protest the judge
そして彼は裁判官に抗議しようとしました
but the gendarmes stopped his mouth
しかし、憲兵は彼の口を止めた
they didn't want to lose any time

彼らは時間を無駄にしたくなかった
and they carried him off to the prison
そして、彼らは彼を牢獄に連れて行きました
And there he remained for four long months
そして、彼はそこに4ヶ月という長い期間滞在しました
and he would have remained there even longer
そして、彼はさらに長くそこに留まっていたでしょう
but puppets do sometimes have good fortune too
しかし、人形には幸運もあることがあります
a young King ruled over the Trap for Blockheads
若き王がブロックヘッドの罠を支配していた
he had won a splendid victory in battle
彼は戦いで見事な勝利を収めた
because of this he ordered great public rejoicings
このため、彼は大衆の喜びを命じました
There were illuminations and fireworks
イルミネーションや花火もありました
and there were horse and velocipede races
そして、馬とベロシペードのレースがありました
the King was so happy he released all prisoners
王様はとても喜んで、すべての囚人を解放しました
Pinocchio was very happy at this news
ピノキオはこのニュースにとても喜んでいました
"if they are freed, then so am I"
「彼らが解放されたら、私も解放される」
but the jailor had other orders
しかし、看守には別の命令がありました
"No, not you," said the jailor
「いや、君じゃない」と看守は言った
"because you do not belong to the fortunate class"
「君は幸運な階級に属していないから」
"I beg your pardon," replied Pinocchio
「ご容赦をお願いします」とピノキオは答えた
"I am also a criminal," he proudly said
「私も犯罪者です」と彼は誇らしげに言いました
the jailor looked at Pinocchio again

看守は再びピノキオを見た
"In that case you are perfectly right"
「それなら、君は全く正しい」
and he took off his hat
そして彼は帽子を脱いだ
and he bowed to him respectfully
そして彼は彼にうやうやしくお辞儀をしました
and he opened the prison doors
そして彼は牢獄の扉を開けた
and he let the little puppet escape
そして彼は小さな人形を逃がしました

Pinocchio Goes back to the Fairy's House
ピノキオは妖精の家に戻る

You can imagine Pinocchio's joy
ピノキオの喜びが想像できます
finally he was free after four months
4ヶ月後、ようやく彼は自由の身となった
but he didn't stop in order to celebrate
しかし、彼は祝うために立ち止まりませんでした
instead, he immediately left the town
それどころか、彼はすぐに町を去った
he took the road that led to the Fairy's house
彼は妖精の家に通じる道を進みました
there had been a lot of rain in recent days
ここ数日、雨が多かった
so the road had become a went boggy and marsh
そのため、道路は沼地と沼地になっていました
and Pinocchio sank knee deep into the mud
そしてピノキオは膝を泥に深く沈めました

But the puppet was not one to give up
しかし、人形は諦める人ではありませんでした
he was tormented by the desire to see his father
彼は父親に会いたいという願望に苦しめられていました
and he wanted to see his little sister again too
そして、彼もまた妹に会いたかった
and he ran through the marsh like a greyhound
そして彼はグレイハウンドのように沼地を駆け抜けました
and as he ran he was splashed with mud
そして彼が走ったとき、彼は泥で飛び散りました
and he was covered from head to foot
そして彼は頭から足まで覆われていました
And he said to himself as he went along:
そして、彼は進みながら自分に言い聞かせました。
"How many misfortunes have happened to me"

「私にはどれだけの不幸が起こったことか」
"But I deserved these misfortunes"
「でも、僕はこんな不幸に値したんだ」
"because I am an obstinate, passionate puppet"
「私は頑固で情熱的な操り人形だから」
"I am always bent upon having my own way"
「私は常に自分の道を歩むことに固執しています」
"and I don't listen to those who wish me well"
「そして、私の幸せを願う人々の言うことは聞かない」
"they have a thousand times more sense than I!"
「彼らは私の千倍も分別がある!」
"But from now I am determined to change"
「でも、これからは変わる決意だ」
"I will become orderly and obedient"
「私は秩序正しく従順になります」
"because I have seen what happened"
「私は何が起こったのかを見てきたから」
"disobedient boys do not have an easy life"
「不従順な少年たちは楽な生活を送っていない」
"they come to no good and gain nothing"
「彼らは何の役にも立たず、何も得られない」
"And has my papa waited for me?"
「それで、パパは僕を待っていたの?」
"Shall I find him at the Fairy's house?"
「妖精の家で彼を見つけようか?」
"it has been so long since I last saw him"
「最後に彼に会ってからずいぶん経ちました」
"I am dying to embrace him again"
「私は彼を再び抱きしめたくてたまりません」
"I can't wait to cover him with kisses!"
「彼をキスで覆うのが待ちきれない!」
"And will the Fairy forgive me my bad conduct?"
「それで、妖精は私の悪い行いを許してくれるの?」
"To think of all the kindness I received from her"
「彼女から受けたすべての親切を考える」
"oh how lovingly did she care for me"

「ああ、彼女はどんなに愛情を込めて私を気にかけてくれたのでしょう」
"that I am now alive I owe to her!"
「私が今生きているのは、彼女のおかげです!」
"could you find a more ungrateful boy"
「もっと恩知らずな男の子を見つけられるか」
"is there a boy with less heart than I have?"
「私よりも心の弱い男の子がいるのだろうか?」
Whilst he was saying this he stopped suddenly
彼がそう言っていると、突然立ち止まりました
he was frightened to death
彼は死ぬほど怯えていました
and he made four steps backwards
そして彼は四歩後ずさった
What had Pinocchio seen?
ピノキオは何を見ていたのか?
He had seen an immense Serpent
彼は巨大な蛇を見た
the snake was stretched across the road
蛇は道路を横切って伸びていました
the snake's skin was a grass green colour
蛇の肌は草緑色をしていました
and it had red eyes in its head
そして、頭の中には赤い目がありました
and it had a long and pointed tail
そして、それは長くて尖った尾を持っていました
and the tail was smoking like a chimney
そして尻尾は煙突のように煙を出していました

It would be impossible to imagine the puppet's terror
人形の恐怖を想像することは不可能でしょう
He walked away to a safe distance
彼は安全な距離まで歩いて立ち去った
and he sat on a heap of stones
そして彼は石の山の上に座っていました
there he waited until the Serpent had finished
そこで彼は蛇が終わるまで待ちました
soon the Serpent's business should be done
すぐに蛇の用事は終わるはずだ
He waited an hour; two hours; three hours
彼は一時間待った。2時間;3時間
but the Serpent was always there
しかし、蛇はいつもそこにいました

even from a distance he could see his fiery eyes
遠くからでも彼の燃えるような目を見ることができた
and he could see the column of smoke
そして彼は煙の柱を見ることができました
the smoke that ascended from the end of his tail
彼の尻尾の先から立ち上る煙
At last Pinocchio tried to feel courageous
ついにピノキオは勇気を出そうとしました
and he approached to within a few steps
そして彼は数歩以内に近づきました
he spoke to the Serpent in a little soft voice
彼は少し柔らかい声で蛇に話しかけました
"Excuse me, Sir Serpent," he insinuated
「すみません、サー・サーペント」彼はほのめかした
"would you be so good as to move a little?"
「ちょっと動いてもいいかな?」
"just a step to the side, if you could"
「できれば、一歩だけ横に」
He might as well have spoken to the wall
彼は壁に向かって話したかもしれない
He began again in the same soft voice:
彼は再び同じ柔らかな声で話し始めた。
"please know, Sir Serpent, I am on my way home"
「サー・サー・サーペント、私は家に帰る途中です」
"my father is waiting for me"
「父が待ってる」
"and it has been such a long time since I saw him!"
「そして、彼に会うのはこんなに久しぶりだ!」
"Will you, therefore, allow me to continue?"
「それでは、続けさせていただけますか?」
He waited for a sign in answer to this request
彼はこの要求に対する答えのサインを待った
but the snake made no answer
しかし、蛇は答えませんでした
up to that moment the serpent had been sprightly
その瞬間まで、蛇は元気だった

up until then it had been full of life
それまでは活気にあふれていました
but now he became motionless and almost rigid
しかし、今や彼は動かなくなり、ほとんど硬直しました
He shut his eyes and his tail ceased smoking
彼は目を閉じ、尻尾は煙を止めた
"Can he really be dead?" said Pinocchio
「彼は本当に死んでいるのだろうか?」とピノキオは言った
and he rubbed his hands with delight
そして彼は喜びで手をこすった
He decided to jump over him
彼は彼を飛び越えることにした
and then he could reach the other side of the road
そして、彼は道路の反対側にたどり着くことができた
Pinocchio took a little run up
ピノキオは少し駆け上がった
and he went to jump over the snake
そして、彼は蛇を飛び越えに行きました
but suddenly the Serpent raised himself on end
しかし、突然、蛇は自分自身を逆さまに起こしました
like a spring set in motion
動き出すバネのように
and the puppet stopped just in time
そして、人形はちょうど間に合うように止まりました
he stopped his feet from jumping
彼は足が跳ねるのを止めた
and he fell to the ground
そして彼は地面に倒れた
he fell rather awkwardly into the mud
彼はかなりぎこちなく泥の中に落ちた
his head got stuck in the mud
彼の頭は泥にはまりました
and his legs went into the air
そして彼の足は宙に浮いた
the Serpent went into convulsions of laughter

蛇は笑い声で痙攣しました
it laughed until he broke a blood-vessel
彼が血管を破るまで笑った
and the snake died from all its laughter
そして蛇はそのすべての笑い声で死にました
this time the snake really was dead
この時、蛇は本当に死んでいました
Pinocchio then set off running again
ピノキオはその後、再び走り始めました
he hoped to reach the Fairy's house before dark
暗くなる前に妖精の家に着くことを望んだ
but soon he had other problems again
しかし、すぐに彼は再び別の問題を抱えました
he began to suffer so dreadfully from hunger
彼は飢えでひどく苦しみ始めました
and he could not bear the hunger any longer
そして、彼はもはや空腹に耐えられませんでした
he jumped into a field by the wayside
彼は道端の野原に飛び込んだ
perhaps there were some grapes he could pick
もしかしたら、彼が摘むことができるブドウがあったのかもしれない
Oh, if only he had never done it!
ああ、彼がそれをやらなかったらいいのに!
He had scarcely reached the grapes
彼はほとんど葡萄にたどり着いていなかった
and then there was a "cracking" sound
そして、「割れる」音がしました
his legs were caught between something
彼の足は何かに挟まれていた
he had stepped into two cutting iron bars
彼は2本の鉄の棒に足を踏み入れた
poor Pinocchio became giddy with pain
かわいそうなピノキオは痛みでめまいがしました
stars of every colour danced before his eyes
彼の目の前で、あらゆる色の星が踊った

The poor puppet had been caught in a trap
哀れな人形は罠にかかっていた
it had been put there to capture polecats
それはケナガイタチを捕まえるために置かれていました

Pinocchio Becomes a Watch-Dog
ピノキオは番犬になる

Pinocchio began to cry and scream
ピノキオは泣き叫び始めました
but his tears and groans were useless
しかし、彼の涙とうめき声は役に立たなかった
because there was not a house to be seen
だって、見るべき家がなかったから
nor did living soul pass down the road
また、生きている魂も道を進んでいきませんでした
At last the night had come on
とうとう夜が明けた
the trap had cut into his leg

罠は彼の足に食い込んでいた
the pain brought him the point of fainting
痛みで彼は失神しそうになりました
he was scared from being alone
彼は一人でいることが怖かった
he didn't like the darkness
彼は暗闇が好きではなかった
Just at that moment he saw a Firefly
ちょうどその瞬間、彼はホタルを見ました
He called to the firefly and said:
彼はホタルに呼びかけて言いました。
"Oh, little Firefly, will you have pity on me?"
「ああ、小さなホタル、私を憐れんでくれる？」
"please liberate me from this torture"
「どうか私をこの拷問から解放してください」
"Poor boy!" said the Firefly
「かわいそうに！」とホタルは言いました
the Firefly stopped and looked at him with compassion
ホタルは立ち止まり、同情の目で彼を見つめました
"your legs have been caught by those sharp irons"
「あの鋭い鉄に足が引っかかっちゃった」
"how did you get yourself into this trap?
「どうやってこの罠にかかったの？
"I came into the field to pick grapes"
「ぶどうを摘みに畑に来た」
"But where did you plant your grapes?"
「でも、ブドウはどこに植えたの？」
"No, they were not my grapes"
「いや、僕のぶどうじゃない」
"who taught you to carry off other people's property?"
「他人の財産を持ち去ることを誰が教えてくれたの？」
"I was so hungry," Pinocchio whimpered
「すごくお腹が空いていた」とピノキオは泣き叫んだ
"Hunger is not a good reason"
「飢餓は正当な理由ではない」
"we cannot appropriated what does not belong to us"

「私たちは自分のものにならないものを流用することはできません」

"That is true, that is true!" said Pinocchio, crying
「それは本当だ、それは本当だ!」ピノキオは泣きながら言った

"I will never do it again," he promised
「もう二度とやらない」と彼は約束した

At this moment their conversation was interrupted
この瞬間、彼らの会話は中断されました

there was a slight sound of approaching footsteps
近づいてくる足音がわずかに聞こえた

It was the owner of the field coming on tiptoe
それは、つま先立ちで来たフィールドのオーナーだった

he wanted to see if he had caught a polecat
彼はケナガイタチを捕まえたかどうか確かめたかった

the polecat that ate his chickens in the night
夜に鶏を食べたケナガイタチ

but he was surprised by what was in his trap
しかし、彼は自分の罠に何が潜んでいるのかに驚いていました

instead of a polecat, a boy had been captured
ケナガイタチの代わりに、男の子が捕らえられていた

"Ah, little thief," said the angry peasant,
「ああ、ちっちゃい泥棒だ」と怒った農夫は言いました。

"then it is you who carries off my chickens?"
「じゃあ、私の鶏を運び去るのはお前だろ?」

"No, I have not been carrying off your chickens"
「いいえ、私はあなたの鶏を運び去っていません」

"I only came into the field to take two grapes!"
「畑に来たのは、ぶどうを二つ取るためだけだよ!」

"He who steals grapes can easily steal chicken"
「ぶどうを盗む者は簡単に鶏肉を盗むことができる」

"Leave it to me to teach you a lesson"
「私にレッスンを教える」

"and you won't forget this lesson in a hurry"

「そして、この教訓をすぐに忘れることはありません」
Opening the trap, he seized the puppet by the collar
罠を開けると、彼は人形の襟をつかんだ
and he carried him to his house like a young lamb
そして、彼は若い子羊のように彼を家に運びました
they reached the yard in front of the house
彼らは家の前の庭に着きました
and he threw him roughly on the ground
そして彼は彼を乱暴に地面に投げつけた
he put his foot on his neck and said to him:
彼は自分の首に足を乗せて言った。
"It is late and I want to go to bed"
「遅くなって寝たい」
"we will settle our accounts tomorrow"
「明日、決算を行います」
"the dog who kept guard at night died today"
「夜に見張りをしていた犬が今日死んだ」
"you will live in his place from now"
「これから彼の場所で暮らすんだよ」
"You shall be my watch-dog from now"
「これからはお前が俺の番犬になるんだ」
he took a great dog collar covered with brass knobs
彼は真鍮のノブで覆われた素晴らしい犬の首輪を取りました
and he strapped the dog collar around Pinocchio's neck
そして彼は犬の首輪をピノキオの首に巻き付けました
it was so tight that he could not pull his head out
それは彼が頭を抜くことができないほどきつかった
the dog collar was attached to a heavy chain
犬の首輪は重いチェーンに取り付けられていました
and the heavy chain was fastened to the wall
そして、重い鎖が壁に固定されました
"If it rains tonight you can go into the kennel"
「今夜雨が降ったら、犬小屋に入ってもいいよ」
"my poor dog had a little bed of straw in there"
「かわいそうな犬は、そこに小さな藁のベッドを持って

いました」
"remember to keep your ears pricked for robbers"
「強盗に耳を澄ましておくことを忘れないでください」
"and if you hear robbers, then bark loudly"
「そして、強盗の声が聞こえたら、大声で吠えなさい」
Pinocchio had received his orders for the night
ピノキオは彼の夜の命令を受け取っていた
and the poor man finally went to bed
そして、かわいそうな男はついに寝ました

Poor Pinocchio remained lying on the ground
かわいそうなピノキオは地面に横たわったままでした
he felt more dead than he felt alive
彼は生きているというよりも死んでいるように感じた
the cold, and hunger, and fear had taken all his energy
寒さ、飢え、恐怖が彼の全エネルギーを奪ってしまった
From time to time he put his hands angrily to the go collar
時々、彼は怒ってゴーカラーに手を入れました
"It serves me right!" he said to himself

「それは正しいことだ!」彼は自分自身に言い聞かせました
"I was determined to be a vagabond"
「私は放浪者になると決めていた」
"I wanted to live the life of a good-for-nothing"
「何の役にも立たない人生を生きたかった」
"I used to listen to bad companions"
「昔は下手な仲間の話を聞いていた」
"and that is why I always meet with misfortunes"
「だから私はいつも不幸に遭遇する」
"if only I had been a good little boy"
「もし私が良い子だったら」
"then I would not be in the midst of the field"
「それなら、私は野原の真ん中にはいないだろう」
"I wouldn't be here if I had stayed at home"
「家にいたら、私はここにいなかったでしょう」
"I wouldn't be a watch-dog if I had stayed with my papa"
「もしパパと一緒にいたら、僕は番犬にはならなかっただろう」
"Oh, if only I could be born again!"
「ああ、もし私が生まれ変わればいいのに!」
"But now it is too late to change anything"
「でも、今となっては何も変えるには遅すぎる」
"the best thing to do now is having patience!"
「今やるべき最善のことは、忍耐を持つことです!」
he was relieved by this little outburst
彼はこの小さな爆発に安堵した
because it had come straight from his heart
なぜなら、それは彼の心から直接出てきたものだったからだ
and he went into the dog-kennel and fell asleep
そして彼は犬小屋に入り、眠りに落ちました

Pinocchio Discovers the Robbers
ピノキオは強盗を発見する

He had been sleeping heavily for about two hours
彼は約2時間、ぐっすり眠っていました
then he was aroused by a strange whispering
その時、彼は奇妙なささやき声に目を覚ましました
the strange voices were coming from the courtyard
奇妙な声が中庭から聞こえてきました
he put the point of his nose out of the kennel
彼は鼻の先を犬小屋から出しました
and he saw four little beasts with dark fur
そして、黒い毛皮を着た四匹の小さな獣を見ました
they looked like cats making a plan
彼らは計画を立てている猫のように見えました
But they were not cats, they were polecats
しかし、彼らは猫ではなく、ケナガイタチでした
what polecats are are carnivorous little animals
ケナガイタチとは肉食性の小動物です
they are especially greedy for eggs and young chickens
彼らは特に卵と若い鶏に貪欲です
One of the polecats came to the opening of the kennel
ケナガイタチの1匹が犬小屋の開口部に来ました
he spoke in a low voice, "Good evening, Melampo"
彼は低い声で「こんばんは、メランポ」と言った。
"My name is not Melampo," answered the puppet
「私の名前はメランポではありません」と人形は答えました
"Oh! then who are you?" asked the polecat
「ああ!じゃあ、お前は誰だ?」とケナガイタチは尋ねました
"I am Pinocchio," answered Pinocchio
「私はピノキオです」とピノキオは答えました
"And what are you doing here?"
「それで、ここで何をしているの?」

"I am acting as watch-dog," confirmed Pinocchio
「私は番犬として行動しています」とピノキオは確認しました

"Then where is Melampo?" wondered the polecat
「じゃあ、メランポはどこだ?」とケナガイタチは不思議に思いました

"Where is the old dog who lived in this kennel?"
「この犬小屋に住んでいた老犬はどこにいるの?」

"He died this morning," Pinocchio informed
「彼は今朝亡くなった」とピノキオは告げた

"Is he dead? Poor beast! He was so good"
「彼は死んだのか?かわいそうな獣!彼はとても良かったです」

"but I would say that you were also a good dog"
「でも、君も良い犬だったと思うよ」

"I can see it in your face"
「君の顔にそれが見える」

"I beg your pardon, I am not a dog"
「ご容赦ください、私は犬ではありません」

"Not a dog? Then what are you?"
「犬じゃないの?じゃあ、お前は何だ?」

"I am a puppet," corrected Pinocchio
「私は操り人形です」とピノキオは訂正した

"And you are acting as watch-dog?"
「それで、君は番犬として行動しているのか?」

"now you understand the situation"
「これで状況がわかりましたね」

"I have been made to be a watch dog as a punishment"
「罰として番犬にさせられてしまった」

"well, then we shall tell you what the deal is"
「じゃあ、取引の内容を教えてあげよう」

"the same deal we had with the deceased Melampo"
「亡くなったメランポと同じ取引」

"I am sure you will be agree to the deal"
「きっと取引に同意していただけると思います」

"What are the conditions of this deal?"

"one night a week we will visit the poultry-yard"
「週に一度、私たちは養鶏場を訪れます」
"and you will allow us to carry off eight chickens"
「そして、あなたは私たちに八羽の鶏を運び去ることを許可してください」
"Of these chickens seven are to be eaten by us"
「このうち7羽は私たちが食べることになっている」
"and we will give one chicken to you"
「そして、私たちはあなたに一羽の鶏を差し上げます」
"your end of the bargain is very easy"
「お買い得品の結末はとても簡単です」
"all you have to do is pretend to be asleep"
「あなたがしなければならないのは眠ったふりをすることだけです」
"and don't get any ideas about barking"
「そして、吠えることについて何も考えないでください」
"you are not to wake the peasant when we come"
「私たちが来たときに農民を起こさないでください」
"Did Melampo act in this manner?" asked Pinocchio
「メランポはこんなふうに行動したの?」ピノキオが尋ねた
"that is the deal we had with Melampo"
「それがメランポとの取引だ」
"and we were always on the best terms with him
「そして、私たちはいつも彼と最高の関係にありました
"sleep quietly and let us do our business"
「静かに眠って、自分たちの仕事をさせてください」
"and in the morning you will have a beautiful chicken"
「そして朝には美しい鶏が手に入る」
"it will be ready plucked for your breakfast tomorrow"
「明日の朝食のために摘み取る準備ができています」
"Have we understood each other clearly?"
「私たちはお互いをはっきり理解できたのだろうか?」
"Only too clearly!" answered Pinocchio

「はっきりしすぎているだけだよ!」ピノキオは答えた
and he shook his head threateningly
そして彼は脅すように首を振った
as if to say: "You shall hear of this shortly!"
まるで「このことはすぐに聞くでしょう!」と言わんばかりに。
the four polecats thought that they had a deal
4匹のポールキャットは、自分たちが取引をしたと思った
so they continued to the poultry-yard
それで彼らは養鶏場に進みました
first they opened the gate with their teeth
まず、彼らは歯で門を開けました
and then they slipped in one by one
そして、彼らは一人ずつ滑り込みました
they hadn't been in the chicken-coup for long
彼らはチキンクーデターに長く関わっていなかった
but then they heard the gate shut behind them
しかし、その時、背後で門が閉まる音が聞こえた
It was Pinocchio who had shut the gate
門を閉めたのはピノキオだった
and Pinocchio took some extra security measures
そしてピノキオはいくつかの追加のセキュリティ対策を講じました
he put a large stone against the gate
彼は大きな石を門に立てかけました
this way the polecats couldn't get out again
これでは、ケナガイタチは再び外に出ることができませんでした
and then Pinocchio began to bark like a dog
そしてピノキオは犬のように吠え始めました
and he barked exactly like a watch-dog barks
そして、彼は番犬が吠えるように正確に吠えました
the peasant heard Pinocchio barking
農民はピノキオの吠え声を聞いた
he quickly awoke and jumped out of bed

彼はすぐに目を覚まし、ベッドから飛び降りました
with his gun he came to the window
彼は銃を持って窓のところに来た
and from the window he called to Pinocchio
そして窓からピノキオに呼びかけた
"What is the matter?" he asked the puppet
「どうしたの?」彼は人形に尋ねました
"There are robbers!" answered Pinocchio
「強盗がいる!」ピノキオは答えた
"Where are they?" he wanted to know
「彼らはどこにいるの?」彼は知りたかった
"they are in the poultry-yard," confirmed Pinocchio
「彼らは養鶏場にいます」とピノキオは確認しました
"I will come down directly," said the peasant
「直接降りてきます」と農夫は言いました
and he came down in a great hurry
そして彼は大急ぎで降りてきました
it would have taken less time to say "Amen"
「アーメン」と言うのにもっと時間がかからなかったでしょう
He rushed into the poultry-yard
彼は養鶏場に駆け込んだ
and quickly he caught all the polecats
そしてすぐに彼はすべてのケナガイタチを捕まえました
and then he put the polecats into a sack
そして、彼はケナガイタチを袋に入れました
he said to them in a tone of great satisfaction:
彼は非常に満足した口調で彼らに言った。
"At last you have fallen into my hands!"
「とうとうお前が私の手に落ちた!」
"I could punish you, if I wanted to"
「お前を罰してやるよ、もしそうしたいなら」
"but I am not so cruel," he comforted them
「でも、僕はそんなに残酷じゃない」と彼は彼らを慰めた
"I will content myself in other ways"

「他の方法で自分を満足させる」
"I will carry you in the morning to the innkeeper"
「朝になったら宿の主人のところまで運びます」
"he will skin and cook you like hares"
「彼はあなたをウサギのように皮を剥ぎ、料理します」
"and you will be served with a sweet sauce"
「そして、甘いソースが添えられます」
"It is an honour that you don't deserve"
「それはあなたが受けるに値しない名誉です」
"you're lucky I am so generous with you"
「君はラッキーだよ。僕が君にとても寛大だよ」
He then approached Pinocchio and stroked him
それから彼はピノキオに近づき、彼を撫でました
"How did you manage to discover the four thieves?"
「どうやって四人の泥棒を見つけたの?」
"my faithful Melampo never found out anything!"
「私の忠実なメランポは何も見つけられませんでした!」
The puppet could then have told him the whole story
その人形は、彼にすべての話を話すことができたでしょう
he could have told him about the treacherous deal
彼は彼に裏切り取引について話すことができたはずだ
but he remembered that the dog was dead
しかし、彼は犬が死んでいたことを思い出した
and the puppet thought to himself:
そして人形は心の中で考えました:
"of what use it it accusing the dead?"
「死者を責めるのに何の役に立つの?」
"The dead are no longer with us"
「死者はもう私たちと一緒にいない」
"it is best to leave the dead in peace!"
「死者を安らかに放置するのが最善です!」
the peasant went on to ask more questions
農民はさらに質問を続けました
"were you sleeping when the thieves came?"

「泥棒が来たとき、君は寝ていたのか?」
"I was asleep," answered Pinocchio
「眠っていたんだ」とピノキオは答えた
"but the polecats woke me with their chatter"
「でも、ケナガイタチはおしゃべりで私を起こした」
"one of the polecats came to the kennel"
「ケナガイタチの1匹が犬小屋に来た」
he tried to make a terrible deal with me
彼は私とひどい取引をしようとしました
"promise not to bark and we'll give you fine chicken"
「吠えないと約束してくれ。そうすれば、ちゃんとした鶏肉をあげるよ」
"I was offended by such an underhanded offer"
「こんなに卑劣な申し出に腹を立てた」
"I can admit that I am a naughty puppet"
「私はいたずらな人形であることを認めることができます」
"but there is one thing I will never be guilty of"
「でも、絶対に罪を犯さないことが一つあるんだ」
"I will not make terms with dishonest people!"
「私は不誠実な人々と折り合いをつけません!」
"and I will not share their dishonest gains"
「そして、私は彼らの不誠実な利益を分け与えません」
"Well said, my boy!" cried the peasant
「よく言った、お坊ちゃん!」と農夫は叫びました
and he patted Pinocchio on the shoulder
そして彼はピノキオの肩を叩いた
"Such sentiments do you great honour, my boy"
「そのような感情は、君にとって非常に名誉なことだ、我が子よ」
"let me show you proof of my gratitude to you"
「君への感謝の証を見せてあげよう」
"I will at once set you at liberty"
「すぐにお前を自由にしてやる」
"and you may return home as you please"
「そして、お好きなだけ家に帰っていただいて構いませ

ん」
And he removed the dog-collar from Pinocchio
そして、ピノキオから犬の首輪を外した

Pinocchio Flies to the Seashore
ピノキオが海岸に飛ぶ

a dog-collar had hung around Pinocchio's neck
ピノキオの首には犬の首輪がぶら下がっていました
but now Pinocchio had his freedom again
しかし、今やピノキオは再び自由を手に入れました
and he wore the humiliating dog-collar no more
そして、彼はもう屈辱的な犬の首輪を着けていませんでした
he ran off across the fields
彼は野原を横切って走り去った
and he kept running until he reached the road
そして、彼は道路にたどり着くまで走り続けました
the road that led to the Fairy's house
妖精の家に通じる道
in the woods he could see the Big Oak tree
森の中で彼は大きな樫の木を見ることができました
the Big Oak tree to which he had been hung
彼が吊るされていた大きな樫の木
Pinocchio looked around in every direction
ピノキオは四方八方を見回した
but he couldn't see his sister's house
しかし、彼は妹の家を見ることができませんでした
the house of the beautiful Child with blue hair
青い髪の美しい子供の家
Pinocchio was seized with a sad presentiment
ピノキオは悲しい予感にとらわれました
he began to run with all the strength he had left
彼は残された力をすべて振り絞って走り始めました

in a few minutes he reached the field
数分後、彼はフィールドに着きました
he was where the little house had once stood
彼はかつて小さな家が立っていた場所にいました
But the little white house was no longer there
しかし、小さな白い家はもうそこにはありませんでした
Instead of the house he saw a marble stone
家の代わりに大理石の石が見えた
on the stone were engraved these sad words:
石にはこれらの悲しい言葉が刻まれていました。
"Here lies the child with the blue hair"
「ここに青い髪の子供がいます」
"she was abandoned by her little brother Pinocchio"
「彼女は弟のピノキオに捨てられた」
"and from the sorrow she succumbed to death"
「そして、その悲しみから彼女は死に屈した」
with difficulty he had read this epitaph
彼はこの墓碑銘を読むのに苦労しました
I leave you to imagine the puppet's feelings
人形の気持ちを想像するのは君に任せます
He fell with his face on the ground
彼は顔を地面につけて倒れた
he covered the tombstone with a thousand kisses
彼は墓石を千のキスで覆った
and he burst into an agony of tears
そして彼は泣き崩れました
He cried for all of that night
彼はその夜ずっと泣いていました
and when morning came he was still crying
そして朝が来ても、彼はまだ泣いていました
he cried although he had no tears left
彼は涙が残っていなかったにもかかわらず、泣いた
his lamentations were heart-breaking
彼の嘆きは心を痛めるものでした
and his sobs echoed in the surrounding hills
そして彼のすすり泣きが周囲の丘に響き渡った

And while he was weeping he said:
そして、彼が泣いている間、彼は言いました。
"Oh, little Fairy, why did you die?"
「あら、小さな妖精、どうして死んだの?」
"Why did I not die instead of you?"
「なぜ私はあなたの代わりに死ななかったのですか?」
"I who am so wicked, whilst you were so good"
「私はとても邪悪なのに、あなたはとても良かったのに」
"And my papa? Where can he be?"
「パパは?彼はどこにいるのだろう?」
"Oh, little Fairy, tell me where I can find him"
「ああ、小さな妖精、どこで見つけられるか教えて」
"for I want to remain with him always"
「いつも彼と一緒にいたいから」
"and I never want to leave him ever again!"
「そして、もう二度と彼から離れたくない!」
"tell me that it is not true that you are dead!"
「あなたが死んだというのは本当じゃないって言って!」
"If you really love your little brother, come to life again"
「本当に弟を愛しているなら、また生き返って」
"Does it not grieve you to see me alone in the world?"
「この世で私が一人ぼっちなのを見るのは、悲しくないの?」
"does it not sadden you to see me abandoned by everybody?"
「私がみんなに見捨てられるのを見るのは悲しくないですか?」
"If assassins come they will hang me from the tree again"
「暗殺者が来たら、また木から吊るす」
"and this time I would die indeed"
「そして今度は本当に死ぬだろう」
"What can I do here alone in the world?"
「世界でここで一人で何ができるの?」

"I have lost you and my papa"
「君とパパを失った」
"who will love me and give me food now?"
「今、誰が私を愛し、食べ物をくれるのだろう?」
"Where shall I go to sleep at night?"
「夜はどこで寝ようか?」
"Who will make me a new jacket?"
「誰が新しいジャケットを作ってくれるの?」
"Oh, it would be better for me to die also!"
「ああ、私も死んだ方がいい!」
"not to live would be a hundred times better"
「生きない方が百倍もましだ」
"Yes, I want to die," he concluded
「はい、私は死にたいです」と彼は結論付けました
And in his despair he tried to tear his hair
そして絶望の中で、彼は髪を引き裂こうとしました
but his hair was made of wood
しかし、彼の髪は木でできていました
so he could not have the satisfaction
だから彼は満足感を得ることができなかった
Just then a large Pigeon flew over his head
ちょうどその時、大きな鳩が彼の頭上を飛んできた
the pigeon stopped with distended wings
鳩は翼を広げて止まった
and the pigeon called down from a great height
そして鳩は高いところから呼びました
"Tell me, child, what are you doing there?"
「教えて、子供、そこで何をしているの?」
"Don't you see? I am crying!" said Pinocchio
「わからないの?泣いちゃった!」とピノキオは言いました
and he raised his head towards the voice
そして彼は声に向かって顔を上げた
and he rubbed his eyes with his jacket
そして彼はジャケットで目をこすった
"Tell me," continued the Pigeon

「教えてくれ」と鳩は続けました
"do you happen to know a puppet called Pinocchio?"
「ピノキオという人形をご存知ですか?」
"Pinocchio? Did you say Pinocchio?" repeated the puppet
「ピノキオ?ピノキオと言ったの?」と人形は繰り返しました
and he quickly jumped to his feet
そして彼はすぐに立ち上がった
"I am Pinocchio!" he exclaimed with hope
「俺はピノキオだ!」彼は希望を込めて叫んだ
At this answer the Pigeon descended rapidly
この答えで、鳩は急速に降りました
He was larger than a turkey
彼は七面鳥よりも大きかった
"Do you also know Geppetto?" he asked
「君もゼペットを知っているのか?」と彼は尋ねた
"Do I know him! He is my poor papa!"
「彼を知っているの!!彼は私のかわいそうなパパです!」
"Has he perhaps spoken to you of me?"
「彼はもしかして、私のことをあなたに話したの?」
"Will you take me to him?"
「彼のところに連れて行ってくれる?」
"Is he still alive?"
「彼はまだ生きているの?」
"Answer me, for pity's sake"
「答えてください、同情のために」
"is he still alive??"
「彼はまだ生きているの??」
"I left him three days ago on the seashore"
「3日前に彼を海辺に置き去りにした」
"What was he doing?" Pinocchio had to know
「彼は何をしていたの?」ピノキオは知らなければならなかった
"He was building a little boat for himself"

「彼は自分のために小さなボートを作っていた」
"he was going to cross the ocean"
「彼は海を渡るつもりだった」
"that poor man has been going all round the world"
「あの可哀想な男は世界中を回っている」
"he has been looking for you"
「彼は君を探していた」
"but he had no success in finding you"
「でも、彼は君を見つけることに成功しなかった」
"so now he will go to the distant countries"
「だから今、彼は遠い国に行くでしょう」
"he will search for you in the New World"
「彼は新世界であなたを探す」
"How far is it from here to the shore?"
「ここから岸まではどれくらい離れているの?」
"More than six hundred miles"
「600マイル以上」
"Six hundred miles?" echoed Pinocchio
「600マイル?」ピノキオがこだました
"Oh, beautiful Pigeon," pleaded Pinocchio
「ああ、美しい鳩」とピノキオは嘆願した
"what a fine thing it would be to have your wings!"
「あなたの翼があるなんて、なんて素晴らしいことでしょう!」
"If you wish to go, I will carry you there"
「行きたいなら、私が運びます」
"How could you carry me there?"
「どうやって私をそこに運べるんだ?」
"I can carry you on my back"
「君を背負ってもいいよ」
"Do you weigh much?"
「体重は多いですか?」
"I weigh next to nothing"
「体重はほぼゼロ」
"I am as light as a feather"
「私は羽のように軽い」

Pinocchio didn't hesitate for another moment
ピノキオは一瞬も躊躇しなかった
and he jumped at once on the Pigeon's back
そして彼はすぐに鳩の背中に飛び乗りました
he put a leg on each side of the pigeon
彼は鳩の両側に足を置きました
just like men do when they're riding horseback
男性が馬に乗っているときと同じように
and Pinocchio exclaimed joyfully:
そしてピノキオは嬉しそうに叫びました。
"Gallop, gallop, my little horse"
「ギャロップ、ギャロップ、私の小さな馬」
"because I am anxious to arrive quickly!"
「早く到着したいから!」
The Pigeon took flight into the air
鳩は空中に飛び立ちました
and in a few minutes they almost touched the clouds
そして数分で、彼らはほとんど雲に触れました

now the puppet was at an immense height
今や人形は途方もない高さにありました
and he became more and more curious
そして彼はますます好奇心をそそられました
so he looked down to the ground
だから彼は地面を見下ろした
but his head spun round in dizziness
しかし、彼の頭はめまいでぐるぐる回った
he became ever so frightened of the height
彼はますます高さに怯えるようになった
and he had to save himself from the danger of falling
そして、彼は転倒の危険から身を守らなければなりませんでした
and so held tightly to his feathered steed
そして、彼の羽毛の馬にしっかりと握りしめられている
They flew through the skies all of that day
彼らはその日一日中空を飛んでいました
Towards evening the Pigeon said:
夕方近くになると、鳩は言いました。
"I am very thirsty from all this flying!"
「こんなに飛んでるから、とても喉が渇いちゃった!」
"And I am very hungry!" agreed Pinocchio
「そして、とてもお腹が空いています!」ピノキオは同意しました
"Let us stop at that dovecote for a few minutes"
「あの鳩小屋で数分間立ち止まりましょう」
"and then we will continue our journey"
「そして、私たちは旅を続ける」
"then we may reach the seashore by dawn tomorrow"
「じゃあ、明日の夜明けまでには海岸に着くかもしれない」
They went into a deserted dovecote
彼らは人けのない鳩小屋に入った
here they found nothing but a basin full of water
ここでは、水でいっぱいの洗面器以外は何も見つかりませんでした

and they found a basket full of vetch
そして、ベッチでいっぱいのバスケットを見つけました
The puppet had never in his life been able to eat vetch
人形は彼の人生でベッチを食べることができませんでした
according to him it made him sick
彼によると、それは彼を病気にしたという
That evening, however, he ate to repletion
しかし、その夜、彼はお腹いっぱい食べました
and he nearly emptied the basket of it
そして、彼はその籠をほとんど空にしそうになった
and then he turned to the Pigeon and said to him:
そして、鳩の方を向いて言いました。
"I never could have believed that vetch was so good!"
「ベッチがこんなに上手いなんて信じられなかった!」
"Be assured, my boy," replied the Pigeon
「安心しろ、坊や」と鳩は答えました
"when hunger is real even vetch becomes delicious"
「空腹が本当なら、ベッチも美味しくなる」
"Hunger knows neither caprice nor greediness"
「飢餓は気まぐれも貪欲も知らない」
the two quickly finished their little meal
二人はすぐに小さな食事を終えました
and they recommenced their journey and flew away
そして、彼らは再び旅を再開し、飛び去った
The following morning they reached the seashore
翌朝、彼らは海岸に到着しました
The Pigeon placed Pinocchio on the ground
鳩はピノキオを地面に置きました
the pigeon did not wish to be troubled with thanks
鳩は感謝に悩まされることを望まなかった
it was indeed a good action he had done
それは確かに彼が行った良い行動だった
but he had done it out the goodness of his heart
しかし、彼は自分の心の善良さからそれを成し遂げた
and Pinocchio had no time to lose

そしてピノキオには一刻の猶予もありませんでした
so he flew quickly away and disappeared
それで彼はすぐに飛んで行って消えました
The shore was crowded with people
海岸は人で賑わっていました
the people were looking out to sea
人々は海を眺めていました
they shouting and gesticulating at something
彼らは何かに向かって叫び、身振り手振りをします
"What has happened?" asked Pinocchio of an old woman
「どうしたの?」ピノキオは老婆に尋ねた
"there is a poor father who has lost his son"
「息子を亡くした可哀想な父がいる」
"he has gone out to sea in a little boat"
「彼は小さなボートで海に出た」
"he will search for him on the other side of the water"
「彼は水の向こう側で彼を探すだろう」
"and today the sea is most tempestuous"
「そして今日、海は最も荒れ狂っています」
"and the little boat is in danger of sinking"
「そして、その小さなボートは沈没の危機に瀕している」
"Where is the little boat?" asked Pinocchio
「その小さなボートはどこにあるの?」とピノキオは尋ねた
"It is out there in a line with my finger"
「私の指で一列に並んでいる」
and she pointed to a little boat
そして彼女は小さなボートを指差しました
and the little boat looked like a little nutshell
そして、小さなボートは小さな一言のように見えました
a little nutshell with a very little man in it
とても小さな男が入っている小さな一言で言えば
Pinocchio fixed his eyes on the little nutshell
ピノキオは小さな一言で言えば、目を凝らしました
after looking attentively he gave a piercing scream:

注意深く見た後、彼は鋭い叫び声を上げた。
"It is my papa! It is my papa!"
「私のパパです!私のパパです!」
The boat, meanwhile, was being beaten by the fury of the waves
一方、ボートは波の猛威に打ちのめされていました
at one moment it disappeared in the trough of the sea
ある瞬間、それは海の谷に消えました
and in the next moment the boat came to the surface again
そして次の瞬間、ボートは再び水面に浮かびました
Pinocchio stood on the top of a high rock
ピノキオは高い岩の頂上に立っていました
and he kept calling to his father
そして彼は父親に電話をかけ続けました
and he made every kind of signal to him
そして、彼は彼にあらゆる種類の合図をしました
he waved his hands, his handkerchief, and his cap
彼は手を振り、ハンカチを振り、帽子を振った
Pinocchio was very far away from him
ピノキオは彼から非常に遠く離れていました
but Geppetto appeared to recognize his son
しかし、ゼペットは息子を認識しているように見えた
and he also took off his cap and waved it
そして彼も帽子を脱いで振った
he tried by gestures to make him understand
彼は身振り手振りで理解させようとした
"I would have returned if it were possible"
「可能であれば、私も戻っていただろう」
"but the sea is most tempestuous"
「しかし、海は最も荒れ狂う」
"and my oars won't take me to the shores again"
「そして、私のオールは二度と私を岸に連れて行ってくれません」
Suddenly a tremendous wave rose out of the sea
突然、海からすさまじい波が立ち上りました
and then the the little nutshell disappeared

そして、小さな一言で言えば消えました
They waited, hoping the boat would come again to the surface
彼らは、ボートが再び水面に浮かぶことを願って待っていました
but the little boat was seen no more
しかし、その小さなボートはもう見えませんでした
the fisherman had assembled at the shore
漁師は岸に集まっていた
"Poor man!" they said of him, and murmured a prayer
「かわいそうな人だ!」彼らは彼のことを言い、祈りをつぶやきました
and then they turned to go home
そして、彼らは家に帰ろうと向きを変えました
Just then they heard a desperate cry
ちょうどその時、彼らは必死の叫び声を聞いた
looking back, they saw a little boy
振り返ると、小さな男の子がいました
"I will save my papa," the boy exclaimed
「パパを救うよ」と少年は叫びました
and he jumped from a rock into the sea
そして彼は岩から海に飛び込みました
as you know Pinocchio was made of wood
ご存知のように、ピノキオは木でできていました
so he floated easily on the water
だから彼は簡単に水に浮かびました
and he swam as well as a fish
そして、彼は魚のように泳ぎました
At one moment they saw him disappear under the water
ある瞬間、彼らは彼が水面下に消えるのを見た
he was carried down by the fury of the waves
彼は波の猛威に押し流された
and in the next moment he reappeared to the surface of the water
そして次の瞬間、彼は再び水面に現れた
he struggled on swimming with a leg or an arm

彼は足や腕で泳ぐのに苦労しました
but at last they lost sight of him
しかし、ついに彼らは彼を見失った
and he was seen no more
そして彼はもう見られませんでした
and they offered another prayer for the puppet
そして、彼らは人形のために別の祈りを捧げました

Pinocchio Finds the Fairy Again
ピノキオは再び妖精を見つける

Pinocchio wanted to be in time to help his father
ピノキオは父親を助けるために間に合うようにしたかった
so he swam all through the night
だから彼は一晩中泳ぎました
And what a horrible night it was!
そして、それは何と恐ろしい夜だったことでしょう。
The rain came down in torrents
雨は激しく降り注いだ
it hailed and the thunder was frightful
それは雹を鳴らし、雷は恐ろしかった
the flashes of lightning made it as light as day
稲妻の閃光が昼のように明るくなりました

Towards morning he saw a long strip of land
朝になると、彼は長い土地を見ました
It was an island in the midst of the sea
海の真ん中に浮かぶ島でした
He tried his utmost to reach the shore
彼は岸にたどり着くために全力を尽くしました
but his efforts were all in vain
しかし、彼の努力はすべて無駄でした
The waves raced and tumbled over each other
波は競い合い、転がり落ちました
and the torrent knocked Pinocchio about
そして激流はピノキオを叩きのめしました
it was as if he had been a wisp of straw
それはまるで彼が藁の切れ端のようだった
At last, fortunately for him, a billow rolled up
ついに、彼にとって幸運なことに、うねりが巻き上げられました
it rose with such fury that he was lifted up
それは彼が持ち上げられるほどの怒りで立ち上がった
and finally he was thrown on to the sands

そして最後に、彼は砂の上に投げ出されました
the little puppet crashed onto the ground
小さな人形は地面に墜落しました
and all his joints cracked from the impact
そして彼のすべての関節は衝撃でひび割れました
but he comforted himself, saying:
しかし、彼は自分を慰めて言った。
"This time also I have made a wonderful escape!"
「今回も素晴らしい脱出ができました!」
Little by little the sky cleared
少しずつ空が晴れ渡ってきた
the sun shone out in all his splendour
太陽は彼のすべての輝きで輝いていました
and the sea became as quiet and smooth as oil
そして海は油のように静かで滑らかになりました
The puppet put his clothes in the sun to dry
人形は自分の服を太陽の下に置き、乾かしました
and he began to look in every direction
そして彼はあらゆる方向を見始めました
somewhere on the water there must be a little boat
水上のどこかに小さなボートがあるはずです
and in the boat he hoped to see a little man
そして、ボートの中で彼は小さな男に会うことを望んでいました
he looked out to sea as far as he could see
彼は見渡す限り海を見渡しました
but all he saw was the sky and the sea
しかし、彼が見たのは空と海だけだった
"If I only knew what this island was called!"
「この島の名前さえ知っていたらいいのに!」
"If I only knew whether it was inhabited"
「人が住んでいるかどうかさえ知っていれば」
"perhaps civilized people do live here"
「もしかしたら、文明人がここに住んでいるのかもしれない」
"people who do not hang boys from trees"

「男の子を木から吊るさない人」
"but whom can I ask if there is nobody?"
「でも、誰もいないのに、誰に聞けばいいの?」
Pinocchio didn't like the idea of being all alone
ピノキオは、一人ぼっちになるのが好きではありませんでした
and now he was alone on a great uninhabited country
そして今、彼は大きな無人の国に一人でいました
the idea of it made him melancholy
その考えが彼を憂鬱にさせた
he was just about to to cry
彼はちょうど泣きそうでした
But at that moment he saw a big fish swimming by
しかし、その瞬間、彼は大きな魚が泳いでいるのを見ました
the big fish was only a short distance from the shore
大きな魚は岸からほんの少しのところにいました
the fish was going quietly on its own business
魚は静かに自分の仕事で進んでいました
and it had its head out of the water
そして、それは頭を水から出していました
Not knowing its name, the puppet called to the fish
その名前を知らなかった人形は、魚に呼びかけた
he called out in a loud voice to make himself heard:
彼は自分の声を聞かせるために大声で叫んだ。
"Eh, Sir Fish, will you permit me a word with you?"
「ええ、サー・フィッシュ、お話しさせていただけますか?」
"Two words, if you like," answered the fish
「もしよろしければ、二言」と魚は答えました
the fish was in fact not a fish at all
その魚は実際にはまったく魚ではありませんでした
what the fish was was a Dolphin
魚が何だったかはイルカでした
and you couldn't have found a politer dolphin
そして、あなたはもっと穏やかなイルカを見つけること

ができなかったでしょう
"Would you be kind enough to tell:"
「教えてもらえますか?」
"is there are villages in this island?"
「この島に村はあるの?」
"and might there be something to eat in these villages?"
「そして、この村には何か食べるものがあるのかな?」
"and is there any danger in these villages?"
「そして、これらの村に危険はあるのか?」
"might one get eaten in these villages?"
「この村で食べられるかもしれない?」
"there certainly are villages," replied the Dolphin
「確かに村はあるよ」とイルカは答えました
"Indeed, you will find one village quite close by"
「確かに、すぐ近くに一つの村があるでしょう」
"And what road must I take to go there?"
「それで、そこに行くにはどんな道を行けばいいの?」
"You must take that path to your left"
「その道を左に進まなければなりません」
"and then you must follow your nose"
「そして、鼻をたどらなければならない」
"Will you tell me another thing?"
「もう一つ教えてくれないか?」
"You swim about the sea all day and night"
「君は昼も夜も海を泳いでいる」
"have you by chance met a little boat"
「Have You by chance met a little boat」
"a little boat with my papa in it?"
「パパが乗った小さなボート?」
"And who is your papa?"
「それで、あなたのパパは誰なの?」
"He is the best papa in the world"
「彼は世界で最高のパパです」
"but it would be difficult to find a worse son than I am"
「でも、僕よりひどい息子を見つけるのは難しいだろう

」

The fish regretted to tell him what he feared
魚は彼が恐れていることを彼に話すことを後悔しました
"you saw the terrible storm we had last night"
「昨夜のひどい嵐を見たでしょう」
"the little boat must have gone to the bottom"
「小さなボートは底に落ちたに違いない」
"And my papa?" asked Pinocchio
「それで、私のパパは?」ピノキオが尋ねた
"He must have been swallowed by the terrible Dog-Fish"
「彼は恐ろしいドッグフィッシュに飲み込まれたに違いない」
"of late he has been swimming on our waters"
「最近、彼は私たちの海で泳いでいます」
"and he has been spreading devastation and ruin"
「そして彼は荒廃と破滅を広めてきた」
Pinocchio was already beginning to quake with fear
ピノキオはすでに恐怖に震え始めていました
"Is this Dog-Fish very big?" asked Pinocchio
「このドッグフィッシュはそんなに大きいの?」とピノキオは尋ねました
"oh, very big!" replied the Dolphin
「ああ、すごく大きい!」とイルカは答えました
"let me tell you about this fish"
「この魚について教えてあげよう」
"then you can form some idea of his size"
「それなら、彼の大きさをある程度把握できるよ」
"he is bigger than a five-storied house"
「彼は5階建ての家よりも大きい」
"and his mouth is more enormous than you've ever seen"
「そして、彼の口はあなたが今まで見たことのないほど巨大です」
"a railway train could pass down his throat"
「鉄道列車が彼の喉を通るかもしれない」
"Mercy upon us!" exclaimed the terrified puppet
「我らに慈悲を!」と怯えた人形は叫んだ

and he put on his clothes with the greatest haste
そして、彼は大急ぎで服を着た
"Good-bye, Sir Fish, and thank you"
「さようなら、フィッシュ卿、そしてありがとう」
"excuse the trouble I have given you"
「お手数をおかけして申し訳ありません」
"and many thanks for your politeness"
「そして、あなたの礼儀正しさに感謝します」
He then took the path that had been pointed out to him
それから彼は彼に指し示された道をたどった
and he began to walk as fast as he could
そして、彼はできるだけ速く歩き始めました
he walked so fast, indeed, that he was almost running
彼はとても速く歩いたので、実際、彼はほとんど走っていました
And at the slightest noise he turned to look behind him
そしてわずかな物音で彼は振り返り、後ろを振り返った
he feared that he might see the terrible Dog-Fish
彼は恐ろしい犬の魚を見るかもしれないと恐れた
and he imagined a railway train in its mouth
そして、彼はその口の中に鉄道列車を想像した
a half-hour walk took him to a little village
30分ほど歩くと、彼は小さな村にたどり着きました
the village was The Village of the Industrious Bees
その村は勤勉な蜂の村でした
The road was alive with people
道は人で賑わっていました
and they were running here and there
そして、彼らはあちこち走り回っていました
and they all had to attend to their business
そして、彼らは皆、自分たちの仕事に気を配らなければなりませんでした
all were at work, all had something to do
全員が仕事中で、何かやることがありました
You could not have found an idler or a vagabond
怠惰な人や放浪者を見つけることはできなかったでしょ

う

even if you searched for him with a lighted lamp
あなたが火のついたランプで彼を探しても

"Ah!" said that lazy Pinocchio at once
「ああ!」と、怠惰なピノキオはすぐに言いました

"I see that this village will never suit me!"
「この村は私には絶対に似合わないわね!」

"I wasn't born to work!"
「私は働くために生まれてきたのではない!」

In the meanwhile he was tormented by hunger
その間、彼は飢えに苦しめられていました

he had eaten nothing for twenty-four hours
彼は二十四時間何も食べていなかった

he had not even eaten vetch
彼はベッチさえ食べていなかった

What was poor Pinocchio to do?
かわいそうなピノキオは何をしましたか?

There were only two ways to obtain food
食料を手に入れる方法は2つしかありませんでした

he could either get food by asking for a little work
彼は少し仕事を頼むことで食べ物を手に入れることができました

or he could get food by way of begging
あるいは、物乞いによって食べ物を手に入れることもできた

someone might be kind enough to throw him a nickel
誰かが親切にも彼にニッケルを投げてくれるかもしれません

or they might give him a mouthful of bread
あるいは、彼らは彼に一口のパンを与えるかもしれません

generally Pinocchio was ashamed to beg
一般的にピノキオは物乞いを恥ずかしがっていました

his father had always preached him to be industrious
彼の父はいつも彼に勤勉であるように説いていました

he taught him no one had a right to beg

彼は彼に、誰も物乞いをする権利はないと教えた
except the aged and the infirm
高齢者や虚弱な人を除いて
The really poor in this world deserve compassion
この世で本当に貧しい人々は、同情を受けるに値する
the really poor in this world require assistance
この世界で本当に貧しい人々は援助を必要としています
only those who are aged or sick
高齢または病気の方のみ
those who are no longer able to earn their own bread
自分でパンを稼ぐことができなくなった人
It is the duty of everyone else to work
働くことは、他のすべての人の義務です
and if they don't labour, so much the worse for them
そして、彼らが働かなければ、彼らにとってはるかに悪いことです
let them suffer from their hunger
彼らを飢えに苦しませておいて下さい
At that moment a man came down the road
その時、一人の男が道を降りてきました
he was tired and panting for breath
彼は疲れていて、息を切らしていました
He was dragging two carts full of charcoal
彼は木炭でいっぱいの2台のカートを引きずっていました
Pinocchio judged by his face that he was a kind man
ピノキオは彼の顔から彼が優しい男であると判断しました
so Pinocchio approached the charcoal man
そこでピノキオは炭男に近づいた
he cast down his eyes with shame
彼は恥ずかしそうに目を伏せた
and he said to him in a low voice:
そして、低い声で彼に言った。
"Would you have the charity to give me a nickel?"
「私にニッケルをくれる慈善団体はありますか?」

"because, as you can see, I am dying of hunger"
「だって、見ての通り、僕は飢えで死にかけているんだ」
"You shall have not only a nickel," said the man
「お前はニッケルだけじゃない」と男は言った
"I will give you a dime"
「10セント硬貨あげるよ」
"but for the dime you must do some work"
「でも、10セント硬貨のために、君は何か仕事をしなければならない」
"help me to drag home these two carts of charcoal"
「この2台の木炭のカートを引きずって家に帰るのを手伝って」
"I am surprised at you!" answered the puppet
「びっくりしました!」と人形は答えました
and there was a tone of offense in his voice
そして彼の声には攻撃的なトーンがありました
"Let me tell you something about myself"
「私自身について少し話させてください」
"I am not accustomed to do the work of a donkey"
「ロバの仕事をすることに慣れていない」
"I have never drawn a cart!"
「カートを引いたことない!」
"So much the better for you," answered the man
「君にとっては、それだけのことだ」と男は答えた
"my boy, I see how you are dying of hunger"
「お坊ちゃん、お前が飢えで死んでいるのが見える」
"eat two fine slices of your pride"
「自慢の上質なスライスを2枚食べる」
"and be careful not to get indigestion"
「そして、消化不良にならないように注意してください」
A few minutes afterwards a mason passed by
数分後、一人の石工が通りかかりました
he was carrying a basket of mortar

彼は迫撃砲の入った籠を持っていた
"Would you have the charity to give me a nickel?"
「私にニッケルをくれる慈善団体はありますか?」
"me, a poor boy who is yawning for want of food"
「私、食べ物が足りなくてあくびをしている可哀想な男の子」
"Willingly," answered the man
「喜んで」と男は答えた
"Come with me and carry the mortar"
「私と一緒に来て、迫撃砲を持って」
"and instead of a nickel I will give you a dime"
「そして、ニッケルの代わりに10セント硬貨をあげるよ」
"But the mortar is heavy," objected Pinocchio
「しかし、迫撃砲は重い」とピノキオは異議を唱えた
"and I don't want to tire myself"
「そして、私は自分自身を疲れさせたくない」
"I see you you don't want to tire yourself"
「なるほど、あなたは疲れたくないのですね」
"then, my boy, go amuse yourself with yawning"
「じゃあ、坊や、あくびをして楽しんでください」
In less than half an hour twenty other people went by
30分も経たないうちに、20人の人々が通り過ぎた
and Pinocchio asked charity of them all
そしてピノキオは彼ら全員に慈善を求めました
but they all gave him the same answer
しかし、彼らは皆、彼に同じ答えを出した
"Are you not ashamed to beg, young boy?"
「お前は物乞いを恥ずかしくないのか、少年よ?」
"Instead of idling about, look for a little work"
「ぼんやりしているのではなく、ちょっとした仕事を探してみて」
"you have to learn to earn your bread"
「パンを稼ぐことを学ばなければならない」
finally a nice little woman walked by
最後に、素敵な小さな女性が通りかかりました

she was carrying two cans of water
彼女は2缶の水を持っていました
Pinocchio asked her for charity too
ピノキオは彼女にも慈善を求めました
"Will you let me drink a little of your water?"
「君の水を少し飲ませてもらえないか?」
"because I am burning with thirst"
「渇きで燃えているから」
the little woman was happy to help
小さな女性は喜んで助けてくれました
"Drink, my boy, if you wish it!"
「飲んでください、私の息子、あなたが望むなら!」
and she set down the two cans
そして、彼女は二つの缶を置いた
Pinocchio drank like a fish
ピノキオは魚のように飲んだ
and as he dried his mouth he mumbled:
そして口を乾かしながら、彼はつぶやいた。
"I have quenched my thirst"
「喉の渇きを癒した」
"If I could only appease my hunger!"
「お腹が空いたらいいのに!」
The good woman heard Pinocchio's pleas
善良な女性はピノキオの嘆願を聞きました
and she was only too willing to oblige
そして、彼女はただ義務を負う気が強すぎただけだった
"help me to carry home these cans of water"
「この水缶を家に持ち帰るのを手伝って」
"and I will give you a fine piece of bread"
「そして、私はあなたに一切れのパンを差し上げます」
Pinocchio looked at the cans of water
ピノキオは水の缶を見た
and he answered neither yes nor no
そして、彼は「はい」とも「いいえ」とも答えませんでした
and the good woman added more to the offer

そして、善良な女性はオファーにさらに追加しました
"As well as bread you shall have cauliflower"
「パンだけでなく、カリフラワーも食べましょう」
Pinocchio gave another look at the can
ピノキオは缶をもう一度見た
and he answered neither yes nor no
そして、彼は「はい」とも「いいえ」とも答えませんでした
"And after the cauliflower there will be more"
「そしてカリフラワーの後にはもっとあるでしょう」
"I will give you a beautiful syrup bonbon"
「綺麗なシロップボンボンをあげる」
The temptation of this last dainty was great
この最後の可憐さの誘惑は大きかった
finally Pinocchio could resist no longer
ついにピノキオはもはや抵抗できなくなりました
with an air of decision he said:
彼は決意に満ちた雰囲気で言った。
"I must have patience!"
「我慢しなきゃ!」
"I will carry the water to your house"
「お前の家まで水を運びます」
The water was too heavy for Pinocchio
ピノキオには水が重すぎました
he could not carry it with his hands
彼はそれを手で運ぶことができませんでした
so he had to carry it on his head
だから彼はそれを頭に乗せて運ばなければならなかった
Pinocchio did not enjoy doing the work
ピノキオは仕事をするのが好きではありませんでした
but soon they reached the house
しかし、すぐに彼らは家に着きました
and the good little woman offered Pinocchio a seat
そして、善良な小柄な女性はピノキオに席を提供しました
the table had already been laid

テーブルはすでに置かれていました
and she placed before him the bread
そして、そのパンを彼の前に置きました
and then he got the cauliflower and the bonbon
そして、カリフラワーとボンボンを手に入れました
Pinocchio did not eat his food, he devoured it
ピノキオは彼の食べ物を食べませんでした、彼はそれをむさぼり食いました
His stomach was like an empty apartment
彼の胃袋は空っぽのアパートのようだった
an apartment that had been left uninhabited for months
何ヶ月も無人のまま放置されていたアパート
but now his ravenous hunger was somewhat appeased
しかし今、彼の貪欲な飢えはいくらか和らいでいました
he raised his head to thank his benefactress
彼は顔を上げて、恩人に感謝した
then he took a better look at her
それから彼は彼女をもっとよく見ました
he gave a prolonged "Oh!" of astonishment
彼は驚きの長い「おお!」と言いました
and he continued staring at her with wide open eyes
そして彼は大きく開いた目で彼女を見つめ続けました
his fork was in the air
彼のフォークは宙に浮いていた
and his mouth was full of cauliflower
そして彼の口はカリフラワーでいっぱいでした
it was as if he had been bewitched
まるで魔法にかけられたかのようだった
the good woman was quite amused
善良な女性はかなり面白がっていました
"What has surprised you so much?"
「何がそんなに驚いたの?」
"It is..." answered the puppet
「それは...」人形に答えた
"it's just that you are like..."
「ただ、君が...」

"it's just that you remind me of someone"
「ただ、君が誰かを思い出させるだけだよ」
"yes, yes, yes, the same voice"
「うん、うん、うん、同じ声」
"and you have the same eyes and hair"
「そして、あなたは同じ目と髪をしています」
"yes, yes, yes. you also have blue hair"
「うん、うん、うん。あなたも青い髪をしています」
"Oh, little Fairy! tell me that it is you!"
「ああ、小さな妖精!それがあなただって言って!」
"Do not make me cry anymore!"
「もう私を泣かせないで!」
"If only you knew how much I've cried"
「私がどれだけ泣いたか知っていれば」
"and I have suffered so much"
「そして、私はとても苦しんできました」
And Pinocchio threw himself at her feet
そしてピノキオは彼女の足元に身を投げ出した
and he embraced the knees of the mysterious little woman
そして彼は神秘的な小さな女性の膝を抱きしめました
and he began to cry bitterly
そして彼は激しく泣き始めました

Pinocchio Promises the Fairy he'll be a Good Boy Again
ピノキオは妖精に彼が再び良い子になると約束します

At first the good little woman played innocent
最初、善良な小さな女性は無邪気に振る舞った
she said she was not the little Fairy with blue hair
彼女は自分は青い髪の小さな妖精ではないと言いました
but Pinocchio could not be tricked
しかし、ピノキオはだまされることができませんでした
she had continued the comedy long enough
彼女はコメディを十分に長く続けていた
and so she ended by making herself known
そして、彼女は自分自身を知らしめることで終わりました

"You naughty little rogue, Pinocchio"
「いたずらっ子、ピノキオ」
"how did you discover who I was?"
「どうやって私が誰だったかを知ったの?」
"It was my great affection for you that told me"
「君に対する僕の大きな愛情が僕に言ったんだ」
"Do you remember when you left me?"
「いつ私を置いていったか覚えてる?」
"I was still a child back then"
「あの頃の僕はまだ子供だった」
"and now I have become a woman"
「そして今、私は女性になりました」
"a woman almost old enough to be your mamma"
「あなたのママになるくらいの年齢の女性」
"I am delighted at that"
「それは嬉しいです」
"I will not call you little sister anymore"
「もうお姉さんとは呼ばない」
"from now I will call you mamma"
「これからはママと呼ぶよ」

"all the other boys have a mamma"
「他の男の子たちはみんなママがいる」
"and I have always wished to also have a mamma"
「そして、私もずっとママが欲しいと思っていました」
"But how did you manage to grow so fast?"
「でも、どうやってこんなに早く成長できたの?」
"That is a secret," said the fairy
「それは秘密だよ」と妖精は言った
Pinocchio wanted to know, "teach me your secret"
ピノキオは知りたかった、「あなたの秘密を教えてください」
"because I would also like to grow"
「自分も成長したいから」
"Don't you see how small I am?"
「私がどれだけ小さいかわからないの?」
"I always remain no bigger than a ninepin"
「私はいつもナインピンより大きくないままです」
"But you cannot grow," replied the Fairy
「でも、君は成長できないよ」と妖精は答えました
"Why can't I grow?" asked Pinocchio
「なぜ私は成長できないのですか?」とピノキオは尋ねました
"Because puppets never grow"
「人形は決して成長しないから」
"when they are born they are puppets"
「彼らが生まれたとき、彼らは操り人形である」
"and they live their lives as puppets"
「そして、彼らは操り人形として生きています」
"and when they die they die as puppets"
「そして、彼らが死ぬと、操り人形として死ぬ」
Pinocchio game himself a slap
ピノキオゲーム自身を平手打ち
"Oh, I am sick of being a puppet!"
「ああ、人形になるのはうんざりだ!」
"It is time that I became a man"
「そろそろ男になる時が来た」

"And you will become a man," promised the fairy
「そして、あなたは男になるでしょう」と妖精は約束しました
"but you must know how to deserve it"
「でも、それにふさわしい方法を知っていなければならない」
"Is this true?" asked Pinocchio
「これは本当ですか?」とピノキオは尋ねた
"And what can I do to deserve to be a man?"
「そして、男になるに値するために何ができるの?」
"it is a very easy thing to deserve to be a man"
「男になるに値するのはとても簡単なことだ」
"all you have to do is learn to be a good boy"
「あなたがしなければならないのは、良い子になることを学ぶことだけです」
"And you think I am not a good boy?"
「それで、僕がいい子じゃないと思う?」
"You are quite the opposite of a good boy"
「君はいい子とは正反対だね」
"Good boys are obedient, and you..."
「いい子は従順だ。君は...」
"And I never obey," confessed Pinocchio
「そして、私は決して従わない」とピノキオは告白した
"Good boys like to learn and to work, and you..."
「いい子は学ぶことと働くことが好きです。そして、あなたは...」
"And I instead lead an idle, vagabond life"
「そして、私は代わりに怠惰で放浪的な生活を送っています」
"Good boys always speak the truth"
「いい子はいつも真実を話す」
"And I always tell lies," admitted Pinocchio
「そして、私はいつも嘘をつきます」とピノキオは認めました
"Good boys go willingly to school"

「いい子は進んで学校に行く」
"And school gives me pain all over the body"
「そして学校は私に全身の痛みを与えます」
"But from today I will change my life"
「でも、今日から僕は人生を変える」
"Do you promise me?" asked the Fairy
「約束しますか?」と妖精は尋ねました
"I promise that I will become a good little boy"
「いい子になることを約束する」
"and I promise be the consolation of my papa"
「そして、私は父の慰めになることを約束します」
"Where is my poor papa at this moment?"
「今、私のかわいそうなパパはどこにいるの?」
but the fairy didn't know where his papa was
しかし、妖精はパパがどこにいるのか知りませんでした
"Shall I ever have the happiness of seeing him again?"
「彼に再び会える幸せはあるのだろうか?」
"will I ever kiss him again?"
「彼にまたキスすることはあるの?」
"I think so; indeed, I am sure of it"
「そう思います。確かに、私はそれを確信しています」
At this answer Pinocchio was delighted
この答えにピノキオは喜びました
he took the Fairy's hands
彼は妖精の手を取りました
and he began to kiss her hands with great fervour
そして彼は彼女の手に熱心にキスをし始めました
he seemed beside himself with joy
彼は喜びで我を忘れているように見えた
Then Pinocchio raised his face
それからピノキオは顔を上げた
and he looked at her lovingly
そして彼は彼女を愛おしそうに見つめました
"Tell me, little mamma:"
「教えて、小さなママ」
"then it was not true that you were dead?"

「では、あなたが死んだというのは本当ではなかったのですか?」
"It seems not," said the Fairy, smiling
「そうじゃないみたいだね」と妖精は微笑みながら言った
"If you only knew the sorrow I felt"
「私が感じた悲しみをあなたが知っていたら」
"you can't imagined the tightening of my throat"
「私の喉が締め付けられるなんて想像もつかない」
"reading what was on that stone almost broke my heart"
「あの石に書かれていたものを読んで、心が折れそうになりました」
"I know what it did to you"
「それが君に何をしたか知ってるよ」
"and that is why I have forgiven you"
「だから私はあなたを許した」
"I saw it from the sincerity of your grief"
「君の悲しみの真摯さから見た」
"I saw that you have a good heart"
「君が善良な心を持っているのを見た」
"boys with good hearts are not lost"
「善良な心を持つ少年たちは迷わない」
"there is always something to hope for"
「いつだって希望がある」
"even if they are scamps"
「たとえ彼らがスキャンプであっても」
"and even if they have got bad habits"
「そして、たとえ彼らが悪い習慣を持っていても」
"there is always hope they change their ways"
「彼らが自分のやり方を変える希望は常にあります」
"That is why I came to look for you here"
「だから君をここに探しに来たんだ」
"I will be your mamma"
「君のママになるよ」
"Oh, how delightful!" shouted Pinocchio
「ああ、なんて楽しいんだろう!」とピノキオは叫んだ

and the little puppet jumped for joy
そして、小さな人形は喜びのあまり飛び跳ねました
"You must obey me, Pinocchio"
「お前は俺に従わなきゃ、ピノキオ」
"and you must do everything that I bid you"
「そして、私があなたに命じたことはすべてやらなければならない」
"I will willingly obey you"
「私は喜んであなたに従います」
"and I will do as I'm told!"
「そして、言われたとおりにする!」
"Tomorrow you will begin to go to school"
「明日から学校に行き始めるよ」
Pinocchio became at once a little less joyful
ピノキオはすぐに少し喜びを失った
"Then you must choose a trade to follow"
「それなら、フォローする取引を選択する必要があります」
"you most choose a job according to your wishes"
「あなたは最も自分の希望に応じて仕事を選びます」
Pinocchio became very grave at this
ピノキオはこれで非常に深刻になりました
the Fairy asked him in an angry voice:
妖精は怒った声で彼に尋ねました。
"What are you muttering between your teeth?"
「歯の間で何をつぶやいているの?」
"I was saying..." moaned the puppet in a low voice
「言ってたんだけど...」人形は低い声でうめき声を上げた
"it seems to me too late for me to go to school now"
「今、学校に行くには遅すぎるように思えます」
"No, sir, it is not too late for you to go to school"
「いいえ、先生、あなたが学校に行くのに遅すぎることはありません」
"Keep it in mind that it is never too late"
「遅すぎることはないということを心に留めておいてく

ださい」
"we can always learn and instruct ourselves"
「私たちは常に学び、自分自身を指導することができます」
"But I do not wish to follow a trade"
「でも、私は取引を追いたくない」
"Why do you not wish to follow an trade?"
「なぜ取引をしたくないのですか?」
"Because it tires me to work"
「仕事が疲れるから」
"My boy," said the Fairy lovingly
「お坊ちゃん」と妖精は愛情を込めて言いました
"there are two kinds of people who talk like that"
「そんな風に話す人には2種類ある」
"there are those that are in prison"
「刑務所にいる者がいる」
"and there are those that are in hospital"
「そして、病院にいる人たちもいます」
"Let me tell you one thing, Pinocchio;"
「一つ言わせてもらうよ、ピノキオ」
"every man, rich or poor, is obliged work"
「金持ちも貧乏人も、すべての人は働く義務がある」
"he has to occupy himself with something"
「彼は何かで自分を占有しなければならない」
"Woe to those who lead slothful lives"
「怠惰な生活を送る者には災いあれ」
"Sloth is a dreadful illness"
「ナマケモノは恐ろしい病気です」
"it must be cured at once, in childhood"
「それは子供の頃にすぐに治らなければならない」
"because it can never be cured once you are old"
「だって、一度年をとったら治らないから」
Pinocchio was touched by these words
ピノキオはこの言葉に感動しました
lifting his head quickly, he said to the Fairy:
彼は素早く頭を上げて、妖精に言いました。

"I will study and I will work"
「勉強して、働く」
"I will do all that you tell me"
「君の言うことは全部やる」
"for indeed I have become weary of being a puppet"
「確かに、私は操り人形であることにうんざりしてしまった」
"and I wish at any price to become a boy"
「そして、どんな犠牲を払っても男の子になりたい」
"You promised me that I can become a boy, did you not?"
「男の子になれるって約束したでしょ?」
"I did promise you that you can become a boy"
「君が男の子になれるって約束したよね」
"and whether you become a boy now depends upon yourself"
「そして、あなたが今男の子になるかどうかはあなた自身にかかっています」

The Terrible Dog-Fish
ひどい犬の魚

The following day Pinocchio went to school
翌日、ピノキオは学校に行きました
you can imagine the delight of all the little rogues
あなたはすべての小さな悪党の喜びを想像することができます
a puppet had walked into their school!
人形が彼らの学校に入ってきたのだ!
They set up a roar of laughter that never ended
彼らは笑い声を上げ、それは決して止まりませんでした
They played all sorts of tricks on him
彼らは彼にあらゆる種類のいたずらをしました
One boy carried off his cap
一人の男の子が帽子を脱いでいた
another boy pulled Pinocchio's jacket over him
別の男の子がピノキオのジャケットを引っ張った
one tried to give him a pair of inky mustachios
一人は彼に真っ黒な口ひげを生やそうとしました
another boy attempted to tie strings to his feet and hands
別の少年は、彼の足と手に紐を結ぼうと試みた
and then he tried to make him dance
そして、彼は彼を踊らせようとした
For a short time Pinocchio pretended not to care
しばらくの間、ピノキオは気にしないふりをしました
and he got on as well with school as he could
そして、彼はできる限り学校でうまくやっていました
but at last he lost all his patience
しかし、ついに彼はすべての忍耐力を失いました
he turned to those who were teasing him most
彼は自分を最もからかっている人たちに目を向けた
"Beware, boys!" he warned them
「気をつけろ、少年たち!」彼は彼らに警告した
"I have not come here to be your buffoon"

「私はあなたの道化師になるためにここに来たのではありません」
"I respect others," he said
「私は他人を尊重します」と彼は言った
"and I intend to be respected"
「そして、私は尊敬されるつもりです」
"Well said, boaster!" howled the young rascals
「よく言った、自慢屋!」若い悪党たちは吠えました
"You have spoken like a book!"
「君は本のように話した!」
and they convulsed with mad laughter
そして彼らは狂った笑い声で痙攣した
there was one boy more impertinent than the others
他の少年よりも生意気な少年が一人いた
he tried to seize the puppet by the end of his nose
彼は鼻の先で人形をつかもうとしました
But he could not do so quickly enough
しかし、彼はそれを十分に迅速に行うことができませんでした
Pinocchio stuck his leg out from under the table
ピノキオはテーブルの下から足を突き出した
and he gave him a great kick on his shins
そして彼は彼のすねに素晴らしい蹴りを与えた
the boy roared in pain
少年は苦痛に吠えた
"Oh, what hard feet you have!"
「ああ、なんて硬い足なんだ!」
and he rubbed the bruise the puppet had given him
そして、人形が彼に与えたあざをこすった
"And what elbows you have!" said another
「そして、あなたは何の肘を持っているんだ!」と別の人が言いました
"they are even harder than his feet!"
「奴の足よりも硬いんだ!」
this boy had also played rude tricks on him
この少年は彼にも無礼ないたずらをしていた

and he had received a blow in the stomach
そして彼は胃を打たれていた
But, nevertheless, the kick and the blow acquired sympathy
しかし、それにもかかわらず、蹴りと打撃は同情を呼びました
and Pinocchio earned the esteem of the boys
そしてピノキオは少年たちの尊敬を集めました
They soon all made friends with him
彼らはすぐに彼と友達になりました
and soon they liked him heartily
そしてすぐに彼らは彼を心から好きになりました
And even the master praised him
そして、マスターでさえ彼を褒めました
because Pinocchio was attentive in class
ピノキオがクラスで気配りが良かったから
he was a studious and intelligent student
彼は勉強熱心で知的な学生でした
and he was always the first to come to school
そして、彼はいつも最初に学校に来ました
and he was always the last to leave when school was over
そして、学校が終わるといつも最後に帰るのは彼でした
But he had one fault; he made too many friends
しかし、彼には一つの欠点がありました。彼は友達を作りすぎた
and amongst his friends were several rascals
そして彼の友人の中には何人かの悪党がいました
these boys were well known for their dislike of study
これらの少年たちは、勉強が嫌いなことでよく知られていました
and they especially loved to cause mischief
そして、彼らは特にいたずらをするのが大好きでした
The master warned him about them every day
マスターは毎日彼にそれらについて警告しました
even the good Fairy never failed to tell him:
善良な妖精でさえ、彼に言うのを怠りませんでした。
"Take care, Pinocchio, with your friends!"

「お元気で、ピノキオ、友達と一緒に!」
"Those bad school-fellows of yours are trouble"
「あんたの悪い学校の仲間たちは厄介者だよ」
"they will make you lose your love of study"
「彼らはあなたに勉強への愛を失わせるでしょう」
"they may even bring upon you some great misfortune"
「彼らはあなたに何か大きな不幸をもたらすかもしれません」
"There is no fear of that!" answered the puppet
「そんな心配はないよ!」と人形は答えました
and he shrugged his shoulders and touched his forehead
そして彼は肩をすくめ、額に触れた
"There is so much sense here!"
「ここにはたくさんのセンスがある!」

one fine day Pinocchio was on his way to school
ある晴れた日、ピノキオは学校に行く途中だった
and he met several of his usual companions
そして、彼はいつもの仲間の何人かに会った
coming up to him, they asked:
彼に近づいて、彼らは尋ねました。
"Have you heard the great news?"
「いい知らせを聞いたか?」
"No, I have not heard the great news"
「いや、いい知らせは聞いていない」
"In the sea near here a Dog-Fish has appeared"
「この近くの海に犬の魚が現れた」
"he is as big as a mountain"
「彼は山のように大きい」
"Is it true?" asked Pinocchio
「それは本当ですか?」ピノキオは尋ねた
"Can it be the same Dog-Fish?"
「もしかして、同じドッグフィッシュなの?」
"The Dog-Fish that was there when my papa drowned"
「パパが溺れたときにそこにいた犬の魚」
"We are going to the shore to see him"
「彼に会うために岸に行くんだ」
"Will you come with us?"
「一緒に来てくれませんか?」
"No; I am going to school"
「いいえ。学校に行くよ」
"of what great importance is school?"
「学校って何の大事なの?」
"We can go to school tomorrow"
「明日学校に行けるよ」
"one lesson more or less doesn't matter"
「1つのレッスンが多かれ少なかれ重要ではない」
"we shall always remain the same donkeys"
「私たちはいつも同じロバのままです」
"But what will the master say?"
「でも、ご主人様は何とおっしゃいますか?」

"The master may say what he likes"
「ご主人様は好きなことを言ってもいい」
"He is paid to grumble all day"
「彼は一日中不平を言うためにお金をもらっている」
"And what will my mamma say?"
「それで、ママは何て言うの?」
"Mammas know nothing," answered the bad little boys
「ママは何も知らない」と悪い男の子たちは答えました
"Do you know what I will do?" said Pinocchio
「私が何をするか分かっているか?」とピノキオは言った
"I have reasons for wishing to see the Dog-Fish"
「ドッグフィッシュを見たい理由があるんだ」
"but I will go and see him when school is over"
「でも、学校が終わったら彼に会いに行くよ」
"Poor donkey!" exclaimed one of the boys
「かわいそうなロバ!」と少年の一人が叫びました
"Do you suppose a fish of that size will wait your convenience?"
「あんな大きさの魚が君の都合を待ってくれると思うか?」
"when he is tired of being here he will go another place"
「彼がここにいるのに疲れたら、彼は別の場所に行くだろう」
"and then it will be too late"
「そして、手遅れになる」
the Puppet had to think about this
人形はこれについて考えなければなりませんでした
"How long does it take to get to the shore?"
「岸までどれくらいかかるの?」
"We can be there and back in an hour"
「1時間で行って戻ってくるよ」
"Then off we go!" shouted Pinocchio
「じゃあ、出発だ!」ピノキオが叫んだ
"and he who runs fastest is the best!"

「そして、一番速く走る者が最高だ!」
and the boys rushed off across the fields
そして、少年たちは野原を駆け抜けていきました
and Pinocchio was always the first
そしてピノキオは常に最初でした
he seemed to have wings on his feet
彼は足に翼があるように見えました
From time to time he turned to jeer at his companions
時折、彼は仲間を嘲笑うようになった
they were some distance behind
彼らは少し遅れていました
he saw them panting for breath
彼は彼らが息を切らしているのを見た
and they were covered with dust
そして、それらはほこりで覆われていました
and their tongues were hanging out of their mouths
そして、彼らの舌は口から垂れ下がっていました
and Pinocchio laughed heartily at the sight
そしてピノキオはその光景に心から笑いました
The unfortunate boy did not know what was to come
不幸な少年は、これから何が起こるのかわかりませんでした
the terrors and horrible disasters that were coming!
迫り来る恐怖と恐ろしい災害!

Pinocchio is Arrested by the Gendarmes
ピノキオは憲兵に逮捕される

Pinocchio arrived at the shore
ピノキオは岸に到着しました
and he looked out to sea
そして彼は海を眺めました
but he saw no Dog-Fish
しかし、彼は犬の魚を見ませんでした
The sea was as smooth as a great crystal mirror
海は大きな水晶鏡のように滑らかでした
"Where is the Dog-Fish?" he asked
「ドッグフィッシュはどこだ?」と彼は尋ねた
and he turned to his companions
そして彼は仲間に向き直った
all the boys laughed together
男の子たちはみんな一緒に笑った
"He must have gone to have his breakfast"
「彼は朝食を食べに行ったに違いない」
"Or he has thrown himself on to his bed"
「それとも、彼はベッドに身を投げた」
"yes, he's having a little nap"
「うん、ちょっと昼寝してるよ」
and they laughed even louder
そして、彼らはさらに大きな声で笑った
their answers seemed particularly absurd
彼らの答えは特にばかげているように見えました
and their laughter was very silly
そして、彼らの笑い声はとてもばかげていました
Pinocchio looked around at his friends
ピノキオは友達を見回しました
his companions seemed to be making a fool of him
彼の仲間は彼を馬鹿にしているように見えた
they had induced him to believe a tale
彼らは彼に物語を信じるように仕向けたのだ

but there was no truth to the tale
しかし、その話には真実はありませんでした
Pinocchio did not take the joke well
ピノキオは冗談をうまく受け取らなかった
and he spoke angrily with the boys
そして彼は少年たちと怒って話しました
"And now??" he shouted
「そして今??」彼は叫んだ
"you told me a story of the Dog-Fish"
「犬の魚の話をしてくれたね」
"but what fun did you find in deceiving me?"
「でも、私を騙すことに何の楽しみがあったの?」
"Oh, it was great fun!" answered the little rascals
「ああ、すごく楽しかった!」と小さな悪党たちは答えました
"And in what did this fun consist of?"
「そして、この楽しみは何から成り立っていたのでしょうか?」
"we made you miss a day of school"
「私たちはあなたに学校の一日を逃しました」
"and we persuaded you to come with us"
「そして、私たちと一緒に来るようにあなたを説得しました」
"Are you not ashamed of your conduct?"
「自分の行いを恥じていないのですか?」
"you are always so punctual to school"
「君はいつも学校に時間厳守だね」
"and you are always so diligent in class"
「そして、あなたはいつもクラスでとても勤勉です」
"Are you not ashamed of studying so hard?"
「そんなに一生懸命勉強して恥ずかしくないの?」
"so what if I study hard?"
「じゃあ、一生懸命勉強したらどうなるの?」
"what concern is it of yours?"
「それはあなたの何の懸念ですか?」

"It concerns us excessively"
「それは私たちを過度に懸念しています」
"because it makes us appear in a bad light"
「それは私たちを悪い光に映し出すから」
"Why does it make you appear in a bad light?"
「なんで嫌な顔をされるの?」
"there are those of us who have no wish to study"
「勉強をしない気持ちがない人もいる」
"we have no desire to learn anything"
「何も学ぼうとは思わない」
"good boys make us seem worse by comparison"
「良い子は、それに比べて私たちを悪く見せる」
"And that is too bad for you"
「そして、それはあなたにとって残念です」
"We, too, have our pride!"
「私たちも誇りを持っている!」
"Then what must I do to please you?"
「じゃあ、君を喜ばせるために僕は何をすればいいの?」
"You must follow our example"
「私たちの例に倣わなければなりません」
"you must hate school like us"
「お前は私たちのような学校が嫌いなのだろう」
"you must rebel in the lessons"
「レッスンでは反抗しなければならない」
"and you must disobey the master"
「そして、あなたはマスターに従わなければなりません」
"those are our three greatest enemies"
「この3つは私たちの最大の敵です」
"And if I wish to continue my studies?"
「それで、もし勉強を続けたいのなら?」
"In that case we will have nothing more to do with you"
「その場合、私たちはあなたとこれ以上何も関係がありません」
"and at the first opportunity we will make you pay for it"

「そして、最初の機会に、私たちはあなたにその代償を払わせます」
"Really," said the puppet, shaking his head
「ほんとうに」と人形は首を振って言った
"you make me inclined to laugh"
「君は僕を笑わせる」
"Eh, Pinocchio," shouted the biggest of the boys
「えっ、ピノキオ」と、男の子たちの中で一番大きい子が叫びました
and he confronted Pinocchio directly
そして彼はピノキオと直接対決しました
"None of your superiority works here"
「ここでは、あなたの優位性はどれも機能しません」
"don't come here to crow over us"
「ここに来て、私たちを叩くな」
"if you are not afraid of us, we are not afraid of you"
「あなたが私たちを恐れていないなら、私たちはあなたを恐れていません」
"Remember that you are one against seven"
「お前は1対7だということを忘れないで」
"Seven, like the seven deadly sins," said Pinocchio
「七つ、七つの大罪のように」とピノキオは言った
and he shouted with laughter
そして彼は笑いながら叫んだ
"Listen to him! He has insulted us all!"
「彼の言うことを聞け!彼は私たち全員を侮辱した!」
"He called us the seven deadly sins!"
「彼は私たちを七つの大罪と呼んだ!」
"Take that to begin with," said one of the boys
「まず、それを取りなさい」と少年の一人が言いました
"and keep it for your supper tonight"
「そして、今夜の夕食のために取っておく」
And, so saying, he punched him on the head
そして、そう言って、彼は彼の頭を殴った
But it was a give and take
しかし、それはギブアンドテイクでした

because the puppet immediately returned the blow
なぜなら、人形はすぐに打撃を返したからです
this was no big surprise
これは大きな驚きではありませんでした
and the fight quickly got desperate
そして、戦いはすぐに絶望的になりました
it is true that Pinocchio was alone
ピノキオが一人だったのは事実です
but he defended himself like a hero
しかし、彼は英雄のように自分を守った
He used his feet, which were of the hardest wood
彼は最も硬い木でできた足を使った
and he kept his enemies at a respectful distance
そして彼は敵を敬意を持って距離を置いた
Wherever his feet touched they left a bruise
彼の足が触れたところには、あざが残った
The boys became furious with him
少年たちは彼に激怒した
hand to hand they couldn't match the puppet
手と手をつないで、彼らは人形に匹敵することができませんでした
so they took other weapons into their hands
そこで彼らは他の武器を手に取った
the boys loosened their satchels
男の子たちは鞄を緩めました
and they threw their school-books at him
そして、彼らは教科書を彼に投げつけた
grammars, dictionaries, and spelling-books
文法、辞書、スペルブック
geography books and other scholastic works
地理学の本と他の学問的作品
But Pinocchio was quick to react
しかし、ピノキオはすぐに反応した
and he had sharp eyes for these things
そして、彼はこれらのことに対して鋭い目を持っていました

he always managed to duck in time
彼はいつも時間内に身をかがめることができました
so the books passed over his head
それで、本は彼の頭の上を通り過ぎました

and instead the books fell into the sea
それどころか、本は海に落ちてしまいました
Imagine the astonishment of the fish!
魚の驚きを想像してみてください!
they thought the books were something to eat
彼らは本を食べるものだと思っていました
and they all arrived in large shoals of fish
そして、彼らは皆、大きな魚の群れに到着しました
but they tasted a couple of the pages
しかし、彼らはいくつかのページを味わいました
and they quickly spat the paper out again
そして、彼らはすぐに再び紙を吐き出しました

and the fish made wry faces
そして魚は苦笑いを浮かべました
"this isn't food for us at all"
「これは私たちの食べ物では全然ありません」
"we are accustomed to something much better!"
「私たちはもっと良いものに慣れています!」
The battle meantime had become fiercer than ever
その間、戦いはかつてないほど激しくなっていた
a big crab had come out of the water
大きなカニが水から出てきた
and he had climbed slowly up on the shore
そして彼はゆっくりと岸に登った
he called out in a hoarse voice
彼はかすれた声で叫んだ
it sounded like a trumpet with a bad cold
ひどい風邪をひいたトランペットのような音でした
"enough of your fighting, you young ruffians"
「お前の戦いはもうたくさんだ、若き悪党ども」
"because you are nothing other than ruffians!"
「だって、お前たちはただの悪党だからだ!」
"These fights between boys seldom finish well"
「男の子同士の喧嘩はめったにうまく終わらない」
"Some disaster is sure to happen!"
「何か災難は必ず起こる!」
but the poor crab should have saved himself the trouble
しかし、かわいそうなカニは自分で面倒を省くべきだった
He might as well have preached to the wind
彼は風に向かって説教したかのようだった
Even that young rascal, Pinocchio, turned around
あの若い悪党、ピノキオでさえ振り返った
he looked at him mockingly and said rudely:
彼は嘲笑うように彼を見て、無礼に言った。
"Hold your tongue, you tiresome crab!"
「舌を押さえて、うんざりするカニめ!」
"You had better suck some liquorice lozenges"

「甘草のトローチを吸った方がいいよ」
"cure that cold in your throat"
「喉の風邪を治して」
Just then the boys had no more books
ちょうどその時、男の子たちはもう本を持っていませんでした
at least, they had no books of their own
少なくとも、彼らは自分の本を持っていませんでした
they spied at a little distance Pinocchio's bag
彼らは少し離れたところでピノキオのバッグを覗き見しました
and they took possession of his things
そして、彼らは彼の物を手に入れました
Amongst his books there was one bound in card
彼の本の中には、カードで綴じられたものがありました
It was a Treatise on Arithmetic
それは算術に関する論文でした
One of the boys seized this volume
少年の一人がこの本をつかんだ
and he aimed the book at Pinocchio's head
そして彼はその本をピノキオの頭に向けました
he threw it at him with all his strength
彼は全力でそれを投げつけた
but the book did not hit the puppet
しかし、その本は人形に当たらなかった
instead the book hit a companion on the head
それどころか、その本は仲間の頭を直撃した
the boy turned as white as a sheet
少年はシーツのように白くなった
"Oh, mother! help, I am dying!"
「ああ、お母さん！助けて、私は死にます！」
and he fell his whole length on the sand
そして、彼は全身を砂の上に倒れた
the boys must have thought he was dead
少年たちは彼が死んだと思ったに違いありません
and they ran off as fast as their legs could run

そして、彼らは足が走れる限りの速さで走り去りました
in a few minutes they were out of sight
数分で彼らは見えなくなりました
But Pinocchio remained with the boy
しかし、ピノキオは少年と一緒にいました
although he would have rather ran off too
彼もむしろ逃げたかったのですが
because his fear was also great
なぜなら、彼の恐怖も大きかったからです
nevertheless, he ran over to the sea
それにもかかわらず、彼は海に走った
and he soaked his handkerchief in the water
そしてハンカチを水に浸しました
he ran back to his poor school-fellow
彼は貧しい学校の仲間のところに走って戻った
and he began to bathe his forehead
そして彼は額を洗い始めました
he cried bitterly in despair
彼は絶望して激しく泣いた
and he kept calling him by name
そして彼は彼を名前で呼び続けました
and he said many things to him:
そして、彼は彼に多くのことを言いました。
"Eugene! my poor Eugene!"
「ユージン！私のかわいそうなユージン！」
"Open your eyes and look at me!"
「目を開けて、私を見て！」
"Why do you not answer?"
「なぜ答えないのですか？」
"I did not do it to you"
「君にやったんじゃない」
"it was not I that hurt you so!"
「君をそんなに傷つけたのは僕じゃない！」
"believe me, it was not me!"
「信じてください、それは私ではありませんでした！」
"Open your eyes, Eugene"

「目を開けて、ユージン」
"If you keep your eyes shut I shall die, too"
「目を閉じていたら、私も死ぬよ」
"Oh! what shall I do?"
「ああ!どうしたらいいの?」
"how shall I ever return home?"
「どうやって家に帰ればいいの?」
"How can I ever have the courage to go back to my good mamma?"
「どうして私は、良い母の元に戻る勇気を持つことができるのだろう?」
"What will become of me?"
「私はどうなるの?」
"Where can I fly to?"
「どこに飛べる?」
"had I only gone to school!"
「学校にさえ行けばよかったのに!」
"Why did I listen to my companions?"
「なぜ私は仲間の言うことを聞いていたのだろう?」
"they have been my ruin"
「彼らは私の破滅だった」
"The master said it to me"
「マスターが言ったんだ」
"and my mamma repeated it often"
「そして、私の母はそれをよく繰り返しました」
'Beware of bad companions!'
「悪い仲間には気をつけろ!」
"Oh, dear! what will become of me?"
「あら、なんてこった!私はどうなるのだろう?」
And Pinocchio began to cry and sob
そしてピノキオは泣き始め、すすり泣き始めました
and he struck his head with his fists
そして彼は拳で頭を打った
Suddenly he heard the sound of footsteps
突然、足音が聞こえた

He turned and saw two soldiers
彼が振り返ると、二人の兵士が見えた
"What are you doing there?"
「そこで何をしているの?」
"why are you lying on the ground?"
「なんで地面に寝転がってるの?」
"I am helping my school-fellow"
「私は学校の仲間を助けています」
"Has he been hurt?"
「彼は怪我をしたの?」
"It seems he has been hurt"
「彼は怪我をしたようです」
"Hurt indeed!" said one of them
「本当に痛い!」と彼らの一人が言いました
and he stooped down to examine Eugene closely
そして彼は身をかがめてユージンをじっくりと調べた
"This boy has been wounded on the head"
「この男の子は頭に傷を負っている」
"Who wounded him?" they asked Pinocchio
「誰が彼を傷つけたのですか?」彼らはピノキオに尋ねました
"Not I," stammered the puppet breathlessly
「俺じゃない」人形は息を切らしてどもった
"If it was not you, who then did it?"
「もし君でなかったら、誰がやったんだ?」
"Not I," repeated Pinocchio
「私は違う」とピノキオは繰り返した
"And with what was he wounded?"
「それで、彼は何で傷ついたのですか?」
"he was hurt with this book"
「彼はこの本で傷ついていた」
And the puppet picked up from the ground his book
そして人形は地面から彼の本を拾い上げました
the Treatise on Arithmetic
算術に関する論文
and he showed the book to the soldier

そして彼はその本を兵士に見せました
"And to whom does this belong?"
「それで、これは誰のものなの?」
"It belongs to me," answered Pinocchio, honestly
「それは私のものです」とピノキオは正直に答えた
"That is enough, nothing more is wanted"
「もう十分だ、これ以上何も欲しくない」
"Get up and come with us at once"
「さっさと起きて、すぐに一緒に来て」
"But I..." Pinocchio tried to object
「でも、僕は……」ピノキオは異議を唱えようとした
"Come along with us!" they insisted
「私たちと一緒に来てください!」と彼らは主張しました
"But I am innocent" he pleaded
「しかし、私は無実です」と彼は嘆願した
but they didn't listen. "Come along with us!"
しかし、彼らは耳を貸さなかった。「一緒に来て!」
Before they left, the soldiers called a passing fishermen
彼らが去る前に、兵士たちは通りすがりの漁師たちを呼びました
"We give you this wounded boy"
「この傷ついた少年を差し上げます」
"we leave him in your care"
「彼を君に任せよう」
"Carry him to your house and nurse him"
「彼をあなたの家に運び、看病して」
"Tomorrow we will come and see him"
「明日、私たちは彼に会いに来ます」
They then turned to Pinocchio
その後、彼らはピノキオに目を向けました
"Forward! and walk quickly"
「前進せよ!そして素早く歩く」
"or it will be the worse for you"
「さもないと、君にとってもっと悪いことになるよ」
Pinocchio did not need to be told twice

ピノキオは二度言われる必要はなかった
the puppet set out along the road leading to the village
人形は村に通じる道に沿って出発しました
But the poor little Devil hardly knew where he was
しかし、かわいそうな小悪魔は自分がどこにいるのかほとんど知りませんでした
He thought he must be dreaming
彼は自分が夢を見ているに違いないと思った
and what a dreadful dream it was!
そして、それは何と恐ろしい夢だったことでしょう。
He saw double and his legs shook
彼は二重を見て、足を震わせました
his tongue clung to the roof of his mouth
彼の舌は口の天井にしがみついていた
and he could not utter a word
そして彼は一言も発することができませんでした
And yet, in the midst of his stupefaction and apathy
それなのに、彼の愚痴と無気力の真っ只中に
his heart was pierced by a cruel thorn
彼の心は残酷な棘に貫かれました
he knew where he had to walk past
彼はどこを通り過ぎなければならないかを知っていました
under the windows of the good Fairy's house
良い妖精の家の窓の下で
and she was going see him with the soldiers
そして彼女は兵士たちと一緒に彼に会いに行くつもりだった
He would rather have died
彼はむしろ死にたかった
soon they reached the village
すぐに彼らは村に着きました
a gust of wind blew Pinocchio's cap off his head
一陣の風がピノキオの帽子を頭から吹き飛ばした
"Will you permit me?" said the puppet to the soldiers
「許してもらえますか?」人形は兵士たちに言いました

"can I go and get my cap?"
「帽子を取りに行ってもいいですか?」

"Go, then; but be quick about it"
「じゃあ、行け。しかし、それについては迅速に行ってください」

The puppet went and picked up his cap
人形は帽子を取りに行きました

but he didn't put the cap on his head
しかし、彼は頭に帽子をかぶらなかった

he put the cap between his teeth
彼はキャップを歯の間に挟んだ

and began to run as fast as he could
そして、彼はできるだけ速く走り始めました

he was running back towards the seashore!
彼は海岸に向かって走っていました!

The soldiers thought it would be difficult to overtake him
兵士たちは彼を追い抜くのは難しいと思った

so they sent after him a large mastiff
それで、彼らは大きなマスティフを彼の後に送りました

he had won the first prizes at all the dog races
彼はすべてのドッグレースで一等賞を獲得していました

Pinocchio ran, but the dog ran faster
ピノキオは走ったが、犬は速く走った

The people came to their windows
人々は窓に来ました

and they crowded into the street
そして彼らは通りに群がった

they wanted to see the end of the desperate race
彼らは絶望的なレースの終わりを見たいと思っていました

Pinocchio Runs the Danger of being Fried in a Pan like a Fish
ピノキオは魚のようにフライパンで揚げられる危険を冒しています

the race was not going well for the puppet
レースは人形にとってうまくいきませんでした
and Pinocchio thought he had lost
そしてピノキオは自分が負けたと思った
Alidoro, the mastiff, had run swiftly
マスティフのアリドロは素早く走った
and he had nearly caught up with him
そして、彼はもう少しで彼に追いつくところだった
the dreadful beast was very close behind him
恐ろしい獣は彼のすぐ後ろにいました
he could hear the panting of the dog
犬の息遣いが聞こえた
there was not a hand's breadth between them
二人の間には手の差はなかった
he could even feel the dog's hot breath
犬の熱い息さえ感じることができた
Fortunately the shore was close
幸いなことに、海岸は近かった
and the sea was but a few steps off
そして海はほんの数歩先にありました
soon they reached the sands of the beach
すぐに彼らはビーチの砂浜に到着しました
they got there almost at the same time
彼らはほぼ同時にそこに着きました
but the puppet made a wonderful leap
しかし、人形は素晴らしい飛躍を遂げました
a frog could have done no better
カエルはこれ以上のことはできなかったでしょう
and he plunged into the water
そして彼は水に飛び込みました

Alidoro, on the contrary, wished to stop himself
それどころか、アリドーロは自分を止めたかった
but he was carried away by the impetus of the race
しかし、彼はレースの推進力に夢中になっていた
he also went into the sea
彼も海に入りました
The unfortunate dog could not swim
不幸な犬は泳ぐことができませんでした
but he made great efforts to keep himself afloat
しかし、彼は自分自身を浮かび上がらせるために多大な努力をしました
and he swam as well as he could with his paws
そして、前足でできるだけ上手に泳ぎました
but the more he struggled the farther he sank
しかし、彼がもがけばもがくほど、彼は深く沈んでいきました
and soon his head was under the water
そしてすぐに彼の頭は水の下に落ちました
his head rose above the water for a moment
彼の頭は一瞬水面から浮かび上がった
and his eyes were rolling with terror
そして彼の目は恐怖で転がっていました
and the poor dog barked out:
そして、かわいそうな犬が吠えました。
"I am drowning! I am drowning!"
「溺れてる!溺れそうだ!」
"Drown!" shouted Pinocchio from a distance
「溺れろ!」ピノキオが遠くから叫んだ
he knew that he was in no more danger
彼は自分がもはや危険にさらされていないことを知っていました
"Help me, dear Pinocchio!"
「助けて、親愛なるピノキオ!」
"Save me from death!"
「私を死から救ってください!」
in reality Pinocchio had an excellent heart

実際には、ピノキオは素晴らしい心を持っていました
he heard the agonizing cry from the dog
彼は犬から苦しそうな叫び声を聞いた
and the puppet was moved with compassion
そして人形は同情に動かされました
he turned to the dog, and said:
彼は犬の方を向いて言いました。
"I will save you," said Pinocchio
「お前を救うよ」とピノキオは言った
"but do you promise to give me no further annoyance?"
「でも、これ以上迷惑をかけないと約束してくれるの?」
"I promise! I promise!" barked the dog
「約束するよ!約束するよ!」犬が吠えた
"Be quick, for pity's sake"
「早く、同情のために」
"if you delay another half-minute I shall be dead"
「あと30分遅らせたら、僕は死んでしまう」
Pinocchio hesitated for a moment
ピノキオは一瞬躊躇した
but then he remembered what his father had often told him
しかし、その時、彼は父がよく言っていたことを思い出した
"a good action is never lost"
「良い行動は決して失われない」
he quickly swam over to Alidoro
彼はすぐにアリドーロまで泳ぎました
and he took hold of his tail with both hands
そして彼は両手で彼の尻尾をつかんだ
soon they were on dry land again
すぐに彼らは再び陸地に着きました
and Alidoro was safe and sound
そしてアリドーロは無事でした
The poor dog could not stand
かわいそうな犬は立っていられませんでした
He had drunk a lot of salt water

彼は塩水をたくさん飲んでいた
and now he was like a balloon
そして今、彼は風船のようでした
The puppet, however, didn't entirely trust him
しかし、人形は彼を完全に信頼していたわけではありませんでした
he thought it more prudent to jump again into the water
彼は再び水に飛び込む方が賢明だと思った
he swam a little distance into the water
彼は少し泳いで水の中に入った
and he called out to his friend he had rescued
そして、彼は救出した友人に声をかけた
"Good-bye, Alidoro; a good journey to you"
「さようなら、アリドーロ。あなたにとって良い旅です」
"and take my compliments to all at home"
「そして、私の賛辞を家にいるすべての人に伝えてください」
"Good-bye, Pinocchio," answered the dog
「さようなら、ピノキオ」と犬は答えた
"a thousand thanks for having saved my life"
「私の命を救ってくれてありがとう」
"You have done me a great service"
「あなたは私に素晴らしいサービスを提供してくれました」
"and in this world what is given is returned"
「そして、この世では与えられたものは返ってくる」
"If an occasion offers I shall not forget it"
「機会があれば、私はそれを忘れない」
Pinocchio swam along the shore
ピノキオは岸辺を泳いだ
At last he thought he had reached a safe place
とうとう彼は安全な場所に着いたと思った
so he gave a look along the shore
そこで彼は岸辺を見渡しました
he saw amongst the rocks a kind of cave

彼は岩の間に一種の洞窟を見ました
from the cave there was a cloud of smoke
洞窟からは煙が立ち込めていました
"In that cave there must be a fire"
「あの洞窟には火があるに違いない」
"So much the better," thought Pinocchio
「そんなにいいんだ」とピノキオは思った
"I will go and dry and warm myself"
「行って乾かして温めます」
"and then?" Pinocchio wondered
「それから?」ピノキオは疑問に思いました
"and then we shall see," he concluded
「そして、私たちは見るでしょう」と彼は結論付けました
Having taken the resolution he swam landwards
決意を固めた彼は陸地に向かって泳いだ
he was was about to climb up the rocks
彼は岩を登ろうとしていた
but he felt something under the water
しかし、彼は水面下に何かを感じた
whatever it was rose higher and higher
それが何であれ、どんどん高く上昇していきました
and it carried him into the air
そしてそれは彼を空中に運びました
He tried to escape from it
彼はそれから逃げようとした
but it was too late to get away
しかし、逃げるには遅すぎた
he was extremely surprised when he saw what it was
彼はそれが何であるかを見て非常に驚いた
he found himself enclosed in a great net
彼は自分が大きな網に閉じ込められていることに気づきました
he was with a swarm of fish of every size and shape
彼はあらゆる大きさと形の魚の群れと一緒にいました
they were flapping and struggling around

彼らは羽ばたき、もがいていました
like a swarm of despairing souls
絶望的な魂の群れのように
At the same moment a fisherman came out of the cave
その時、一人の漁師が洞窟から出てきた
the fisherman was horribly ugly
漁師は恐ろしく醜かった
and he looked like a sea monster
そして彼は海の怪物のように見えました
his head was not covered in hair
彼の頭は髪の毛で覆われていませんでした
instead he had a thick bush of green grass
それどころか、彼は緑の草の厚い茂みを持っていました
his skin was green and his eyes were green
彼の肌は緑色で、目は緑色でした
and his long beard came down to the ground
そして彼の長いあごひげは地面に落ちました
and of course his beard was also green
そしてもちろん、彼のあごひげも緑色でした
He had the appearance of an immense lizard
彼は巨大なトカゲのような姿をしていました
a lizard standing on its hind-paws
後ろ足で立っているトカゲ

the fisherman pulled his net out of the sea
漁師は海から網を引き抜きました
"Thank Heaven!" he exclaimed greatly satisfied
「天に感謝します!」彼は大いに満足して叫びました
"Again today I shall have a splendid feast of fish!"
「今日も、私は素晴らしい魚のごちそうをしよう!」
Pinocchio thought to himself for a moment
ピノキオは一瞬考えました
"What a mercy that I am not a fish!"
「私が魚でないなんて、なんと慈悲深いことでしょう!」
and he regained a little courage
そして彼は少し勇気を取り戻しました
The netful of fish was carried into the cave
網一杯の魚が洞窟に運ばれました
and the cave was dark and smoky
そして洞窟は暗くて煙が立ち込めていました
In the middle of the cave was a large frying-pan
洞窟の真ん中には大きなフライパンがありました
and the frying-pan was full of oil
そしてフライパンは油でいっぱいでした
there was a suffocating smell of mushrooms
キノコの息苦しい匂いがしました
but the fisherman was very excited
しかし、漁師はとても興奮していました
"Now we will see what fish we have taken!"
「さあ、どんな魚を釣ったか見てみよう!」
and he put into the net an enormous hand
そして、彼は巨大な手を網に入れました
his hand had the proportions of a baker's shovel
彼の手はパン屋のシャベルのようなプロポーションを持っていました
and he pulled out a handful of fish
そして、一握りの魚を取り出した
"These fish are good!" he said
「この魚はいい!」と彼は言った

and he smelled the fish complacently
そして彼は満足げに魚の匂いを嗅ぎました
And then he threw the fish into a pan without water
そして、水のない鍋に魚を投げ入れました
He repeated the same operation many times
彼は同じ手術を何度も繰り返しました
and as he drew out the fish his mouth watered
そして彼が魚を引き抜くと、彼の口は潤った
and the Fisherman chuckled to himself
そして漁師は独り言で笑いました
"What exquisite sardines I've caught!"
「なんて絶品のイワシを釣ったんだ!」
"These mackerel are going to be delicious!"
「このサバ、きっと美味しくなるぞ!」
"And these crabs will be excellent!"
「そして、このカニは素晴らしいでしょう!」
"What dear little anchovies they are!"
「なんて愛らしい小さなアンチョビなのでしょう!」
The last to remain in the fisher's net was Pinocchio
漁師の網に最後に残ったのはピノキオでした
his big green eyes opened with astonishment
彼の大きな緑色の目は驚きで開きました
"What species of fish is this??"
「これは何種類の魚だ??」
"Fish of this kind I don't remember to have eaten"
「こんな魚は食べた覚えがない」
And he looked at him again attentively
そして彼は再び彼を注意深く見つめました
and he examined him well all over
そして、彼は彼を全身でよく調べました
"I know: he must be a craw-fish"
「わかってるよ。彼はザリガニに違いない」
Pinocchio was mortified at being mistaken for a craw-fish
ピノキオはザリガニと間違えられて悔しかった
"Do you take me for a craw-fish?"
「ザリガニに連れて行ってくれる?」

"that's no way to treat your guests!"
「それはあなたのゲストをもてなす方法ではありません！」
"Let me tell you that I am a puppet"
「言わせてもらうけど、僕は操り人形だって」
"A puppet?" replied the fisherman
「人形ですか?」と漁師は答えた
"then I must tell you the truth"
「それなら、本当のことを言わなきゃ」
"a puppet is quite a new fish to me"
「人形は私にとってまったく新しい魚です」
"but that is even better!"
「でも、それはもっといいことだよ！」
"I shall eat you with greater pleasure"
「お前をもっと喜んで食べよう」
"you can eat me all you want"
「好きなだけ食べていいよ」
"but will you understand that I am not a fish?"
「でも、私が魚ではないと理解してくれるか?」
"Do you not hear that I talk?"
「私が話しているのが聞こえないのか?」
"can you not see that I reason as you do?"
「私があなたと同じように推論しているのがわからないのですか?」
"That is quite true," said the fisherman
「それは全く本当だ」と漁師は言った
"you are indeed a fish with the talent of talking"
「お前は確かに話す才能のある魚だ」
"and you are a fish that can reason as I do"
「そして、あなたは私と同じように推論できる魚です」
"I must treat you with appropriate attention"
「私はあなたに適切な注意を払って接しなければなりません」
"And what would this attention be?"
「それで、この注目は何なのだろう?」
"let me give you a token of my friendship"

「私の友情の証をあげよう」
"and let me show my particular regard"
「そして、私の特別な敬意を示させてください」
"I will let you choose how you would like to be cooked"
「どう料理されたいかは、君に選ばせてあげる」
"Would you like to be fried in the frying-pan?
「フライパンで揚げてみませんか?」
"or would you prefer to be stewed with tomato sauce?"
「それとも、トマトソースで煮込むのが好きですか?」
"let me tell you the truth," answered Pinocchio
「本当のことを言わせてください」とピノキオは答えました
"if I had to choose, I would like to be set free"
「もし選べるなら、自由になりたい」
"You are joking!" laughed the fisherman
「冗談だろ!」と漁師は笑った
"why would I lose the opportunity to taste such a rare fish?"
「なんでこんな珍しい魚を味わう機会を逃すのだろう」
"I can assure you puppet fish are rare here"
「ここでは人形の魚は珍しいと断言できます」
"one does not catch a puppet fish every day"
「人形魚は毎日釣れない」
"Let me make the choice for you"
「君のために選択させてください」
"you will be with the other fish"
「君は他の魚と一緒にいるよ」
"I will fry you in the frying-pan"
「フライパンで炒めます」
"and you will be quite satisfied"
「そして、あなたはかなり満足するでしょう」
"It is always consolation to be fried in company"
「一緒に揚げられるのはいつも慰めになる」
At this speech the unhappy Pinocchio began to cry
この演説で、不幸なピノキオは泣き始めました
he screamed and implored for mercy
彼は叫び、慈悲を懇願した

"How much better it would have been if I had gone to school!"
「学校に行っていたら、どんなに良かっただろう!」
"I shouldn't have listened to my companions"
「仲間の言うことを聞かなくてよかった」
"and now I am paying for it"
「そして今、私はその代償を払っています」
And he wriggled like an eel
そして彼はウナギのように身をよじった
and he made indescribable efforts to slip out
そして、彼は抜け出そうと筆舌に尽くしがたい努力をしました
but he was tight in clutches of the green fisherman
しかし、彼は緑の漁師の手の中でしっかりと握られていました
and all of Pinocchio's efforts were useless
そして、ピノキオの努力はすべて無駄でした
the fisherman took a long strip of rush
漁師は長い急ぎ足を取った
and he bound the puppets hands and feet
そして彼は人形の手と足を縛りました
Poor Pinocchio was tied up like a sausage
かわいそうなピノキオはソーセージのように縛られていました
and he threw him into the pan with the other fish
そして、彼は他の魚と一緒に彼を鍋に投げ入れました
He then fetched a wooden bowl full of flour
それから彼は小麦粉でいっぱいの木のボウルを持ってきました
and one by one he began to flour each fish
そして、一匹一匹の魚に小麦粉をまぶし始めました
soon all the little fish were ready
すぐにすべての小さな魚の準備が整いました
and he threw them into the frying-pan
そして、それらをフライパンに投げ入れました
The first to dance in the boiling oil were the poor whitings

沸騰した油の中で最初に踊ったのは、哀れなホワイティングスでした
the crabs were next to follow the dance
次にカニがダンスを追いかけました
and then the sardines came too
そして、イワシも来ました
and finally the anchovies were thrown in
そして最後にアンチョビが投げ込まれました
at last it had come to Pinocchio's turn
とうとうピノキオの番が来た
he saw the horrible death waiting for him
彼は恐ろしい死が彼を待っていたのを見た
and you can imagine how frightened he was
そして、彼がどれほど怯えていたか想像できるでしょう
he trembled violently and with great effort
彼は激しく、そして多大な努力で震えました
and he had neither voice nor breath left for further entreaties
そして、彼にはそれ以上の懇願のための声も息も残っていなかった
But the poor boy implored with his eyes!
しかし、かわいそうな少年は目で懇願しました!
The green fisherman, however, didn't care the least
しかし、緑の漁師は少しも気にしませんでした
and he plunged him five or six times in the flour
そして、小麦粉に5、6回突っ込みました
finally he was white from head to foot
ついに彼は頭から足まで白くなった
and he looked like a puppet made of plaster
そして彼は石膏でできた人形のように見えました

Pinocchio Returns to the Fairy's House
ピノキオは妖精の家に戻ります

Pinocchio was dangling over the frying pan
ピノキオはフライパンの上にぶら下がっていました
the fisherman was just about to throw him in
漁師はちょうど彼を投げ込もうとしていました
but then a large dog entered the cave
しかし、その時、大きな犬が洞窟に入りました
the dog had smelled the savoury odour of fried fish
犬はフライドフィッシュの香ばしい匂いを嗅いでいました
and he had been enticed into the cave
そして彼は洞窟に誘われていた
"Get out!" shouted the fisherman
「出て行け！」と漁師は叫んだ
he was holding the floured puppet in one hand
彼は片手で粉をまぶした人形を持っていました
and he threatened the dog with the other hand
そして、もう片方の手で犬を脅しました
But the poor dog was as hungry as a wolf
しかし、かわいそうな犬はオオカミのようにお腹が空いていました
and he whined and wagged his tail
そして彼は泣き叫び、尻尾を振った
if he could have talked he would have said:
もし彼が話すことができたなら、彼は言っただろう。
"Give me some fish and I will leave you in peace"
「魚をくれれば、君を安らかに残しておいて」
"Get out, I tell you!" repeated the fisherman
「出て行け、言ってるよ！」漁師は繰り返した
and he stretched out his leg to give him a kick
そして彼は足を伸ばして蹴りを入れた
But the dog would not stand trifling
しかし、犬は些細なことでは立ちはだかりませんでした

he was too hungry to be denied the food
彼は食べ物を拒否されるにはあまりにもお腹が空いていました
he started growling at the fisherman
彼は漁師に向かって唸り始めました
and he showed his terrible teeth
そして彼は彼の恐ろしい歯を見せました
At that moment a little feeble voice called out
その時、小さな弱々しい声が叫んだ
"Save me, Alidoro, please!"
「助けて、アリドーロ、お願い!」
"If you do not save me I shall be fried!"
「私を救わないなら、私は揚げられるぞ!」
The dog recognized Pinocchio's voice
犬はピノキオの声を認識しました
all he saw was the floured bundle in the fisherman's hand
彼が見たのは、漁師の手にある小麦粉の束だけでした
that must be where the voice had come from
その声はどこから来たのでしょう
So what do you think he did?
それで、彼は何をしたと思いますか?
Alidoro sprung up to the fisherman
アリドーロは漁師に飛びつきました
and he seized the bundle in his mouth
そして彼はその束を口に掴んだ
he held the bundle gently in his teeth
彼は包みをそっと歯に挟んだ
and he rushed out of the cave again
そして彼は再び洞窟から急いで出ました
and then he was gone like a flash of lightning
そして、彼は稲妻の閃光のように去っていきました
The fisherman was furious
漁師は激怒しました
the rare puppet fish had been snatched from him
珍しい人形の魚が彼から奪われたのだ
and he ran after the dog

そして彼は犬を追いかけました
he tried to get his fish back
彼は魚を取り戻そうとしました
but the fisherman did not run far
しかし、漁師は遠くまでは走りませんでした
because he had been taken by a fit of coughing
彼は咳き込みに襲われていたからだ

Alidoro ran almost to the village
アリドーロは村まで走りました
when he got to the path he stopped
彼が道に着いたとき、彼は立ち止まりました
he put his friend Pinocchio gently on the ground
彼は友人のピノキオをそっと地面に置きました
"How much I have to thank you for!" said the puppet
「お礼を言わなきゃ!」と人形は言いました
"There is no necessity," replied the dog
「必要ないんだよ」と犬は答えた

"You saved me and I have now returned it"
「あなたが私を救ってくれて、今は返しました」
"You know that we must all help each other in this world"
「この世では、私たち全員が助け合わなければならないことをご存知でしょう」
Pinocchio was happy to have saved Alidoro
ピノキオはアリドーロを救えて嬉しかった
"But how did you get into the cave?"
「でも、どうやって洞窟に入ったの?」
"I was lying on the shore more dead than alive"
「私は生きているというよりも死んでいるように岸に横たわっていました」
"then the wind brought to me the smell of fried fish"
「その時、風が私にフライドフィッシュの匂いをもたらしました」
"The smell excited my appetite"
「匂いが食欲をそそりました」
"and I followed my nose"
「そして私は鼻を追いかけた」
"If I had arrived a second later..."
「もし私が一秒遅れて到着していたら...」
"Do not mention it!" sighed Pinocchio
「そんなことは言わないで!」ピノキオはため息をついた
he was still trembling with fright
彼はまだ恐怖に震えていました
"I would be a fried puppet by now"
「今頃は揚げ人形になっていただろう」
"It makes me shudder just to think of it!"
「考えるだけでゾッとします!」
Alidoro laughed a little at the idea
アリドーロはその考えに少し笑った
but he extended his right paw to the puppet
しかし、彼は右足を人形に伸ばしました
Pinocchio shook his paw heartily
ピノキオは心から前足を振った

and then they went their separate ways
そして、彼らは別々の道を歩みました
The dog took the road home
犬は道を家に持ち帰りました
and Pinocchio went to a cottage not far off
そしてピノキオはそう遠くないコテージに行きました
there was a little old man warming himself in the sun
太陽の下で体を温めている小さな老人がいました
Pinocchio spoke to the little old man
ピノキオは小さな老人に話しかけました
"Tell me, good man," he started
「教えてくれ、いい男だ」彼は話し始めた
"do you know anything of a poor boy called Eugene?"
「ユージンという可哀想な少年について何か知ってる？」
"he was wounded in the head"
「彼は頭を負傷していた」
"The boy was brought by some fishermen to this cottage"
「その少年は、何人かの漁師に連れられてこのコテージに来たんだ」
"and now I do not know what happened to him"
「そして今、彼に何が起こったのかわかりません」
"And now he is dead!" interrupted Pinocchio with great sorrow
「そして今、彼は死んだ！」ピノキオは大きな悲しみで遮った
"No, he is alive," interrupted the fisherman
「いや、彼は生きている」と漁師が遮った
"and he has been returned to his home"
「そして彼は家に戻されました」
"Is it true?" cried the puppet
「本当ですか？」と人形は叫びました
and Pinocchio danced with delight
そしてピノキオは喜びで踊りました
"Then the wound was not serious?"
「では、傷は重傷ではなかったのですか？」

the little old man answered Pinocchio
小さな老人はピノキオに答えた
"It might have been very serious"
「大変だったかもしれない」
"it could even have been fatal"
「致命的だった可能性さえありました」
"they threw a thick book at his head"
「彼らは彼の頭に分厚い本を投げつけた」
"And who threw it at him?"
「それで、誰が彼に投げたの?」
"One of his school-fellows, by the name of Pinocchio"
「彼の学校の仲間の一人、ピノキオという名前で」
"And who is this Pinocchio?" asked the puppet
「それで、このピノキオは誰なの?」と人形は尋ねました
and he pretended his ignorance as best he could
そして、彼はできる限り自分の知らないふりをしました
"They say that he is a bad boy"
「彼らは彼が悪い子だと言っています」
"a vagabond, a regular good-for-nothing"
「放浪者、普通の何の役にも立たない」
"Calumnies! all calumnies!"
「中傷だ!すべての中傷!」
"Do you know this Pinocchio?"
「このピノキオ知ってる?」
"By sight!" answered the puppet
「目視で!」人形は答えました
"And what is your opinion of him?" asked the little man
「それで、彼についてどう思いますか?」と小男は尋ねました
"He seems to me to be a very good boy"
「彼はとてもいい子に思えます」
"he is anxious to learn," added Pinocchio
「彼は学ぶことを切望しています」とピノキオは付け加えました
"and he is obedient and affectionate to his father and family"

「そして、彼は父と家族に対して従順で愛情深い」
the puppet fired off a bunch of lies
人形はたくさんの嘘を放ちました
but then he remembered to touch his nose
しかし、その時、彼は自分の鼻を触ることを思い出した
his nose seemed to have grown by more than a hand
彼の鼻は手一本以上で成長したように見えた
Very much alarmed he began to cry:
彼は非常に驚いて泣き始めました。
"Don't believe me, good man"
「信じるな、いい男」
"what I said were all lies"
「私が言ったことはすべて嘘だった」
"I know Pinocchio very well"
「ピノキオのことはよく知ってる」
"and I can assure you that he is a very bad boy"
「そして、彼がとても悪い子だと断言できます」
"he is disobedient and idle"
「彼は不従順で怠惰です」
"instead of going to school, he runs off with his companions"
「学校に行く代わりに、彼は仲間と一緒に逃げる」
He had hardly finished speaking when his nose became shorter
彼が話し終えたところで、鼻が短くなった
and finally his nose returned to the old size
そしてついに彼の鼻は元のサイズに戻りました
the little old man noticed the boys' colour
小さな老人は男の子の色に気づきました
"And why are you all covered with white?"
「それで、なんでみんな白だらけなの?」
"I will tell you why," said Pinocchio
「なぜか教えてあげるよ」とピノキオは言った
"Without observing it I rubbed myself against a wall"
「それを見ずに、私は壁に自分をこすりつけた」
"little did I know that the wall had been freshly

whitewashed"
「壁が新しく白塗りされていたとは知らなかった」
he was ashamed to confess the truth
彼は真実を告白することを恥じた
in fact he had been floured like a fish
実際、彼は魚のように粉をまぶされていた
"And what have you done with your jacket?"
「それで、上着はどうしたの?」
"where are your trousers, and your cap?"
「ズボンと帽子はどこにあるの?」
"I met some robbers on my journey"
「旅の途中で強盗に会った」
"and they took all my things from me"
「そして、彼らは私からすべてのものを奪った」
"Good old man, I have a favour to ask"
「おじいさん、お願いがあります」
"could you perhaps give me some clothes to return home in?"
「家に帰るための服をくれませんか?」
"My boy, I would like to help you"
「私の息子、私はあなたを助けたいです」
"but I have nothing but a little sack"
「でも、僕には小さな袋しかないんだ」
"it is but a sack in which I keep beans"
「それは私が豆を保管する袋にすぎません」
"but if you have need of it, take it"
「でも、必要なら持って行って」
Pinocchio did not wait to be asked twice
ピノキオは二度も聞かれるのを待たなかった
He took the sack at once
彼はすぐに袋を取りました
and he borrowed a pair of scissors
そして彼はハサミを借りました
and he cut a hole at the end of the sack
そして、袋の端に穴を開けました
at each side, he cut out small holes for his arms

彼は両側に腕のための小さな穴を切り取りました
and he put the sack on like a shirt
そして彼はシャツのように袋をかぶった
And with his new clothing he set off for the village
そして、新しい服を着て村へ出発しました
But as he went he did not feel at all comfortable
しかし、彼が行くと、彼はまったく快適ではありませんでした
for each step forward he took another step backwards
一歩前進するごとに、彼はまた一歩後退した
"How shall I ever present myself to my good little Fairy?"
「どうやって私の善良な小さな妖精に自分を見せればいいの?」
"What will she say when she sees me?"
「彼女は私を見たら何と言うのだろう?」
"Will she forgive me this second escapade?"
「彼女はこの二度目の逃避行を許してくれるのだろうか?」
"Oh, I am sure that she will not forgive me!"
「ああ、きっと許してもらえない!」
"And it serves me right, because I am a rascal"
「そして、それは私に正しい役割を果たします。なぜなら、私は悪党だからです」
"I am always promising to correct myself"
「自分を正すことを常に約束している」
"but I never keep my word!"
「でも、約束は絶対に守らない!」
When he reached the village it was night
彼が村に着いたとき、それは夜でした
and it had gotten very dark
そして、とても暗くなっていました
A storm had come in from the shore
岸から嵐が来ていた
and the rain was coming down in torrents
そして雨は激しく降り注いでいました
he went straight to the Fairy's house

彼はまっすぐ妖精の家に行きました
he was resolved to knock at the door
彼はドアをノックする決心をした
But when he was there his courage failed him
しかし、彼がそこにいたとき、彼の勇気は彼を失望させました
instead of knocking he ran away some twenty paces
彼はノックする代わりに、20歩ほど逃げた
He returned to the door a second time
彼は二度目にドアに戻った
and he held the door knocker in his hand
そして彼はドアノッカーを手に持っていた
trembling, he gave a little knock at the door
震えながら、彼はドアを少しノックした
He waited and waited for his mother to open the door
彼は母親がドアを開けるのを待ち続けました
Pinocchio must have waited no less than half an hour
ピノキオは30分も待ったに違いない
At last a window on the top floor was opened
ついに最上階の窓が開けられました
the house was four stories high
家は4階建てでした
and Pinocchio saw a big Snail
そしてピノキオは大きなカタツムリを見ました
it had a lighted candle on her head to look out
彼女の頭には火のついた蝋燭が置かれていて、外を眺めていました
"Who is there at this hour?"
「この時間に誰がいるの?」
"Is the Fairy at home?" asked the puppet
「妖精は家にいるの?」と人形は尋ねました
"The Fairy is asleep," answered the snail
「妖精は眠っているよ」とカタツムリは答えました
"and she must not be awakened"
「そして、彼女は起こされてはならない」
"but who are you?" asked the Snail

「でも、お前は誰だ?」とカタツムリは尋ねました
"It is I," answered Pinocchio
「私です」とピノキオは答えました
"Who is I?" asked the Snail
「俺は誰だ?」とカタツムリは尋ねました
"It is I, Pinocchio," answered Pinocchio
「私です、ピノキオ」とピノキオは答えました
"And who is Pinocchio?" asked the Snail
「で、ピノキオって誰だ?」とカタツムリは尋ねました
"The puppet who lives in the Fairy's house"
「妖精の家に住む人形」
"Ah, I understand!" said the Snail
「ああ、わかった!」とカタツムリは言いました
"Wait for me there"
「そこで待ってて」
"I will come down and open the door"
「降りてきてドアを開けます」
"Be quick, for pity's sake"
「早く、同情のために」
"because I am dying of cold"
「寒くて死にそうだから」
"My boy, I am a snail"
「私の息子、私はカタツムリです」
"and snails are never in a hurry"
「そしてカタツムリは決して急いでいない」
An hour passed, and then two
1時間が経過し、さらに2時間が経過しました
and the door was still not opened
それでもドアは開いていませんでした
Pinocchio was wet through and through
ピノキオは全身から濡れていました
and he was trembling from cold and fear
そして彼は寒さと恐怖に震えていました
at last he had the courage to knock again
とうとう彼は再びノックする勇気を持っていました
this time he knocked louder than before

今回は前よりも大きな声でノックしました
At this second knock a window on the lower story opened
この二度目のノックで、下層階の窓が開いた
and the same Snail appeared at the window
そして、同じカタツムリが窓に現れました
"Beautiful little Snail," cried Pinocchio
「美しい小さなカタツムリ」とピノキオは叫んだ
"I have been waiting for two hours!"
「2時間も待ってた!」
"two hours on such a night seems longer than two years"
「こんな夜に2時間かかるのは、2年よりも長く感じる」
"Be quick, for pity's sake"
「早く、同情のために」
"My boy," answered the calm little animal
「お坊ちゃん」と穏やかな小動物は答えました
"you know that I am a snail"
「私がカタツムリだって知ってるでしょ」
"and snails are never in a hurry"
「そしてカタツムリは決して急いでいない」
And the window was shut again
そして、窓は再び閉められました
Shortly afterwards midnight struck
その直後、真夜中が襲った
then one o'clock, then two o'clock
その後、1時、次に2時
and the door still remained unopened
そして、ドアはまだ開いていませんでした
Pinocchio finally lost all patience
ピノキオはついにすべての忍耐力を失いました
he seized the door knocker in a rage
彼は激怒してドアノッカーをつかんだ
he intended bang the door as hard as he could
彼はドアを全力で叩くつもりだった
a blow that would resound through the house
家中に響き渡る打撃
the door knocker was made from iron

ドアノッカーは鉄製でした
but suddenly it turned into an eel
でも、いきなりウナギに変わった
and the eel slipped out of Pinocchio's hand
そしてウナギはピノキオの手から滑り落ちました
down the street was a stream of water
通りを下ったところには水の流れがありました
and the eel disappeared down the stream
そして、ウナギは川に消えました
Pinocchio was blinded with rage
ピノキオは怒りで目がくらんでいた
"Ah! so that's the way it is?"
「あぁ!そういうものなの?」
"then I will kick with all my might"
「じゃあ全力で蹴る」
Pinocchio took a little run up to the door
ピノキオはドアまで少し駆け寄った
and he kicked the door with all his might
そして彼は全力でドアを蹴った
it was indeed a mighty strong kick
それは確かに強烈な強烈な蹴りだった
and his foot went through the door
そして彼の足はドアを通り抜けました
Pinocchio tried to pull his foot out
ピノキオは足を引き抜こうとしました
but then he realized his predicament
しかし、彼は自分の苦境に気づきました
it was as if his foot had been nailed down
まるで彼の足が釘付けにされたかのようでした
Think of poor Pinocchio's situation!
かわいそうなピノキオの状況を考えてみてください!
He had to spend the rest of the night on one foot
彼は残りの夜を片足で過ごさなければならなかった
and the other foot was in the air
そしてもう片方の足は宙に浮いていました
after many hours daybreak finally came

何時間も経って、ついに夜明けが来ました
and at last the door was opened
そしてついにドアが開かれました
it had only taken the Snail nine hours
カタツムリ号はたったの9時間しかかからなかった
he had come all the way from the fourth story
彼は4階からずっと来ていた
It is evident that her exertions must have been great
彼女の努力が大きかったに違いないことは明らかです
but she was equally confused by Pinocchio
しかし、彼女はピノキオにも同様に混乱していました
"What are you doing with your foot in the door?"
「ドアに足を突っ込んで何をしているの?」
"It was an accident," answered the puppet
「事故だったよ」と人形は答えました
"oh beautiful snail, please help me"
「ああ、美しいカタツムリ、助けてください」
"try and get my foot out the door"
「ドアから足を出してみてください」
"My boy, that is the work of a carpenter"
「お坊ちゃん、あれは大工の仕事だよ」
"and I have never been a carpenter"
「そして、私は大工になったことがありません」
"in that case please get the Fairy for me!"
「それなら、妖精を連れてきてください!」
"The Fairy is still asleep"
「妖精はまだ眠っている」
"and she must not be awakened"
「そして、彼女は起こされてはならない」
"But what can I do with me foot stuck in the door?"
「でも、ドアに足が引っかかっていて何ができるの?」
"there are many ants in this area"
「この辺りにはアリがたくさんいる」
"Amuse yourself by counting all the little ants"
「小さなアリを全部数えて楽しんでください」
"Bring me at least something to eat"

「せめて何か食べるものを持ってきて」
"because I am quite exhausted and hungry"
「かなり疲れていてお腹が空いているから」
"At once," said the Snail
「すぐに」とカタツムリは言いました
it was in fact almost as fast as she had said
実際、彼女が言ったのとほぼ同じ速さだった
after three hours she returned to Pinocchio
3時間後、彼女はピノキオに戻った
and on her head was a silver tray
そして彼女の頭には銀の盆がありました
The tray contained a loaf of bread
トレイには一斤のパンが入っていました
and there was a roast chicken
そして、ローストチキンもありました
and there were four ripe apricots
そして、熟したアプリコットが4つありました
"Here is the breakfast that the Fairy has sent you"
「これが妖精が送ってくれた朝食です」
these were all things Pinocchio liked to eat
これらはすべてピノキオが好んで食べるものでした
The puppet felt very much comforted at the sight
人形はその光景にとても慰められました
But then he began to eat the food
しかし、その後、彼は食べ物を食べ始めました
and he was most disgusted by the taste
そして、彼はその味に最も嫌悪感を抱いていました
he discovered that the bread was plaster
彼はパンが漆喰であることを発見しました
the chicken was made of cardboard
鶏肉は段ボールでできていました
and the four apricots were alabaster
そして、4つのアプリコットはアラバスターでした
Poor Pinocchio wanted to cry
かわいそうなピノキオは泣きたかった
In his desperation he tried to throw away the tray

彼は必死になってトレイを捨てようとしました
perhaps it was because of his grief
彼の悲しみのせいだったのかもしれません
or it could have been that he was exhausted
あるいは、疲れ果てていたのかもしれない
and the little puppet fainted from the effort
そして、小さな人形はその努力で気を失いました
eventually he regained consciousness
やがて彼は意識を取り戻しました
and he found that he was lying on a sofa
そして、彼は自分がソファに横たわっていることに気づきました
and the good Fairy was beside him
そして、善良な妖精が彼のそばにいました
"I will pardon you once more," the Fairy said
「もう一度許してあげる」と妖精は言った
"but woe to you if you behave badly a third time!"
「でも、三度目でひどい振る舞いをしたら、お前は悲惨だ!」
Pinocchio promised and swore that he would study
ピノキオは勉強することを約束し、誓いました
and he swore he would always conduct himself well
そして、彼は常に自分自身を良く振る舞うことを誓った
And he kept his word for the remainder of the year
そして、彼はその年の残りの期間、その約束を守りました
Pinocchio got very good grades at school
ピノキオは学校で非常に良い成績を収めました
and he had the honour of being the best student
そして、彼は最高の学生であるという名誉を持っていました
his behaviour in general was very praiseworthy
彼の行動は一般的に非常に称賛に値するものでした
and the Fairy was very much pleased with him
そして妖精は彼にとても満足しました
"Tomorrow your wish shall be gratified"

「明日、あなたの願いが叶う」
"what wish was that?" asked Pinocchio
「それは何の願いだったの?」とピノキオは尋ねた
"Tomorrow you shall cease to be a wooden puppet"
「明日、お前は木製の人形ではなくなる」
"and you shall finally become a boy"
「そして、ついに君は男の子になる」
you could not have imagined Pinocchio's joy
ピノキオの喜びは想像もできなかったでしょう
and Pinocchio was allowed to have a party
そしてピノキオはパーティーを開くことを許されました
All his school-fellows were to be invited
彼の学校の仲間全員が招待されることになっていた
there would be a grand breakfast at the Fairy's house
妖精の家では盛大な朝食があります
together they would celebrate the great event
彼らは一緒に素晴らしいイベントを祝いました
The Fairy had prepared two hundred cups of coffee and milk
妖精は200杯のコーヒーとミルクを用意していました
and four hundred rolls of bread were cut
そして、400ロールのパンが切られました
and all the bread was buttered on each side
そして、すべてのパンは両側にバターを塗られました
The day promised to be most happy and delightful
その日は、最も幸せで楽しい日になることを約束しました
but...
だがしかし。。。
Unfortunately in the lives of puppets there is always a "but" that spoils everything
残念ながら、人形の生活には、すべてを台無しにする「しかし」が常にあります

The Land of the Boobie Birds
カツオドリの国

Of course Pinocchio asked the Fairy's permission
もちろん、ピノキオは妖精の許可を求めました
"may I go round the town to give out the invitations?"
「招待状を配るために町を回ってもいいですか?」
and the Fairy said to him:
そして妖精は彼に言いました。
"Go, if you like, you have my permission"
「行って、もしよかったら、私の許可を得てください」
"invite your companions for the breakfast tomorrow"
「明日の朝食に仲間を招待して」
"but remember to return home before dark"
「でも、暗くなる前に家に帰ることを忘れないでください」
"Have you understood?" she checked
「わかった?」彼女は確認した
"I promise to be back in an hour"
「1時間後にまた来ると約束します」
"Take care, Pinocchio!" she cautioned him
「気をつけて、ピノキオ!」彼女は彼に警告した
"Boys are always very ready to promise"
「男の子はいつも約束する準備ができています」
"but generally boys struggle to keep their word"
「でも、一般的に男の子は約束を守るのに苦労するんだ」
"But I am not like other boys"
「でも、僕は他の男の子とは違う」
"When I say a thing, I do it"
「私が何かを言うとき、私はそれをする」
"We shall see if you will keep your promise"
「君が約束を守るかどうか見てみよう」
"If you are disobedient, so much the worse for you"
「もし君が不従順なら、君にとってもっと悪いことだ」

"Why would it be so much the worse for me?"
「どうして僕にとってこんなにひどいことなのだろう？」
"there are boys who do not listen to the advice"
「アドバイスを聞かない男の子がいる」
"advice from people who know more than them"
「自分よりも詳しい人からのアドバイス」
"and they always meet with some misfortune or other"
「そして、彼らはいつも何か不幸に遭遇します」
"I have experienced that," said Pinocchio
「私もそれを経験しました」とピノキオは言いました
"but I shall never make that mistake again"
「でも、もう二度とあの過ちは犯さない」
"We shall see if that is true"
「それが本当かどうか、見てみよう」
and the puppet took leave of his good Fairy
そして人形は彼の良い妖精に別れを告げました
the good Fairy was now like a mamma to him
善良な妖精は、今や彼にとってママのようでした
and he went out of the house singing and dancing
そして、歌ったり踊ったりしながら家を出ました
In less than an hour all his friends were invited
1時間も経たないうちに、彼の友人全員が招待されました
Some accepted at once heartily
何人かはすぐに心から受け入れました
others at first required some convincing
他のものは、最初は説得が必要でした
but then they heard that there would be coffee
しかし、その後、彼らはコーヒーがあると聞きました
and the bread was going to be buttered on both sides
そして、パンは両面にバターを塗る予定でした
"We will come also, to do you a pleasure"
「私たちも来ます、あなたに喜びを与えるために」

Now I must tell you that Pinocchio had many friends
さて、ピノキオには多くの友人がいたと言わざるを得ません

and there were many boys he went to school with
そして、彼が一緒に学校に通った男の子はたくさんいました

but there was one boy he especially liked
しかし、彼が特に気に入った男の子が一人いました

This boy's name was Romeo
この男の子の名前はロミオでした

but he always went by his nickname
しかし、彼はいつも自分のニックネームで通っていました

all the boys called him Candle-wick

男の子たちは皆、彼をキャンドルウィックと呼んでいました
because he was so thin, straight and bright
なぜなら、彼はとても痩せていて、まっすぐで、聡明だったからだ
like the new wick of a little nightlight
小さな常夜灯の新しい芯のように
Candle-wick was the laziest of the boys
蝋燭の芯は男の子たちの中で最も怠惰だった
and he was naughtier than the other boys too
そして、彼は他の男の子たちよりもいたずらでもありました
but Pinocchio was devoted to him
しかし、ピノキオは彼に献身的でした
he had gone to Candle-wick's house before the others
彼は他の者たちよりも先にキャンドルウィックの家に行っていた
but he had not found him
しかし、彼は彼を見つけられなかった
He returned a second time, but Candle-wick was not there
彼は二度目に戻ったが、キャンドルウィックはそこにいなかった
He went a third time, but it was in vain
彼は三度目に行きましたが、無駄でした
Where could he search for him?
どこで彼を探せばいいのだろう？
He looked here, there, and everywhere
彼はここを見て、あそこで、そしてどこでも見ました
and at last he found his friend Candle-wick
そしてついに彼は友人のキャンドルウィックを見つけました
he was hiding on the porch of a peasant's cottage
彼は農民の小屋のポーチに隠れていました
"What are you doing there?" asked Pinocchio
「そこで何をしているの?」とピノキオは尋ねた
"I am waiting for midnight"

「真夜中を待っています」
"I am going to run away"
「逃げちゃう」
"And where are you going?"
「それで、どこに行くの?」
"I am going to live in another country"
「私は別の国で暮らすつもりです」
"the most delightful country in the world"
「世界で最も楽しい国」
"a real land of sweetmeats!"
「本物のお菓子の国!」
"And what is it called?"
「それで、それは何と呼ばれているの?」
"It is called the Land of Boobies"
「おっぱいの国っていうところ」
"Why do you not come, too?"
「どうして君も来ないの?」
"I? No, even if I wanted to!"
「私が?いや、したくても!」
"You are wrong, Pinocchio"
「あなたは間違っています、ピノキオ」
"If you do not come you will repent it"
「来ないなら悔い改める」
"Where could you find a better country for boys?"
「男の子にとってこれ以上の国をどこで見つけることができるでしょうか?」
"There are no schools there"
「そこには学校がない」
"there are no masters there"
「そこにはマスターはいない」
"and there are no books there"
「そしてそこには本がない」
"In that delightful land nobody ever studies"
「あの楽しい土地では、誰も勉強しない」
"On Saturday there is never school"
「土曜日は学校がない」

"every week consists of six Saturdays"
「毎週6つの土曜日から成り立っている」
"and the remainder of the week are Sundays"
「そして、その週の残りは日曜日です」
"think of all the time there is to play"
「遊ぶ時間を常に考えてください」
"the autumn holidays begin on the first of January"
「秋の休みは1月1日から始まります」
"and they finish on the last day of December"
「そして、彼らは12月の最終日に終わります」
"That is the country for me!"
「それが私にとっての国です!」
"That is what all civilized countries should be like!"
「それがすべての文明国のあるべき姿だ!」
"But how are the days spent in the Land of Boobies?"
「でも、おっぱいの国で過ごす日々はどうなの?」
"The days are spent in play and amusement"
「遊びと娯楽に明け暮れる日々」
"you enjoy yourself from morning till night"
「朝から晩まで楽しむ」
"and when night comes you go to bed"
「そして夜になったら寝る」
"and then you recommence the fun the next day"
「そして、次の日から楽しみを再開する」
"What do you think of it?"
「どう思う?」
"Hum!" said Pinocchio thoughtfully
「フム!」ピノキオは思慮深く言った
and he shook his head slightly
そして彼はわずかに首を振った
the gesture did seem to say something
その仕草は何かを言っているように見えた
"That is a life that I also would willingly lead"
「私も喜んでその人生を送りたい」
but he had not accepted the invitation yet
しかし、彼はまだ招待を受け入れていなかった

"Well, will you go with me?"
「じゃあ、一緒に行ってくれないか?」
"Yes or no? Resolve quickly"
「イエスかノーか?すぐに解決してください」
"No, no, no, and no again"
「いや、いや、いや、またや」
"I promised my good Fairy to be good boy"
「いい妖精にいい子になると約束した」
"and I will keep my word"
「そして私は約束を守ります」
"the sun will soon be setting"
「もうすぐ太陽が沈む」
"so I must leave you and run away"
「だから、お前を置いて逃げなきゃ」
"Good-bye, and a pleasant journey to you"
「さようなら、そして楽しい旅を」
"Where are you rushing off to in such a hurry?"
「そんなに急いでどこへ行くの?」
"I am going home," said Pinocchio
「家に帰ります」とピノキオは言いました
"My good Fairy wishes me to be back before dark"
「私の善良な妖精は、暗くなる前に戻ってくることを願っています」
"Wait another two minutes"
「あと2分待って」
"It will make me too late"
「手遅れになっちゃう」
"Only two minutes," Candle-wick pleaded
「たった2分だよ」とキャンドルウィックは懇願した
"And if the Fairy scolds me?"
「妖精に叱られたら?」
"Let her scold you," he suggested
「彼女に叱らせて」と彼は提案した
Candle-wick was quite a persuasive rascal
キャンドルウィックはかなり説得力のある悪党でした
"When she has scolded well she will hold her tongue"

"彼女がよく叱ったとき、彼女は舌を押さえます」
"And what are you going to do?"
「それで、あなたはどうするつもりですか?」
"Are you going alone or with companions?"
「一人で行くの?それとも仲間と一緒に行くの?」
"oh don't worry about that Pinocchio"
「ああ、そのピノキオのことは心配しないで」
"I will not be alone in the Land of Boobies"
「おっぱいの国に一人じゃない」
"there will be more than a hundred boys"
「100人以上の男の子がいるでしょう」
"And do you make the journey on foot?"
「そして、あなたは徒歩で旅をしますか?」
"A coach will pass by shortly"
「すぐ馬車が通り過ぎるよ」
"the carriage will take me to that happy country"
「馬車は私をその幸せな国に連れて行ってくれる」
"What would I not give for the coach to pass by now!"
「今、コーチが通り過ぎるのに、私は何をしないでしょう!」
"Why do you want the coach to come by so badly?"
「どうして馬車がそんなにひどく来るの?」
"so that I can see you all go together"
「君たちが一緒に行くのを見ることができるように」
"Stay here a little longer, Pinocchio"
「もう少しここにいて、ピノキオ」
"stay a little longer and you will see us"
「もう少し滞在すれば、私たちを見ることができます」
"No, no, I must go home"
「いやいや、家に帰らなきゃ」
"just wait another two minutes"
「あと2分待って」
"I have already delayed too long"
「もう遅らせすぎちゃった」
"The Fairy will be anxious about me"
「妖精は私のことを心配するでしょう」

"Is she afraid that the bats will eat you?"
「彼女はコウモリに食べられるのを恐れているの?」
Pinocchio had grown a little curious
ピノキオは少し好奇心が湧いてきました
"are you certain that there are no schools?"
「学校がないって確信してるの?」
"there is not even the shadow of a school"
「学校の影すらない」
"And are there no masters either?"
「そして、マスターもいないのですか?」
"the Land of the Boobies is free of masters"
「おっぱいの国には主人がいない」
"And no one is ever made to study?"
「そして、誰も勉強させられないのですか?」
"Never, never, and never again!"
「絶対に、絶対に、そして二度と!」
Pinocchio's mouth watered at the idea
ピノキオの口は、その考えに潤った
"What a delightful country!" said Pinocchio
「なんて楽しい国なんだろう!」とピノキオは言いました
"I have never been there," said Candle-wick
「私はそこに行ったことがありません」とキャンドルウィックは言いました
"but I can imagine it perfectly well"
「でも、完璧に想像できるよ」
"Why will you not come also?"
「なぜあなたも来ないのですか?」
"It is useless to tempt me"
「私を誘惑しても無駄だ」
"I made a promise to my good Fairy"
「私の良い妖精と約束した」
"I will become a sensible boy"
「良識ある少年になる」
"and I will not break my word"
「そして、私は約束を破りません」

"Good-bye, then," said Candle-wick
「じゃあ、さようなら」とキャンドルウィックは言った
"give my compliments to all the boys at school"
「学校の男の子全員に褒め言葉を」
"Good-bye, Candle-wick; a pleasant journey to you"
「さようなら、キャンドルウィック。あなたに楽しい旅を」
"amuse yourself in this pleasant land"
「この快適な土地で自分を楽しませる」
"and think sometimes of your friends"
「そして時々友達のことを考える」
Thus saying, the puppet made two steps to go
そう言って、人形は二歩進みました
but then he stopped halfway in his track
しかし、彼は途中で止まった
and, turning to his friend, he inquired:
そして、友人の方を向いて尋ねた。
"But are you quite certain about all this?"
「でも、君はこれについて本当に確信しているの?」
"in that country all the weeks consist of six Saturdays?"
「その国では、すべての週は6つの土曜日で構成されていますか?」
"and the rest of the week consists of Sundays?"
「そして、残りの週は日曜日で構成されていますか?」
"all the weekdays most certainly consist of six Saturdays"
「すべての平日は間違いなく6つの土曜日で構成されています」
"and the rest of the days are indeed Sundays"
「そして残りの日は確かに日曜日です」
"and are you quite sure about the holidays?"
「それで、休日については確信が持てるのか?」
"the holidays definitely begin on the first of January?"
「ホリデーシーズンは絶対に1月1日から始まるの?
"and you're sure the holidays finish on the last day of December?"

「それで、本当に12月の最終日に休暇が終わるの?」
"I am assuredly certain that this is how it is"
「きっとこういうものだと確信しています」
"What a delightful country!" repeated Pinocchio
「なんて楽しい国なんだろう!」とピノキオは繰り返した
and he was enchanted by all that he had heard
そして、彼は聞いたことすべてに魅了されました
this time Pinocchio spoke more resolute
この時、ピノキオはより毅然とした口調で話した
"This time really good-bye"
「今回は本当にさようなら」
"I wish you pleasant journey and life"
「楽しい旅と人生をお祈りします」
"Good-bye, my friend," bowed Candle-wick
「さようなら、友よ」キャンドルウィックはお辞儀をした
"When do you start?" inquired Pinocchio
「いつから始めるの?」ピノキオが尋ねた
"I will be leaving very soon"
「もうすぐ出発します」
"What a pity that you must leave so soon!"
「こんなに早く出て行かなければならないなんて、なんて残念なのでしょう!」
"I would almost be tempted to wait"
「待ちたくなりそう」
"And the Fairy?" asked Candle-wick
「それで、妖精は?」とキャンドルウィックは尋ねました
"It is already late," confirmed Pinocchio
「もう遅い」とピノキオは認めた
"I can return home an hour sooner"
「1時間早く帰れる」
"or I can return home an hour later"
「さもないと、一時間後に家に帰ることもできます」

"really it will be all the same"
「本当にそれはすべて同じになるでしょう」
"but what if the Fairy scolds you?"
「でも、妖精に叱られたらどうするの?」
"I must have patience!"
「我慢しなきゃ!」
"I will let her scold me"
「彼女に叱らせてあげる」
"When she has scolded well she will hold her tongue"
「彼女がよく叱ったとき、彼女は舌を押さえます」
In the meantime night had come on
そうこうしているうちに夜が来た
and by now it had gotten quite dark
そして、その頃にはすっかり暗くなっていました
Suddenly they saw in the distance a small light moving
突然、遠くに小さな光が動いているのが見えました

they heard a noise of talking
彼らは話す音を聞いた
and there was the sound of a trumpet
そして、トランペットの音が聞こえました
but the sound was still small and feeble
しかし、その音はまだ小さく、弱々しいものでした
so the sound still resembled the hum of a mosquito
そのため、その音はまだ蚊の鳴き声に似ていました
"Here it is!" shouted Candle-wick, jumping to his feet
「ここだ!」とキャンドルウィックは叫び、飛び跳ねて立ち上がった
"What is it?" asked Pinocchio in a whisper
「それは何だ?」ピノキオはささやき声で尋ねた
"It is the carriage coming to take me"
「私を連れて行くのは馬車です」
"so will you come, yes or no?"
「それで、はい、いいえ、来ますか?」
"But is it really true?" asked the puppet
「でも、それは本当に本当なの?」と人形は尋ねました
"in that country boys are never obliged to study?"
「その国では、男の子は勉強する義務がないの?」
"Never, never, and never again!"
「絶対に、絶対に、そして二度と!」
"What a delightful country!"
「なんて楽しい国なんだろう!」

Pinocchio Enjoys Six Months of Happiness
ピノキオは6ヶ月間の幸せを楽しんでいます

At last the wagon finally arrived
ついにワゴンが到着しました
and it arrived without making the slightest noise
そして、それは少しの音も立てずに到着しました
because its wheels were bound with flax and rags
その車輪は亜麻とぼろきれで縛られていたからです
It was drawn by twelve pairs of donkeys
それは12組のロバによって引かれました
all the donkeys were the same size
ロバはみんな同じ大きさでした
but each donkey was a different colour
しかし、ロバはそれぞれ異なる色をしていました
Some of the donkeys were gray
ロバの中には灰色のものもいました
and some of the donkeys were white
そして、ロバの中には白いものもいました
and some donkeys were brindled like pepper and salt
そして、一部のロバはコショウと塩のようにブリンドルされていました
and other donkeys had large stripes of yellow and blue
そして他のロバは黄色と青の大きな縞模様を持っていました
But there was something most extraordinary about them
しかし、彼らには最も驚くべき何かがありました
they were not shod like other beasts of burden
彼らは他の重荷を背負った獣のようには蹄鉄を履いていなかった
on their feet the donkeys had men's boots
ロバの足元には男性用のブーツを履いていました
"And the coachman?" you may ask
「御者は?」と尋ねるかもしれません
Picture to yourself a little man broader than long

長いよりも幅の広い小さな男を自分自身に想像してください
flabby and greasy like a lump of butter
たるんでバターの塊のように脂っこい
with a small round face like an orange
オレンジのような小さな丸い顔をしています
a little mouth that was always laughing
いつも笑っていた小さな口
and a soft, caressing voice of a cat
そして、猫の柔らかく愛撫する声
All the boys fought for their place in the coach
すべての少年たちは、コーチの地位を争いました
they all wanted to be conducted to the Land of Boobies
彼らは皆、おっぱいの国に連れて行かれることを望んでいました
The carriage was, in fact, quite full of boys
実際、馬車は男の子でいっぱいでした
and all the boys were between eight and fourteen years
そして、すべての男の子は8歳から14歳の間でした
the boys were heaped one upon another
男の子たちは次から次へと山積みにされました
just like herrings are squeezed into a barrel
ニシンが樽に絞られるのと同じように
They were uncomfortable and packed closely together
彼らは不快で、ぎっしりと詰め込まれていました
and they could hardly breathe
そして、彼らはほとんど息をすることができませんでした
but not one of the boys thought of grumbling
しかし、男の子の誰一人として不平を言おうとは思いませんでした
they were consoled by the promises of their destination
彼らは目的地の約束に慰められました
a place with no books, no schools, and no masters
本も学校もマスターもない場所
it made them so happy and resigned

それは彼らをとても幸せにし、諦めさせました
and they felt neither fatigue nor inconvenience
そして、彼らは疲労も不便も感じませんでした
neither hunger, nor thirst, nor want of sleep
飢えも、渇きも、睡眠不足も
soon the wagon had reached them
すぐにワゴンが彼らに到着しました
the little man turned straight to Candle-wick
小男はまっすぐにキャンドルウィックに向き直った
he had a thousand smirks and grimaces
彼は何千回もにやにや笑い、しかめっ面をしていた
"Tell me, my fine boy;"
「教えて、私の立派な子よ」
"would you also like to go to the fortunate country?"
「あなたも幸運な国に行きたいですか?」
"I certainly wish to go"
「もちろん行きたいです」
"But I must warn you, my dear child"
「しかし、私はあなたに警告しなければなりません、私の愛する子」
"there is not a place left in the wagon"
「ワゴン車には一席も残っていない」
"You can see for yourself that it is quite full"
「かなり満員になっていることが自分でわかります」
"No matter," replied Candle-wick
「関係ない」とキャンドルウィックは答えた
"I do not need to sit in the wagon"
「ワゴン車に座る必要はありません」
"I will sit on the arch of the wheel"
「ホイールのアーチに座ります」
And with a leap he sat above the wheel
そして跳躍して彼は車輪の上に座った
"And you, my love!" said the little man
「そして、お前、私の愛する人よ!」と小男は言った
and he turned in a flattering manner to Pinocchio
そして彼はお世辞でピノキオに向き直った

"what do you intend to do?"
「何をするつもりですか?」
"Are you coming with us?
「私たちと一緒に来るの?
"or are you going to remain behind?"
「それとも、君は残るつもりなの?」
"I will remain behind," answered Pinocchio
「私は残るよ」とピノキオは答えた
"I am going home," he answered proudly
「家に帰ります」と彼は誇らしげに答えました
"I intend to study, as all well conducted boys do"
「私は勉強するつもりです。すべての善良な男の子がそうであるように」
"Much good may it do you!"
「それが君にとって良いことでありますように!」
"Pinocchio!" called out Candle-wick
「ピノキオ!」とキャンドルウィックが叫びました
"come with us and we shall have such fun"
「私たちと一緒に来て、とても楽しい時間を過ごそう」
"No, no, and no again!" answered Pinocchio
「いや、いや、またダメだ!」ピノキオは答えました
a chorus of hundred voices shouted from the the coach
馬車から百人の声の合唱が叫ばれた
"Come with us and we shall have so much fun"
「私たちと一緒に来て、とても楽しい時間を過ごそう」
but the puppet was not at all sure
しかし、人形はまったく確信が持てませんでした
"if I come with you, what will my good Fairy say?"
「もし私があなたと一緒に行ったら、私の善良な妖精は何と言うの?」
and he was beginning to yield
そして彼は譲歩し始めていました
"Do not trouble your head with melancholy thoughts"
「憂鬱な考えで頭を悩ませないでください」
"consider only how delightful it will be"
「どれだけ楽しいかだけを考えてください」

"we are going to the Land of the Boobies"
「おっぱいの国に行く」
"all day we shall be at liberty to run riot"
「一日中、私たちは自由に暴動を起こすことができる」
Pinocchio did not answer, but he sighed
ピノキオは答えなかったが、ため息をついた
he sighed again, and then sighed for the third time
彼は再びため息をつき、そして三度目のため息をついた
finally Pinocchio made up his mind
ついにピノキオは決心しました
"Make a little room for me"
「私のために少し部屋を作って」
"because I would like to come, too"
「私も来たいから」
"The places are all full," replied the little man
「場所は全部いっぱいだよ」と小男は答えました
"but, let me show you how welcome you are"
「でも、君がどれだけ歓迎されているか見せてあげるよ」
"I will let you have my seat on the box"
「ボックス席に座らせてあげる」
"And where will you sit?"
「それで、どこに座るのですか?」
"Oh, I will go on foot"
「あ、徒歩で行くよ」
"No, indeed, I could not allow that"
「いや、確かに、それは許せませんでした」
"I would rather mount one of these donkeys"
「私はむしろこのロバの1つに乗りたい」
so Pinocchio went up the the first donkey
それでピノキオは最初のロバに上がった
and he attempted to mount the animal
そして彼は動物に乗ろうとしました
but the little donkey turned on him
しかし、小さなロバは彼に背を向けました
and the donkey gave him a great blow in the stomach

そしてロバは彼の胃に大きな打撃を与えました
and it rolled him over with his legs in the air
そして、それは彼を足で宙に転がしました
all the boys had been watching this
男の子たちはみんなこれを見ていた
so you can imagine the laughter from the wagon
だから、ワゴンからの笑い声を想像することができます
But the little man did not laugh
しかし、小さな男は笑いませんでした
He approached the rebellious donkey
彼は反抗的なロバに近づいた
and at first he pretended to kiss him
そして最初、彼は彼にキスするふりをした
but then he bit off half of his ear
しかし、その後、彼は耳の半分を噛みちぎった
Pinocchio in the meantime had gotten up from the ground
その間にピノキオは地面から立ち上がっていました
he was still very cross with the animal
彼はまだ動物にとても腹が立っていました
but with a spring he jumped onto him
しかし、彼はバネで彼に飛び乗った
and he seated himself on the poor animal's back
そして、彼は哀れな動物の背中に座りました
And he sprang so well that the boys stopped laughing
そして、彼はとても上手に跳ねたので、男の子たちは笑うのをやめました
and they began to shout: "Hurrah, Pinocchio!"
そして彼らは叫び始めました：「万歳、ピノキオ！」
and they clapped their hands and applauded him
そして、彼らは手を叩き、彼に拍手を送りました
soon the donkeys were galloping down the track
すぐにロバが線路を疾走しました
and the wagon was rattling over the stones
そして荷馬車は石の上をガタガタと音を立てていました
but the puppet thought that he heard a low voice
しかし、人形は低い声が聞こえたと思いました

"Poor fool! you should have followed your own way"
「かわいそうな愚か者め!自分の道を歩むべきだった」
"but but you will repent having come!"
「しかし、来てしまったことを後悔するでしょう!」
Pinocchio was a little frightened by what he had heard
ピノキオは聞いたことに少し怖かった
he looked from side to side to see what it was
彼はそれが何であるかを見るために左右を見ました
he tried to see where these words could have come from
彼は、これらの言葉がどこから来たのかを見ようとしました
but regardless of of where he looked he saw nobody
しかし、どこを見ても誰も見えませんでした
The donkeys galloped and the wagon rattled
ロバは疾走し、荷馬車はガタガタと音を立てました
and all the while the boys inside slept
そしてその間ずっと、中の男の子たちは眠っていました
Candle-wick snored like a dormouse
蝋燭の芯がヤマネのようにいびきをかいた
and the little man seated himself on the box
そして、小男は箱に座りました
and he sang songs between his teeth
そして彼は歯の間で歌を歌いました
"During the night all sleep"
「夜はみんな寝る」
"But I sleep never"
「でも、僕は絶対に眠らない」
soon they had gone another mile
すぐに彼らはさらに一歩進んだ
Pinocchio heard the same little low voice again
ピノキオは再び同じ小さな低い声を聞いた
"Bear it in mind, simpleton!"
「覚えておけ、単純者!」
"there are boys who refuse to study"
「勉強を拒む男の子がいる」
"they turn their backs upon books"

「彼らは本に背を向ける」
"they think they're too good to go to school
「彼らは自分たちが学校に行くには良すぎると思っている
"and they don't obey their masters"
「そして、彼らは主人に従わない」
"they pass their time in play and amusement"
「遊びや娯楽で時間を過ごす」
"but sooner or later they come to a bad end"
「しかし、遅かれ早かれ、彼らは悪い終わりを迎えます」
"I know it from my experience"
「自分の経験からわかる」
"and I can tell you how it always ends"
「そして、いつもどう終わるのか教えてあげるよ」
"A day will come when you will weep"
「泣く日が来る」
"you will weep just as I am weeping now"
「私が今泣いているように、あなたも泣くでしょう」
"but then it will be too late!"
「でも、それでは手遅れだよ!」
the words had been whispered very softly
その言葉は、とても静かにささやかれていた
but Pinocchio could be sure of what he had heard
しかし、ピノキオは自分が聞いたことに確信が持てた
the puppet was more frightened than ever
人形はこれまで以上に怯えていました
he sprang down from the back of his donkey
彼はロバの背中から飛び降りた
and he went and took hold of the donkey's mouth
そして、ロバの口をつかみに行きました
you can imagine Pinocchio's surprise at what he saw
ピノキオが見たものに驚いたことは想像に難くありません
the donkey was crying just like a boy!
ロバは男の子のように泣いていました!

"Eh! Sir Coachman," cried Pinocchio
「えっ!御者卿」とピノキオは叫んだ
"here is an extraordinary thing!"
「これは驚くべきことです!」
"This donkey is crying"
「このロバが泣いてる」
"Let him cry," said the coachman
「彼を泣かせてください」と御者は言いました
"he will laugh when he is a bridegroom"
「彼は花婿のとき笑うだろう」
"But have you by chance taught him to talk?"
「でも、たまたま彼に話し方を教えたの?」
"No; but he spent three years with learned dogs"
「いいえ。しかし、彼は3年間、学んだ犬と一緒に過ごしました」
"and he learned to mutter a few words"
「そして彼はいくつかの言葉をつぶやくことを学びました」
"Poor beast!" added the coachman
「かわいそうな獣だ!」と御者が付け加えた
"but don't you worry," said the little man
「でも、心配しないで」と小男は言いました
"don't let us waste time in seeing a donkey cry"
「ロバの泣き声を見て時間を無駄にしないで」
"Mount him and let us go on"
「彼に騎乗して、さっそく行こう」
"the night is cold and the road is long"
「夜は寒くて道が長い」
Pinocchio obeyed without another word
ピノキオは何も言わずに従った

In the morning about daybreak they arrived
夜明け頃の朝、彼らは到着した
they were now safely in the Land of Boobie Birds
彼らは今、無事にカツオドリの国にいました
It was a country unlike any other country in the world
それは世界の他のどの国とも異なる国でした
The population was composed entirely of boys
人口はすべて男の子で構成されていました
The oldest of the boys were fourteen
男の子の中で一番上の子は14歳でした
and the youngest were scarcely eight years old
そして、最年少はわずか8歳でした
In the streets there was great merriment
通りには大いに陽気な雰囲気が漂っていました
the sight of it was enough to turn anybody's head
その光景は、誰もが頭を悩ませるほどでした
There were troops of boys everywhere

いたるところに男の子の軍隊がいました
Some were playing with nuts they had found
見つけたナッツで遊んでいる人もいました
some were playing games with battledores
バトルドールとゲームをしている人もいました
lots of boys were playing football
たくさんの男の子がサッカーをしていました
Some rode velocipedes, others wooden horses
ベロシペードに乗る人もいれば、木馬に乗る人もいました
A party of boys were playing hide and seek
男の子たちの一団がかくれんぼをしていた
a few boys were chasing each other
数人の男の子が追いかけ合っていました
Some were reciting and singing songs
歌を朗読したり歌ったりしている人もいました
others were just leaping into the air
他の人々はただ空中に飛び跳ねていました
Some amused themselves with walking on their hands
手をついて歩くのを楽しんでいる人もいました
others were trundling hoops along the road
他の人々は道路に沿ってフープを踏みつけていました
and some were strutting about dressed as generals
そして、将軍の格好をして闊歩している者もいた
they were wearing helmets made from leaves
彼らは葉っぱで作ったヘルメットをかぶっていました
and they were commanding a squadron of cardboard soldiers
そして、彼らは段ボール兵の戦隊を指揮していました
Some were laughing and some shouting
笑っている人もいれば、叫んでいる人もいました
and some were calling out silly things
そして、馬鹿げたことを叫ぶ人もいました
others clapped their hands, or whistled
他の人は手を叩いたり、口笛を吹いたりしました
some clucked like a hen who has just laid an egg

卵を産んだばかりの雌鶏のように鳴くものもいました
In every square, canvas theatres had been erected
すべての広場に、キャンバス劇場が建てられていました
and they were crowded with boys all day long
そして、彼らは一日中男の子で賑わっていました
On the walls of the houses there were inscriptions
家の壁には碑文が刻まれていました
"Long live the playthings"
「おもちゃ万歳」
"we will have no more schools"
「学校はもうありません」
"down the toilet with arithmetic"
「算数でトイレを下る」
and similar other fine sentiments were written
そして、同様の他の素晴らしい感情が書かれました
of course all the slogans were in bad spelling
もちろん、すべてのスローガンはスペルが間違っていました
Pinocchio, Candle-wick and the other boys went to the town
ピノキオ、キャンドルウィック、そして他の男の子たちは町に行きました
they were in the thick of the tumult
彼らは騒動の真っ只中にいた
and I need not tell you how fun it was
そして、それがどれほど楽しかったかは言うまでもありません
within minutes they acquainted themselves with everybody
数分のうちに、彼らは皆と知り合いになりました
Where could happier or more contented boys be found?
これほど幸せで満足している男の子はどこにいるのでしょうか?
the hours, days and weeks passed like lightning
時間、日、週が稲妻のように過ぎていきました
time flies when you're having fun
楽しんでいると時間があっという間に過ぎます
"Oh, what a delightful life!" said Pinocchio

「ああ、なんて楽しい人生なんだろう!」とピノキオは言いました

"See, then, was I not right?" replied Candle-wick
「じゃあ、僕は間違っていたのか?」とキャンドルウィックは答えた

"And to think that you did not want to come!"
「そして、あなたが来たくなかったと思うとは!」

"imagine you had returned home to your Fairy"
「妖精の家に帰ったと想像してみて」

"you wanted to lose your time in studying!"
「勉強で時間を無駄にしたかったのですね!」

"now you are free from the bother of books"
「これで、本の煩わしさから解放されました」

"you must acknowledge that you owe it to me"
「君はそれを私に借りがあることを認めなければならない」

"only friends know how to render such great services"
「このような素晴らしいサービスを提供する方法は、友人だけが知っている」

"It is true, Candle-wick!" confirmed Pinocchio
「本当だよ、キャンドルウィック!」ピノキオは確認した

"If I am now a happy boy, it is all your doing"
「もし私が今幸せな少年なら、それはすべて君の仕業だ」

"But do you know what the master used to say?"
「でも、マスターがよく言っていたこと知ってる?」

"Do not associate with that rascal Candle-wick"
「あの悪党のキャンドルウィックと関連付けないでください」

"because he is a bad companion for you"
「彼はあなたにとって悪い仲間だからです」

"and he will only lead you into mischief!"
「そして、彼はあなたを悪戯に導くだけだ!」

"Poor master!" replied the other, shaking his head

「かわいそうなご主人様!」もう一人が首を振って答えた

"I know only too well that he disliked me"
「彼が私を嫌っていたことはよくわかっています」

"and he amused himself by making my life hard"
「そして彼は私の人生を困難にすることで自分自身を楽しませた」

"but I am generous, and I forgive him!"
「でも、私は寛大で、彼を許します!」

"you are a noble soul!" said Pinocchio
「お前は高貴な魂だ!」とピノキオは言った

and he embraced his friend affectionately
そして彼は愛情を込めて友人を抱きしめました

and he kissed him between the eyes
そして彼は彼の目の間にキスをした

This delightful life had gone on for five months
この楽しい生活は5ヶ月間続きました

The days had been entirely spent in play and amusement
日々は遊びと娯楽に完全に費やされていました

not a thought was spent on books or school
本や学校には何も考えていませんでした

but one morning Pinocchio awoke to a most disagreeable surprise
しかし、ある朝、ピノキオは最も不愉快な驚きで目を覚ましました

what he saw put him into a very bad humour
彼が見たものは、彼を非常に悪いユーモアに陥らせました

Pinocchio Turns into a Donkey
ピノキオはロバに変わります

when Pinocchio awoke he scratched his head
ピノキオが目を覚ますと、彼は頭を掻いた
when scratching his head he discovered something...
頭を掻いたとき、彼は何かを発見しました...
his ears had grown more than a hand!
彼の耳は手よりも大きくなっていました!
You can imagine his surprise
彼の驚きは想像に難くありません
because he had always had very small ears
なぜなら、彼はいつもとても小さな耳を持っていたからです
He went at once in search of a mirror
彼はすぐに鏡を探しに行きました
he had to have a better look at himself
彼は自分自身をもっとよく見なければなりませんでした
but he was not able to find any kind of mirror
しかし、彼は鏡のようなものを見つけることができませんでした
so he filled the basin with water
そこで彼は洗面器を水で満たしました
and he saw a reflection he never wished to see
そして彼は見たくなかった反射を見た
a magnificent pair of donkey's ears embellished his head!
ロバの耳の見事なペアが彼の頭を飾っていました!
think of poor Pinocchio's sorrow, shame and despair!
かわいそうなピノキオの悲しみ、恥、絶望を考えてみてください!
He began to cry and roar
彼は泣き叫び始めました
and he beat his head against the wall
そして彼は壁に頭を打ち付けた
but the more he cried the longer his ears grew

しかし、泣けば泣くほど、彼の耳は長く伸びていきました
and his ears grew, and grew, and grew
そして彼の耳は成長し、成長し、成長しました
and his ears became hairy towards the points
そして彼の耳はポイントに向かって毛むくじゃらになりました
a little Marmot heard Pinocchio's loud cries
ピノキオの大きな叫び声を聞いた小さなマーモット
Seeing the puppet in such grief she asked earnestly:
人形がとても悲しんでいるのを見て、彼女は真剣に尋ねました。
"What has happened to you, my dear fellow-lodger?"
「親愛なる下宿人、君に何があったんだ?」
"I am ill, my dear little Marmot"
「私は病気です、私の愛する小さなマーモット」
"very ill, and my illness frightens me"
「とても病気で、病気が怖いです」
"Do you understand counting a pulse?"
「脈拍を数えるのがわかりますか?」
"A little," sobbed Pinocchio
「少し」ピノキオはすすり泣いた
"Then feel and see if by chance I have got fever"
「じゃあ、たまたま熱が出ていないか感じて確かめてみて」
The little Marmot raised her right fore-paw
小さなマーモットは彼女の右前足を上げました
and the little Marmot felt Pinocchio's pulse
そして小さなマーモットはピノキオの脈を感じました
and she said to him, sighing:
そして彼女はため息をつきながら彼に言いました。
"My friend, it grieves me very much"
「友よ、それは私をとても悲しませています」
"but I am obliged to give you bad news!"
「でも、悪い知らせを言わざるを得ないんだ!」
"What is it?" asked Pinocchio

"それは何だ?" ピノキオは尋ねた
"You have got a very bad fever!"
「あなたはとてもひどい熱を出しています!」
"What fever is it?"
「何の熱ですか?」
"you have a case of donkey fever"
「ロバ熱にかかったんじゃないか」
"That is a fever that I do not understand"
「あれは私には理解できない熱です」
but he understood it only too well
しかし、彼はそれをあまりにもよく理解していた
"Then I will explain it to you," said the Marmot
「じゃあ、君に説明するよ」とマーモットは言いました
"soon you will no longer be a puppet"
「もうすぐ君は人形ではなくなる」
"it won't take longer than two or three hours"
「2、3時間もかからないよ」
"nor will you be a boy either"
「君も男の子じゃないよ」
"Then what shall I be?"
「じゃあ、僕は何になろうか?」
"you will well and truly be a little donkey"
「あなたは本当に小さなロバになるでしょう」
"a donkey like those that draw the carts"
「荷車を引くようなロバ」
"a donkey that carries cabbages to market"
「キャベツを市場に運ぶロバ」
"Oh, how unfortunate I am!" cried Pinocchio
「ああ、なんて不幸なんだ!」とピノキオは叫んだ
and he seized his two ears with his hands
そして、両手で両耳をつかんだ
and he pulled and tore at his ears furiously
そして彼は猛烈に耳を引っ張り、引き裂いた
he pulled as if they had been someone else's ears
彼はまるで他人の耳のように引っ張った
"My dear boy," said the Marmot

「お坊ちゃん」とマーモットは言いました
and she did her best to console him
そして彼女は彼を慰めるために最善を尽くしました
"you can do nothing about it"
「あなたはそれについて何もできません」
"It is your destiny to become a donkey"
「ロバになるのは君の運命だ」
"It is written in the decrees of wisdom"
「知恵の定めに書いてある」
"it happens to all boys who are lazy"
「怠惰な男の子はみんなに起こること」
"it happens to the boys that dislike books"
「本が嫌いな男の子にはよくあることだ」
"it happens to the boys that don't go to schools"
「学校に行かない男の子にも起こること」
"and it happens to boys who disobey their masters"
「そして、それは彼らの主人に従わない少年に起こります」
"all boys who pass their time in amusement"
「娯楽で時間を過ごすすべての男の子」
"all the boys who play games all day"
「一日中ゲームをする男の子たち」
"boys who distract themselves with diversions"
「気晴らしで気を紛らわせる男の子」
"the same fate awaits all those boys"
「同じ運命がすべての少年たちを待っています」
"sooner or later they become little donkeys"
「遅かれ早かれ、彼らは小さなロバになる」
"But is it really so?" asked the puppet, sobbing
「でも、本当にそうなのか?」人形はすすり泣きながら尋ねた
"It is indeed only too true!"
「それは確かに真実すぎる!」
"And tears are now useless"
「そして、涙はもう無駄です」
"You should have thought of it sooner!"

「もっと早く考えるべきだった!」
"But it was not my fault; believe me, little Marmot"
「でも、それは私のせいではありません。信じて、小さなマーモット」
"the fault was all Candle-wick's!"
「欠点は全部キャンドルウィックのせいだ!」
"And who is this Candle-wick?"
「で、このキャンドルウィックは誰だ?」
"Candle-wick is one of my school-fellows"
「キャンドルウィックは私の学校の仲間の一人です」
"I wanted to return home and be obedient"
「家に帰って従順になりたかった」
"I wished to study and be a good boy"
「勉強していい子になりたかった」
"but Candle-wick convinced me otherwise"
「しかし、キャンドルウィックはそうではないと私を説得しました」
'Why should you bother yourself by studying?'
「なんでわざわざ勉強しなきゃ」
'Why should you go to school?'
「なんで学校に行かなくちゃいけないの?」
'Come with us instead to the Land of Boobies Birds'
「代わりに私たちと一緒におっぱいの鳥の国に来てください」
'there we shall none of us have to learn'
「そこでは、誰も学ぶ必要はない」
'we will amuse ourselves from morning to night'
「私たちは朝から晩まで自分たちを楽しませます」
'and we shall always be merry'
「そして、私たちはいつも陽気でいられるでしょう」
"that friend of yours was false"
「君の友達は嘘だった」
"why did you follow his advice?"
「なぜ彼のアドバイスに従ったのですか?」
"Because, my dear little Marmot, I am a puppet"
「だって、私の愛する小さなマーモット、私は人形だか

"I have no sense and no heart"
「私にはセンスも心もない」
"if I had had a heart I would never have left"
「もし心があったら、決して離れなかっただろう」
"I left my good Fairy who loved me like a mamma"
「私をママのように愛してくれた良き妖精と別れました」
"the good Fairy who had done so much for me!"
「私のためにたくさんのことをしてくれた善良な妖精!」
"And I was going to be a puppet no longer"
「そして、私はもう人形にはならない」
"I would by this time have become a little boy"
「この頃、僕は小さな男の子になっていただろう」
"and I would be like the other boys"
「そして、僕も他の男の子たちと同じになるだろう」
"But if I meet Candle-wick, woe to him!"
「でも、もしキャンドルウィックに会ったら、彼には災いが降りかかるよ!」
"He shall hear what I think of him!"
「彼は私が彼についてどう思うか聞くでしょう!」
And he turned to go out
そして彼は外に出ようと振り返った
But then he remembered he had donkey's ears
しかし、その時、彼は自分がロバの耳を持っていたことを思い出しました
of course he was ashamed to show his ears in public
もちろん、人前で耳を見せるのは恥ずかしかったです
so what do you think he did?
それで、彼は何をしたと思いますか?
He took a big cotton hat
彼は大きな綿の帽子をかぶった
and he put the cotton hat on his head
そして、綿の帽子を頭にかぶせました
and he pulled the hat well down over his nose

そして彼は帽子を鼻の上でしっかりと引っ張りました
He then set out in search of Candle-wick
その後、彼はキャンドルウィックを探しに出かけました
He looked for him in the streets
彼は通りで彼を探しました
and he looked for him in the little theatres
そして彼は小さな劇場で彼を探しました
he looked in every possible place
彼はあらゆる場所を探しました
but he could not find him wherever he looked
しかし、どこを見ても彼を見つけることができませんでした
He inquired for him of everybody he met
彼は出会ったすべての人について尋ねました
but no one seemed to have seen him
しかし、誰も彼を見ていないようだった
He then went to seek him at his house
それから彼は彼の家に彼を探しに行きました
and, having reached the door, he knocked
そして、ドアにたどり着くと、彼はノックしました
"Who is there?" asked Candle-wick from within
「そこにいるのは誰だ?」とキャンドルウィックが中から尋ねた
"It is I!" answered the puppet
「私だ!」と人形は答えました
"Wait a moment and I will let you in"
「ちょっと待ってください。入れます」
After half an hour the door was opened
30分後、ドアが開けられました
now you can imagine Pinocchio's feeling at what he saw
今、ピノキオが見たものに対する気持ちを想像することができます
his friend also had a big cotton hat on his head
彼の友人も頭に大きな綿の帽子をかぶっていました
At the sight of the cap Pinocchio felt almost consoled
帽子を見て、ピノキオはほとんど慰められたように感じ

ました
and Pinocchio thought to himself:
そしてピノキオは心の中で考えました。
"Has my friend got the same illness that I have?"
「私の友人は私と同じ病気にかかっているの?」
"Is he also suffering from donkey fever?"
「彼もロバ熱にかかっているの?」
but at first Pinocchio pretended not to have noticed
しかし、最初はピノキオは気づかなかったふりをしていました
he just casually asked him a question, smiling:
彼はただ微笑みながら、何気なく彼に質問をした。
"How are you, my dear Candle-wick?"
「お元気ですか、私の親愛なるキャンドルウィック?」
"as well as a mouse in a Parmesan cheese"
「パルメザンチーズのネズミのように」
"Are you saying that seriously?"
「そんなことを本気で言ってるの?」
"Why should I tell you a lie?"
「なぜ嘘をつく必要があるのですか?」
"but why, then, do you wear a cotton hat?"
「でも、じゃあ、どうして綿の帽子をかぶっているの?」
"is covers up all of your ears"
「耳を全部覆う」
"The doctor ordered me to wear it"
「医者から着るように言われた」
"because I have hurt this knee"
「この膝を痛めてしまったから」
"And you, dear puppet," asked Candle-wick
「そして、あなた、親愛なる人形」とキャンドルウィックは尋ねました
"why have you pulled that cotton hat passed your nose?"
「なんであの綿帽子を引っ張って鼻を通したの?」
"The doctor prescribed it because I have grazed my foot"

「医者が処方したのは、足をかすめてしまったからだ」
"Oh, poor Pinocchio!" - "Oh, poor Candle-wick!"
「ああ、かわいそうなピノキオ!」-
「ああ、かわいそうなキャンドルウィック!」
After these words a long silence followed
この言葉の後、長い沈黙が続いた
the two friends did nothing but look mockingly at each other
二人の友人は、お互いを嘲笑うように見つめ合うだけでした
At last the puppet said in a soft voice to his companion:
とうとう人形は小さな声で仲間に言いました。
"Satisfy my curiosity, my dear Candle-wick"
「私の好奇心を満たしてください、私の愛するキャンドルウィック」
"have you ever suffered from disease of the ears?"
「耳の病気にかかったことはありますか?」
"I have never suffered from disease of the ears!"
「耳の病気にかかったことがない!」
"And you, Pinocchio?" asked Candle-wick
「それで、ピノキオ、君は?」とキャンドルウィックが尋ねた
"have you ever suffered from disease of the ears?"
「耳の病気にかかったことはありますか?」
"I have never suffered from that disease either"
「私もその病気にかかったことはありません」
"Only since this morning one of my ears aches"
「今朝から耳が痛い」
"my ear is also paining me"
「耳も痛い」
"And which of your ears hurts you?"
「それで、あなたのどちらの耳が痛いの?」
"Both of my ears happen to hurt"
「たまたま両耳が痛い」
"And what about you?"

「それで、君はどうだ?」
"Both of my ears happen to hurt too"
「たまたま両耳も痛い」
Can we have got the same illness?"
私たちは同じ病気にかかったのでしょうか?」
"I fear we might have caught a fever"
「熱が出たのではないかと心配しています」
"Will you do me a kindness, Candle-wick?"
「親切にしてくれるか、キャンドルウィック?」
"Willingly! With all my heart"
「喜んで!心を込めて」
"Will you let me see your ears?"
「君の耳を見せてくれる?」
"Why would I deny your request?"
「なぜ私はあなたの要求を拒否するのですか?」
"But first, my dear Pinocchio, I should like to see yours"
「でもその前に、親愛なるピノキオ、君のものを見たいんだ」
"No: you must do so first"
「いいえ、最初にそうしなければなりません」
"No, dear. First you and then I!"
「いや、ねえ。まず君、次に僕だ!」
"Well," said the puppet
「まあ」と人形は言いました
"let us come to an agreement like good friends"
「仲良しのように合意に至ろう」
"Let me hear what this agreement is"
「この契約が何であるかを聞かせてください」
"We will both take off our hats at the same moment"
「二人同時に帽子を脱ぎます」
"Do you agree to do it?"
「あなたはそれに同意しますか?」
"I agree, and you have my word"
「私も同意します。そして、あなたは私の言葉を持っています」

And Pinocchio began to count in a loud voice:
そしてピノキオは大声で数え始めました。
"One, two, three!" he counted
「1、2、3!」彼は数えた
At "Three!" the two boys took off their hats
「スリー!」と、二人の少年は帽子を脱いだ
and they threw their hats into the air
そして、彼らは帽子を空中に投げました
and you should have seen the scene that followed
そして、その後のシーンを見るべきだった
it would seem incredible if it were not true
もしそれが真実でなかったら、信じられないように思えるでしょう
they saw they were both struck by the same misfortune
彼らは、自分たちが同じ不幸に見舞われたことを悟った
but they felt neither mortification nor grief
しかし、彼らは悔しさも悲しみも感じませんでした
instead they began to prick their ungainly ears
それどころか、彼らは不格好な耳を刺し始めました
and they began to make a thousand antics
そして、彼らは千のふざけた行動を始めました
they ended by going into bursts of laughter
彼らは爆笑して終わりました
And they laughed, and laughed, and laughed
そして、彼らは笑い、笑い、笑った
until they had to hold themselves together
彼らが一緒に保たなければならなくなるまで

But in the midst of their merriment something happened
しかし、彼らが歓喜している最中に、何かが起こりました

Candle-wick suddenly stopped laughing and joking
キャンドルウィックは突然笑ったり冗談を言ったりするのをやめました

he staggered around and changed colour
彼はよろめきながら歩き回り、色を変えた

"Help, help, Pinocchio!" he cried
「助けて、助けて、ピノキオ!」彼は叫んだ

"What is the matter with you?"
「どうしたの?」

"Alas, I cannot any longer stand upright"
「ああ、もう直立できない」

"Neither can I," exclaimed Pinocchio
「私もできません」とピノキオは叫びました

and he began to totter and cry
そして彼はよろめき、泣き始めました
And whilst they were talking, they both doubled up
そして、彼らが話している間、彼らは両方とも倍増しました
and they began to run round the room on their hands and feet
そして、彼らは手と足で部屋の中を走り回り始めました
And as they ran, their hands became hoofs
そして、彼らが走ると、彼らの手はひづめになりました
their faces lengthened into muzzles
彼らの顔は銃口に引き伸ばされた
and their backs became covered with a light gray hairs
そして彼らの背中は薄い灰色の毛で覆われるようになりました
and their hair was sprinkled with black
そして、彼らの髪には黒が散りばめられていました
But do you know what was the worst moment?
しかし、最悪の瞬間は何だったか知っていますか?
one moment was worse than all the others
ある瞬間は他のどの瞬間よりもひどかった
both of the boys grew donkey tails
男の子は両方ともロバの尻尾を育てました
the boys were vanquished by shame and sorrow
少年たちは恥と悲しみに打ちのめされました
and they wept and lamented their fate
そして、彼らは泣き、自分たちの運命を嘆き悲しんだ
Oh, if they had but been wiser!
ああ、彼らがもっと賢かったら!
but they couldn't lament their fate
しかし、彼らは自分たちの運命を嘆くことができなかった
because they could only bray like asses
なぜなら、彼らはロバのようにしか泣くことができなかったからだ
and they brayed loudly in chorus: "Hee-haw!"

そして、彼らは大声で「ヒッホー!」と叫んだ。
Whilst this was going on someone knocked at the door
これが進行している間に、誰かがドアをノックしました
and there was a voice on the outside that said:
そして、外側から声がしました。
"Open the door! I am the little man"
「ドアを開けて!私は小さな男です」
"I am the coachman who brought you to this country"
「私はあなたをこの国に連れてきた御者です」
"Open at once, or it will be the worse for you!"
「すぐに開けてください。さもないと、もっとひどいことになるよ!」

Pinocchio gets Trained for the Circus
ピノキオはサーカスのために訓練を受ける

the door wouldn't open at his command
彼の命令でドアは開かなかった
so the little man gave the door a violent kick
それで、小さな男はドアを激しく蹴りました
and the coachman burst into the room
そして御者が部屋に飛び込んできました
he spoke with his usual little laugh:
彼はいつもの小さな笑い声で話した。
"Well done, boys! You brayed well"
「よくやった、男の子たち!よく祈ってくれたね」
"and I recognized you by your voices"
「そして、私はあなたの声であなたを認識しました」
"That is why I am here"
「だから僕はここにいるんだ」
the two little donkeys were quite stupefied
2頭の小さなロバはすっかり呆然としていました
they stood with their heads down
彼らは頭を下げて立っていました

they had their ears lowered
彼らは耳を下げていました
and they had their tails between their legs
そして、彼らは尻尾を足の間に持っていました
At first the little man stroked and caressed them
最初、小男は彼らを撫でて愛撫しました
then he took out a currycomb
それから彼はカレーコームを取り出しました
and he currycombed the donkeys well
そして彼はロバを上手にカレーコーミングしました
by this process he had polished them
このプロセスによって、彼はそれらを磨き上げました
and the two donkeys shone like two mirrors
そして、二頭のロバは二つの鏡のように輝いていました
he put a halter around their necks
彼は彼らの首にホルターをつけた
and he led them to the market-place
そして彼は彼らを市場に導きました

he was in hopes of selling them
彼はそれらを売ることを期待していました
he thought he could get a good profit
彼は良い利益を得ることができると思った
And indeed there were buyers for the donkeys
そして確かにロバの買い手がいました
Candle-wick was bought by a peasant
キャンドル芯は農民が買いました
his donkey had died the previous day
彼のロバは前日に死んでいた
Pinocchio was sold to the director of a company
ピノキオは会社の取締役に売却されました
they were a company of buffoons and tight-rope dancers
彼らは道化師と綱渡りの踊り手の会社でした
he bought him so that he might teach him to dance
彼は彼にダンスを教えるために彼を買った
he could dance with the other circus animals
彼は他のサーカスの動物たちと踊ることができた
And now, my little readers, you understand
そして今、私の小さな読者の皆さん、あなたは理解しています
the little man was just a businessman
その小さな男はただのビジネスマンだった
and it was a profitable business that he led
そして、彼が率いたのは収益性の高いビジネスでした
The wicked little monster with a face of milk and honey
ミルクと蜂蜜の顔をした邪悪な小さなモンスター
he made frequent journeys round the world
彼は頻繁に世界中を旅しました
he promised and flattered wherever he went
彼はどこへ行っても約束し、お世辞を言いました
and he collected all the idle boys
そして、彼はすべての怠惰な少年たちを集めました
and there were many idle boys to collect
そして、集めるべき怠惰な男の子がたくさんいました
all the boys who had taken a dislike to books

本が嫌いだった男の子たちはみんな
and all the boys who weren't fond of school
そして、学校が好きではなかったすべての男の子
each time his wagon filled up with these boys
そのたびに、彼の荷馬車はこれらの少年たちでいっぱいになりました
and he took them all to the Land of Boobie Birds
そして、彼は彼ら全員をカツオドリの国に連れて行きました
here they passed their time playing games
ここで彼らはゲームをして時間を過ごしました
and there was uproar and much amusement
そして、騒ぎと大いに楽しんだ
but the same fate awaited all the deluded boys
しかし、惑わされたすべての少年たちと同じ運命が待っていました
too much play and no study turned them into donkeys
遊びすぎて勉強がなかったため、彼らはロバになってしまいました
then he took possession of them with great delight
それから彼は大喜びでそれらを手に入れました
and he carried them off to the fairs and markets
そして、彼はそれらを見本市や市場に運びました
And in this way he made heaps of money
このようにして、彼は大金を稼ぎました
What became of Candle-wick I do not know
キャンドルウィックがどうなったのかはわかりません
but I do know what happened to poor Pinocchio
しかし、私はかわいそうなピノキオに何が起こったのか知っています
from the very first day he endured a very hard life
彼は最初の日から非常に厳しい生活に耐えました
Pinocchio was put into his stall
ピノキオは彼の屋台に入れられました
and his master filled the manger with straw
そして主人は飼い葉桶に藁を詰めました

but Pinocchio didn't like eating straw at all
しかし、ピノキオは藁を食べるのが全く好きではありませんでした
and the little donkey spat the straw out again
そして、小さなロバは再びわらを吐き出しました
Then his master, grumbling, filled the manger with hay
すると主人は不平を言いながら、飼い葉桶に干し草を入れました
but hay did not please Pinocchio either
しかし、干し草はピノキオも喜ばなかった
"Ah!" exclaimed his master in a passion
「あっ!」主人は激怒して叫んだ
"Does not hay please you either?"
「干し草も君を喜ばせないのか?」
"Leave it to me, my fine donkey"
「私に任せて、私の立派なロバ」
"I see you are full of caprices"
「気まぐれだなぁ」
"but worry not, I will find a way to cure you!"
「でも心配しないで、君を治す方法を見つけるよ!」
And he struck the donkey's legs with his whip
そして、彼は鞭でロバの足を叩きました
Pinocchio began to cry and bray with pain
ピノキオは痛みで泣き叫び始めました
"Hee-haw! I cannot digest straw!"
「ヒホー!藁が消化できない!」
"Then eat hay!" said his master
「じゃあ、干し草を食べろ!」と主人は言った
he understood perfectly the asinine dialect
彼はアシニン方言を完全に理解していた
"Hee-haw! hay gives me a pain in my stomach"
「ヒホー!干し草は私に胃の痛みを与えます」
"I see how it is little donkey"
「なるほど、ちっちゃいロバだな」
"you would like to be fed with capons in jelly"
「ゼリーに入ったカポンを食べさせたい」

and he got more and more angry
そして彼はますます怒った
and he whipped poor Pinocchio again
そして彼は再び哀れなピノキオを鞭打ちました
the second time Pinocchio held his tongue
ピノキオが舌を噛んだのは二度目
and he learned to say nothing more
そして彼はそれ以上何も言わないことを学びました
The stable was then shut
その後、厩舎は閉鎖されました
and Pinocchio was left alone
そしてピノキオは一人取り残されました
He had not eaten for many hours
彼は何時間も食べていなかった
and he began to yawn from hunger
そして、彼は空腹からあくびをし始めました
his yawns seemed as wide as an oven
彼のあくびはオーブンのように広く見えた
but he found nothing else to eat
しかし、彼は他に食べるものを見つけられませんでした
so he resigned himself to his fate
だから彼は自分の運命に身を任せた
and he gave in and chewed a little hay
そして彼は諦めて、少し干し草を噛みました
he chewed the hay well, because it was dry
彼は干し草をよく噛んだ、なぜならそれは乾いていたからだ
and he shut his eyes and swallowed it
そして彼は目を閉じてそれを飲み込んだ
"This hay is not bad," he said to himself
「この干し草は悪くない」と彼は独り言を言いました
"but better would have been if I had studied!"
「でも、勉強していればもっと良かったのに!」
"Instead of hay I could now be eating bread"
「干し草の代わりに、パンを食べることができるようになった」

"and perhaps I would have been eating fine sausages"
「そして、おそらく私は上質なソーセージを食べていたでしょう」
"But I must have patience!"
「でも、我慢しなきゃ!」
The next morning he woke up again
翌朝、彼は再び目を覚ました
he looked in the manger for a little more hay
彼は飼い葉桶の中でもう少し干し草を探しました
but there was no more hay to be found
しかし、もう干し草は見つかりませんでした
for he had eaten all the hay during the night
彼は夜の間に干し草を全部食べてしまったからです
Then he took a mouthful of chopped straw
それから彼は刻んだストローを口に含んだ
but he had to acknowledge the horrible taste
しかし、彼はその恐ろしい味を認めざるを得なかった
it tasted not in the least like macaroni or pie
マカロニやパイのような味は少しもありませんでした
"I hope other naughty boys learn from my lesson"
「他のいたずらっ子たちが私のレッスンから学べるといいな」
"But I must have patience!"
「でも、我慢しなきゃ!」
and the little donkey kept chewing the straw
そして、小さなロバは藁を噛み続けました
"Patience indeed!" shouted his master
「本当に忍耐強い!」と主人は叫んだ
he had come at that moment into the stable
彼はその瞬間、厩舎に来ていた
"but don't get too comfortable, my little donkey"
「でも、あまり気にしないで、私の小さなロバ」
"I didn't buy you to give you food and drink"
「食べ物や飲み物をあげるために買ったんじゃない」
"I bought you to make you work"
「お前を働かせるために買った」

"I bought you so that you earn me money"
「お金を稼ぐために君を買った」
"Up you get, then, at once!"
「さあ、すぐに起きてるぞ!」
"you must come with me into the circus"
「私と一緒にサーカスに来てください」
"there I will teach you to jump through hoops"
「そこでフープを飛び越える方法を教えてあげる」
"you will learn to stand upright on your hind legs"
「後ろ足で直立することを学びます」
"and you will learn to dance waltzes and polkas"
「そして、ワルツとポルカの踊りを学びます」
Poor Pinocchio had to learn all these fine things
かわいそうなピノキオは、これらすべての素晴らしいことを学ばなければなりませんでした
and I can't say it was easy to learn
そして、学ぶのは簡単だったとは言えません
it took him three months to learn the tricks
彼がトリックを学ぶのに3ヶ月かかりました
he got many a whipping that nearly took off his skin
彼は何度も鞭打ちを受け、皮膚が剥がれそうになりました
At last his master made the announcement
ついに彼の主人が発表をしました
many coloured placards stuck on the street corners
街角に貼られた色とりどりのプラカードの数々
"Great Full Dress Representation"
「グレートフルドレス表現」
"TONIGHT will Take Place the Usual Feats and Surprises"
「今夜はいつもの偉業と驚きが起こります」
"Performances Executed by All the Artists and horses"
「すべてのアーティストと馬が行うパフォーマンス」
"and moreover; The Famous LITTLE DONKEY PINOCCHIO"
「そしてさらに;名物の「リトルロバ ピノキオ」
"THE STAR OF THE DANCE"

「ダンスのスター」
"the theatre will be brilliantly illuminated"
「劇場は燦然と照らされます」
you can imagine how crammed the theatre was
劇場がどれほど詰め込まれていたか想像できるでしょう
The circus was full of children of all ages
サーカスはあらゆる年齢の子供たちでいっぱいでした
all came to see the famous little donkey Pinocchio dance
誰もが有名な小さなロバのピノキオの踊りを見に来ました
the first part of the performance was over
パフォーマンスの前半は終了しました
the director of the company presented himself to the public
会社の取締役は自分自身を一般に公開しました
he was dressed in a black coat and white breeches
彼は黒いコートと白いズボンを着ていました
and big leather boots that came above his knees
そして彼の膝の上に来た大きな革のブーツ
he made a profound bow to the crowd
彼は群衆に向かって深々とお辞儀をした
he began with much solemnity a ridiculous speech:
彼は非常に厳粛にばかげた演説を始めました。
"Respectable public, ladies and gentlemen!"
「立派な公衆の皆さん、紳士淑女の皆さん!」
"it is with great honour and pleasure"
「大変光栄に思います」
"I stand here before this distinguished audience"
「私はこの著名な聴衆の前にここに立っています」
"and I present to you the celebrated little donkey"
「そして、私はあなたに有名な小さなロバをプレゼントします」
"the little donkey who has already had the honour"
「すでに名誉ある小さなロバ」
"the honour of dancing in the presence of His Majesty"
「陛下の前で踊る光栄」
"And, thanking you, I beg of you to help us"

「そして、ありがとう、どうか助けていただきたい」
"help us with your inspiring presence"
「あなたの感動的な存在を助けてください」
"and please, esteemed audience, be indulgent to us"
「そして、尊敬する観客の皆さん、どうか私たちに甘やかしてください」
This speech was received with much laughter and applause
このスピーチは、多くの笑いと拍手で受け止められました
but the applause soon was even louder than before
しかし、拍手はすぐに以前よりもさらに大きくなりました
the little donkey Pinocchio made his appearance
小さなロバのピノキオが登場しました
and he stood in the middle of the circus
そして彼はサーカスの真ん中に立っていました
He was decked out for the occasion
彼はその機会のために着飾っていました
He had a new bridle of polished leather
彼は磨かれた革の新しい手綱を持っていました
and he was wearing brass buckles and studs
そして彼は真鍮のバックルとスタッズをつけていました
and he had two white camellias in his ears
そして、彼の耳には二本の白い椿が入っていました
His mane was divided and curled
彼のたてがみは裂けて丸まっていました
and each curl was tied with bows of coloured ribbon
そして、それぞれのカールは色とりどりのリボンのリボンで結ばれていました
He had a girth of gold and silver round his body
彼は体の周りに金と銀の胴回りを持っていました
his tail was plaited with amaranth and blue velvet ribbons
彼の尻尾はアマランサスと青いベルベットのリボンで編まれていました
He was, in fact, a little donkey to fall in love with!
実際、彼は恋に落ちる小さなロバでした！

The director added these few words:
監督は、以下の言葉を付け加えた。

"My respectable auditors!"
「私の尊敬すべき監査役たち!」

"I am not here to tell you falsehoods"
「私はあなたに嘘を言うためにここにいるのではありません」

"there were great difficulties I had to overcome"
「乗り越えなければならなかった大きな困難がありました」

"I understood and subjugated this mammifer"
「このマミファーを理解して討伐した」

"he was grazing at liberty amongst the mountains"
「彼は山の中で自由に草を食んでいた」

"he lived in the plains of the torrid zone"
「彼は灼熱地帯の平原に住んでいた」

"I beg you will observe the wild rolling of his eyes"
「彼の荒々しい目の動きを観察してください」

"Every means had been tried in vain to tame him"
「彼を飼いならすためにあらゆる手段を講じたが無駄だった」

"I have accustomed him to the life of domestic quadrupeds"
「私は彼を国内の四足動物の生活に慣れさせました」

"and I spared him the convincing argument of the whip"
「そして、私は彼に鞭の説得力のある議論を免れた」

"But all my goodness only increased his viciousness"
「しかし、私のすべての善良さは彼の悪意を増すだけだった」

"However, I discovered in his cranium a bony cartilage"
「しかし、彼の頭蓋骨に骨の軟骨を発見しました」

"I had him inspected by the Faculty of Medicine of Paris"
「パリの医学部に検査してもらった」

"I spared no cost for my little donkey's treatment"
「私は小さなロバの治療に費用を惜しまなかった」

"in him the doctors found the regenerating cortex of dance"
「彼の中に、医者はダンスの再生皮質を見つけた」

"For this reason I have not only taught him to dance"
「だから、私は彼にダンスを教えただけではない」
"but I also taught him to jump through hoops"
「でも、フープを飛び越える方法も教えたよ」
"Admire him, and then pass your opinion on him!"
「彼を賞賛し、それから彼にあなたの意見を伝えてください!」
"But before taking my leave of you, permit me this;"
「でも、お前と別れる前に、これを許してくれ」
"ladies and gentlemen, esteemed members of the crowd"
「紳士淑女の皆様、尊敬される群衆の一員」
"I invite you to tomorrow's daily performance"
「明日の日常公演にご招待します」
Here the director made another profound bow
ここで監督は再び深々とお辞儀をした
and, then turning to Pinocchio, he said:
そして、ピノキオの方を向いて言った。
"Courage, Pinocchio! But before you begin:"
「勇気を出せ、ピノキオ!しかし、始める前に:
"bow to this distinguished audience"
「この著名な聴衆にお辞儀をする」
Pinocchio obeyed his master's commands
ピノキオは主人の命令に従った
and he bent both his knees till they touched the ground
そして、両膝が地面に触れるまで曲げた
the director cracked his whip and shouted:
監督は鞭を鳴らして叫んだ。
"At a foot's pace, Pinocchio!"
「足の速さで、ピノキオ!」
Then the little donkey raised himself on his four legs
それから小さなロバは彼の4本の足で体を起こしました
and he began to walk round the theatre
そして彼は劇場の周りを歩き始めました
and the whole time he kept at a foot's pace
そして、その間ずっと彼は足の速さでい続けた
After a little time the director shouted again:

しばらくして、監督が再び叫んだ。
"Trot!" and Pinocchio, obeyed the order
「トロット!」とピノキオは命令に従った
and he changed his pace to a trot
そして彼は歩調を速歩に変えた
"Gallop!" and Pinocchio broke into a gallop
「ギャロップ!」とピノキオがギャロップに突入しました
"Full gallop!" and Pinocchio went full gallop
「全速力で!」とピノキオは全速力で走りました
he was running round the circus like a racehorse
彼は競走馬のようにサーカスの周りを走り回っていました
but then the director fired off a pistol
しかし、その後、監督はピストルを発砲した
at full speed he fell to the floor
全速力で彼は床に倒れた
and the little donkey pretended to be wounded
そして、小さなロバは怪我をしたふりをしました
he got up from the ground amidst an outburst of applause
彼は拍手喝采の中、地面から立ち上がった
there were shouts and clapping of hands
叫び声と手を叩く声が響き渡った
and he naturally raised his head and looked up
そして彼は自然に頭を上げて見上げました
and he saw in one of the boxes a beautiful lady
そして、彼は箱の一つに美しい女性を見つけました
she wore round her neck a thick gold chain
彼女は首に太い金のチェーンを巻いていました
and from the chain hung a medallion
そしてチェーンからはメダリオンがぶら下がっていました
On the medallion was painted the portrait of a puppet
メダリオンには人形の肖像画が描かれていました
"That is my portrait!" realized Pinocchio
「これが私の肖像画だ!」とピノキオは悟った

"That lady is the Fairy!" said Pinocchio to himself
「あの女性が妖精だ!」ピノキオは独り言を言いました
Pinocchio had recognized her immediately
ピノキオはすぐに彼女に気づいた
and, overcome with delight, he tried to call her
そして、喜びに圧倒され、彼は彼女に電話をかけようとしました
"Oh, my little Fairy! Oh, my little Fairy!"
「ああ、私の小さな妖精!ああ、私の小さな妖精!」
But instead of these words a bray came from his throat
しかし、その言葉の代わりに、彼の喉から一本の祈りが湧いてきた
a bray so prolonged that all the spectators laughed
観客全員が笑うほど長引くブレイ
and all the children in the theatre especially laughed
そして、劇場にいた子供たちは皆、特に笑いました
Then the director gave him a lesson
それから、監督は彼にレッスンをしました
it is not good manners to bray before the public
公衆の面前で祈るのはマナーが良くありません
with the handle of his whip he smacked the donkey's nose
彼は鞭の柄でロバの鼻を叩きました
The poor little donkey put his tongue out an inch
かわいそうな小さなロバは舌を出しました
and he licked his nose for at least five minutes
そして、彼は少なくとも5分間鼻を舐めました
he thought perhaps that it would ease the pain
彼はおそらくそれが痛みを和らげると思った
But how he despaired when looking up a second time
しかし、二度目に顔を上げたとき、彼はどれほど絶望したことでしょう
he saw that the seat was empty
彼は座席が空いているのを見た
the good Fairy of his had disappeared!
彼の善良な妖精は消えてしまったのだ!
He thought he was going to die

彼は死ぬと思った
his eyes filled with tears and he began to weep
彼の目には涙があふれ、彼は泣き始めました
Nobody, however, noticed his tears
しかし、誰も彼の涙に気づかなかった
"Courage, Pinocchio!" shouted the director
「勇気を出せ、ピノキオ!」監督が叫んだ
"show the audience how gracefully you can jump through the hoops"
「観客に、どれだけ優雅にフープを飛び越えられるかを見せて」
Pinocchio tried two or three times
ピノキオは2、3回試しました
but going through the hoop is not easy for a donkey
しかし、ロバにとってフープを通過するのは簡単ではありません
and he found it easier to go under the hoop
そして、彼はフープの下に入るのが簡単だと感じました
At last he made a leap and went through the hoop
とうとう彼は跳躍して、輪をくぐりました
but his right leg unfortunately caught in the hoop
しかし、残念ながら彼の右足はフープに引っかかりました
and that caused him to fall to the ground
そして、それが彼を地面に倒す原因となりました
he was doubled up in a heap on the other side
彼は反対側の山に倍増させられました
When he got up he was lame
彼が起きたとき、彼は足が不自由でした
only with great difficulty did he return to the stable
彼は非常に困難を伴ってのみ、厩舎に戻りました
"Bring out Pinocchio!" shouted all the boys
「ピノキオを連れてこい!」と男の子たちはみんな叫びました
"We want the little donkey!" roared the theatre
「小さなロバが欲しい!」劇場が叫びました

they were touched and sorry for the sad accident
彼らは感動し、悲しい事故を悔やみました
But the little donkey was seen no more that evening
しかし、その夜、その小さなロバはもう見られませんでした
The following morning the veterinary paid him a visit
翌朝、獣医は彼を訪ねました
the vets are doctors to the animals
獣医は動物の医者です
and he declared that he would remain lame for life
そして彼は、一生足が不自由なままでいると宣言した
The director then said to the stable-boy:
それから、監督は厩舎の少年に言いました。
"What do you suppose I can do with a lame donkey?"
「足の不自由なロバで何ができると思う?」
"He will eat food without earning it"
「彼はそれを稼ぐことなく食べ物を食べる」
"Take him to the market and sell him"
「彼を市場に連れて行き、売る」
When they reached the market a purchaser was found at once
彼らが市場に着いたとき、すぐに購入者が見つかりました
He asked the stable-boy:
彼は馬小屋の少年に尋ねました。
"How much do you want for that lame donkey?"
「あの足の不自由なロバにいくら欲しいの?」
"Twenty dollars and I'll sell him to you"
「20ドルで、彼を君に売るよ」
"I will give you two dollars"
「2ドルあげる」
"but don't suppose that I will make use of him"
「でも、私が彼を利用するとは思わないでください」
"I am buying him solely for his skin"
「私は彼の肌のためだけに彼を買っている」
"I see that his skin is very hard"

「彼の肌はとても硬いのが見えます」
"I intend to make a drum with him"
「彼と一緒にドラムを作るつもりだ」
he heard that he was destined to become a drum!
彼は自分が太缶になる運命にあると聞きました！
you can imagine poor Pinocchio's feelings
可哀想なピノキオの気持ちが想像できます
the two dollars were handed over
2ドルが手渡されました
and the man was given his donkey
そして、その男はロバを与えられた
he led the little donkey to the seashore
彼は小さなロバを海辺に連れて行きました
he then put a stone round his neck
それから彼は首に石を巻き付けました
and he gave him a sudden push into the water
そして彼は突然彼を水に押し込みました
Pinocchio was weighted down by the stone
ピノキオは石によって重くのしかかりました
and he went straight to the bottom of the sea
そして、彼はまっすぐ海の底に落ちていきました
his owner kept tight hold of the cord
彼の所有者はコードをしっかりと握っていました
he sat down quietly on a piece of rock
彼は静かに岩の上に座った
and he waited until the little donkey was drowned
そして、小さなロバが溺れるまで待ちました
and then he intended to skin him
そして、彼は彼を皮を剥ぐつもりだった

Pinocchio gets Swallowed by the Dog-Fish
ピノキオは犬の魚に飲み込まれる

Pinocchio had been fifty minutes under the water
ピノキオは50分間水面下にいた

his purchaser said aloud to himself:
彼の購入者は大声で独り言を言いました。

"My little lame donkey must by now be quite drowned"
「私の小さな足の不自由なロバは、もうかなり溺れているに違いない」

"I will therefore pull him out of the water"
「だから、彼を水から引き上げよう」

"and I will make a fine drum of his skin"
「そして、彼の皮で立派な太鼓を作る」

And he began to haul in the rope
そして、彼はロープを引き抜き始めました

the rope he had tied to the donkey's leg
彼がロバの足に結んでいたロープ

and he hauled, and hauled, and hauled
そして、彼は引っ張って、引っ張って、引っ張った

he hauled until at last...
彼はついに...

what do you think appeared above the water?
水面上に何が現れたと思いますか？

he did not pull a dead donkey to land
彼は死んだロバを引っ張って着陸させませんでした

instead he saw a living little puppet
それどころか、彼は生きている小さな人形を見た

and this little puppet was wriggling like an eel!
そして、この小さな人形はウナギのようにうごめいていました!
the poor man thought he was dreaming
貧しい男は夢を見ていると思った
and he was struck dumb with astonishment
そして彼は驚きで唖然としました
he eventually recovered from his stupefaction
彼は最終的に彼の愚痴から立ち直りました
and he asked the puppet in a quavering voice:
そして、彼は震える声で人形に尋ねました。
"where is the little donkey I threw into the sea?"
「海に投げ込んだ小さなロバはどこにいるの?」
"I am the little donkey!" said Pinocchio
「私は小さなロバだ!」とピノキオは言った
and Pinocchio laughed at being a puppet again
そしてピノキオは再び人形になったことを笑った

"How can you be the little donkey??"
「どうして小さなロバになれるの??」
"I was the little donkey," answered Pinocchio
「私は小さなロバでした」とピノキオは答えました
"and now I'm a little puppet again"
「そして今、私は再び小さな人形になりました」
"Ah, a young scamp is what you are!!"
「ああ、若きスキャンプがお前だ!!」
"Do you dare to make fun of me?"
「あえて私をからかうの?」
"To make fun of you?" asked Pinocchio
「あなたをからかうために?」ピノキオは尋ねた
"Quite the contrary, my dear master?"
「むしろ逆です、私の親愛なるご主人様?」
"I am speaking seriously with you"
「君と真剣に話してるよ」
"a short time ago you were a little donkey"
「さっきまで君は小さなロバだった」
"how can you have become a wooden puppet?"
「どうして木の人形になれたの?」
"being left in the water does not do that to a donkey!"
「水の中に放置されても、ロバにはそんなことはしない!」
"It must have been the effect of sea water"
「海水の影響だったんだろうな」
"The sea causes extraordinary changes"
「海は驚くべき変化をもたらす」
"Beware, puppet, I am not in the mood!"
「気をつけて、人形、私は気分じゃない!」
"Don't imagine that you can amuse yourself at my expense"
「私の費用で自分を楽しませることができるなんて想像しないでください」
"Woe to you if I lose patience!"
「我慢できなくなったら、お前は災いだ!」
"Well, master, do you wish to know the true story?"

「さて、ご主人様、本当の話を知りたいのですか?」
"If you set my leg free I will tell it you"
「もし君が僕の足を自由にするなら、君に言うよ」
The good man was curious to hear the true story
善良な男は本当の話を聞きたくてたまりませんでした
and he immediately untied the knot
そして彼はすぐに結び目をほどきました
Pinocchio was again as free as a bird in the air
ピノキオは再び空を飛ぶ鳥のように自由になった
and he commenced to tell his story
そして彼は自分の話をし始めました
"You must know that I was once a puppet"
「私がかつて操り人形だったことを知ってるはずだ」
"that is to say, I wasn't always a donkey"
「つまり、私は昔からロバだったわけではない」
"I was on the point of becoming a boy"
「男の子になる寸前だった」
"I would have been like the other boys in the world"
「僕も世界の他の男の子たちと同じだっただろう」
"but like other boys, I wasn't fond of study"
「でも、他の男の子たちと同じように、勉強が好きではなかった」
"and I followed the advice of bad companions"
「そして、悪い仲間のアドバイスに従った」
"and finally I ran away from home"
「そしてついに家出をした」
"One fine day when I awoke I found myself changed"
「ある晴れた日、目が覚めたとき、自分が変わっていることに気づきました」
"I had become a donkey with long ears"
「耳の長いロバになっちゃった」
"and I had grown a long tail too"
「そして、私も長い尻尾を生やしていました」
"What a disgrace it was to me!"
「それは私にとって何という恥ずべきことだったのでしょう!」

"even your worst enemy would not inflict it upon you!"
「最悪の敵でさえ、お前にはそれを負わせないだろう！」
"I was taken to the market to be sold"
「売られるために市場に連れて行かれた」
"and I was bought by an equestrian company"
「そして、乗馬会社に買われてしまった」
"they wanted to make a famous dancer of me"
「彼らは私を有名なダンサーにしたかった」
"But one night during a performance I had a bad fall"
「でも、ある夜、パフォーマンス中にひどい転倒をしてしまった」
"and I was left with two lame legs"
「そして、足が不自由になった」
"I was of no use to the circus no more"
「私はもうサーカスには役に立たなかった」
"and again I was taken to the market
「そしてまた、私は市場に連れて行かれました
"and at the market you were my purchaser!"
「そして市場では、君が私の購入者だったんだ！」
"Only too true," remembered the man
「あまりにも真実だ」と男は思い出した
"And I paid two dollars for you"
「そして、君に2ドル払ったんだ」
"And now, who will give me back my good money?"
「さて、誰が私の良いお金を返してくれるの？」
"And why did you buy me?"
「それで、なぜ私を買ったの？」
"You bought me to make a drum of my skin!"
「私の皮でドラム缶を作るために買ったのね！」
"Only too true!" said the man
「あまりにも真実だ！」と男は言った
"And now, where shall I find another skin?"
「さて、別の皮はどこで見つけようか？」
"Don't despair, master"

「絶望しないで、ご主人様」
"There are many little donkeys in the world!"
「世界にはたくさんの小さなロバがいる!」
"Tell me, you impertinent rascal;"
「教えてくれ、生意気な悪党め」
"does your story end here?"
「あなたの話はここで終わりですか?」
"No," answered the puppet
「いいえ」と人形は答えました
"I have another two words to say"
「あと2つ言いたいことがあるんだ」
"and then my story shall have finished"
「そして、私の物語は終わるでしょう」
"you brought me to this place to kill me"
「お前は私を殺すためにこの場所に連れてきた」
"but then you yielded to a feeling of compassion"
「でも、その後、君は同情の気持ちに屈してしまった」
"and you preferred to tie a stone round my neck
「そして、君は私の首に石を巻くことを好んだ
"and you threw me into the sea"
「そして、あなたは私を海に投げ込んだ」
"This humane feeling does you great honour"
「この人間的な気持ちは、あなたに大きな名誉をもたらします」
"and I shall always be grateful to you"
「そして、私はいつもあなたに感謝します」
"But, nevertheless, dear master, you forgot one thing"
「しかし、それにもかかわらず、親愛なるご主人様、あなたは一つ忘れていたことがあります」
"you made your calculations without considering the Fairy!"
「妖精のことを考えずに計算したのか!」
"And who is the Fairy?"
「で、その妖精は誰だ?」
"She is my mamma," replied Pinocchio
「彼女は私のママです」とピノキオは答えました
"and she resembles all other good mammas"

"and all good mammas care for their children"
「そして、彼女は他のすべての良いママに似ています」
「そして、すべての良いママは子供たちの世話をします」
"mammas who never lose sight of their children""
「子どもを見失わないママたち」
"mammas who help their children lovingly"
「子どもを愛おしそうに助けるママたち」
"and they love them even when they deserve to be abandoned"
「そして、彼らは見捨てられるに値するときでさえ、彼らを愛しています」
"my good mamma kept me in her sight"
「私の良いママは私を彼女の視界に留めていました」
"and she saw that I was in danger of drowning"
「そして彼女は私が溺れる危険にさらされているのを見ました」
"so she immediately sent an immense shoal of fish"
「それで彼女はすぐに巨大な魚の群れを送りました」
"first they really thought I was a little dead donkey"
「最初、彼らは本当に私が少し死んだロバだと思った」
"and so they began to eat me in big mouthfuls"
「それで、彼らは私を大口で食べ始めました」
"I never knew fish were greedier than boys!"
「魚が男の子よりも貪欲だとは知らなかった!」
"Some ate my ears and my muzzle"
「私の耳と銃口を食べた者もいた」
"and other fish my neck and mane"
「そして他の魚は私の首とたてがみ」
"some of them ate the skin of my legs"
「私の足の皮を食べた者もいた」
"and others took to eating my fur"
「そして他の人々は私の毛皮を食べることになりました」
"Amongst them there was an especially polite little fish"
「その中に、特に丁寧な小魚がいました」

"and he condescended to eat my tail"
「そして彼は私の尻尾を食べようと見下した」
the purchaser was horrified by what he heard
購入者は彼が聞いたことにぞっとしました
"I swear that I will never touch fish again!"
「もう二度と魚には触れないと誓います!」
"imagine opening a mullet and finding a donkey's tail!"
「ボラを開けてロバの尻尾を見つけるところを想像してみてください!」
"I agree with you," said the puppet, laughing
「私も同感です」と人形は笑いながら言いました
"However, I must tell you what happened next"
「しかし、次に何が起こったのかを話さなければなりません」
"the fish had finished eating the donkey's hide"
「魚がロバの皮を食べ終わった」
"the donkey's hide that had covered me"
「私を覆っていたロバの皮」
"then they naturally reached the bone"
「それから彼らは自然に骨に到達しました」
"but it was not bone, but rather wood"
「でも、それは骨ではなく、木だった」
"for, as you see, I am made of the hardest wood"
「見ての通り、私は最も硬い木でできているのです」
"they tried to take a few more bites"
「彼らはさらに何口か噛もうとしました」
"But they soon discovered I was not for eating"
「でも、彼らはすぐに私が食べるのが苦手だと気づいた」
"disgusted with such indigestible food, they swam off"
「そのような難消化性の食べ物にうんざりして、彼らは泳ぎ去った」
"and they left without even saying thank you"
「そして、彼らはお礼を言わずに去っていきました」
"And now, at last, you have heard my story"
「そして今、ついに、あなたは私の話を聞いた」

"and that is why you didn't find a dead donkey"
「だから君は死んだロバを見つけられなかったんだ」
"and instead you found a living puppet"
「そして、その代わりに、あなたは生きている人形を見つけた」
"I laugh at your story," cried the man in a rage
「君の話には笑っちゃうよ」と男は激怒して叫んだ
"I only know that I spent two dollars to buy you"
「私が知っているのは、君を買うために2ドル使ったことだけだ」
"and I will have my money back"
「そして、お金を取り戻します」
"Shall I tell you what I will do?"
「私が何をするか教えてあげようか?」
"I will take you back to the market"
「市場に連れ戻します」
"and I will sell you by weight as seasoned wood"
「そして、私はあなたを味付けされた木として重量で売ります」
and the purchaser can light fires with you"
そして購入者はあなたと一緒に火をつけることができます」
Pinocchio was not too worried about this
ピノキオはこれについてあまり心配していませんでした
"Sell me if you like; I am content"
「もしよろしければ、私を売ってください。私は満足しています」
and he plunged back into the water
そして彼は再び水に飛び込みました
he swam gaily away from the shore
彼は岸から陽気に泳ぎ去った
and he called to his poor owner
そして彼は彼の貧しい所有者に呼びかけました
"Good-bye, master, don't forget me"
「さようなら、マスター、私を忘れないで」
"the wooden puppet you wanted for its skin"

「あなたが肌に欲しかった木製の人形」
"and I hope you get your drum one day"
「そして、いつか君がドラム缶を手に入れることを願っている」
And he laughed and went on swimming
そして彼は笑い、泳ぎ続けました
and after a while he turned around again
そしてしばらくして、彼は再び振り返った
"Good-bye, master," he shouted louder
「さようなら、マスター」彼は大声で叫んだ
"and remember me when you need well seasoned wood"
「そして、よく味付けされた木材が必要なときは、私を覚えておいて」
"and think of me when you're lighting a fire"
「そして、火をつけているとき、私のことを考えてください」
soon Pinocchio had swam towards the horizon
すぐにピノキオは地平線に向かって泳ぎました
and now he was scarcely visible from the shore
そして今、彼は岸からほとんど見えなくなりました
he was a little black speck on the surface of the sea
彼は海面に浮かぶ小さな黒い斑点だった
from time to time he lifted out of the water
時々、彼は水から浮き上がった
and he leaped and capered like a happy dolphin
そして彼は幸せなイルカのように跳び跳ねました
Pinocchio was swimming and he knew not whither
ピノキオは泳いでいて、どこが泳いでいるのかわからなかった
he saw in the midst of the sea a rock
彼は海の真ん中に岩を見ました
the rock seemed to be made of white marble
岩は白い大理石でできているように見えました
and on the summit there stood a beautiful little goat
そして頂上には美しい小さなヤギが立っていました
the goat bleated lovingly to Pinocchio

ヤギはピノキオに愛情を込めて血を流しました
and the goat made signs to him to approach
そしてヤギは彼に近づくように合図をしました
But the most singular thing was this:
しかし、最も特異なことはこれでした。
The little goat's hair was not white nor black
小さなヤギの毛は白くも黒くもありませんでした
nor was it a mixture of two colours
また、2つの色が混ざっているわけでもありません
this is usual with other goats
これは他のヤギでは普通のことです
but the goat's hair was a very vivid blue
しかし、ヤギの毛はとても鮮やかな青でした
a vivid blue like the hair of the beautiful Child
美しい子供の髪の毛のような鮮やかなブルー
imagine how rapidly Pinocchio's heart began to beat
ピノキオの心臓がどれほど速く鼓動し始めたか想像してみてください
He swam with redoubled strength and energy
彼は倍増した力とエネルギーで泳ぎました
and in no time at all he was halfway there
そして、あっという間に彼は半分まで来ました
but then he saw something came out the water
しかし、その後、彼は何かが水から出てきたのを見ました
the horrible head of a sea-monster!
海の怪物の恐ろしい頭!
His mouth was wide open and cavernous
彼の口は大きく開いており、海綿状になっていました
there were three rows of enormous teeth
巨大な歯が三列に並んでいました
even a picture of if would terrify you
IFの写真でさえあなたを怖がらせるでしょう
And do you know what this sea-monster was?
そして、この海の怪物が何だったか知っていますか?
it was none other than that gigantic Dog-Fish

それは他ならぬ巨大なドッグフィッシュでした
the Dog-Fish mentioned many times in this story
この話で何度も言及されている犬の魚
I should tell you the name of this terrible fish
この恐ろしい魚の名前を教えてあげよう
Attila of Fish and Fishermen
魚と漁師のアッティラ
on account of his slaughter and insatiable voracity
彼の殺戮と飽くなき貪欲さのために
think of poor Pinocchio's terror at the sight
哀れなピノキオの恐怖を思い浮かべてください
a true sea monster was swimming at him
本物の海の怪物が彼に向かって泳いでいた
He tried to avoid the Dog-Fish
彼はドッグフィッシュを避けようとしました
he tried to swim in other directions
彼は他の方向に泳ごうとしました
he did everything he could to escape
彼は逃げるためにできる限りのことをしました
but that immense wide-open mouth was too big
しかし、その大きく開いた口は大きすぎました
and it was coming with the velocity of an arrow
そしてそれは矢の速度で来ていました
the beautiful little goat tried to bleat
美しい小さなヤギは鳴き声を出そうとしました
"Be quick, Pinocchio, for pity's sake!"
「早くしろ、ピノキオ。同情のために!」
And Pinocchio swam desperately with all he could
そしてピノキオは全力で必死に泳ぎました
his arms, his chest, his legs, and his feet
彼の腕、胸、足、そして彼の足
"Quick, Pinocchio, the monster is close upon you!"
「早く、ピノキオ、怪物がお前に迫っている!」
And Pinocchio swam quicker than ever
そしてピノキオはかつてないほど速く泳ぎました
he flew on with the rapidity of a ball from a gun

彼は銃から弾丸を放つような速さで飛び続けた
He had nearly reached the rock
彼はもう少しで岩にたどり着くところだった
and he had almost reached the little goat
そして、彼はもう少しで小さなヤギにたどり着くところだった
and the little goat leaned over towards the sea
そして、小さなヤギは海に向かって身を乗り出しました
she stretched out her fore-legs to help him
彼女は彼を助けるために前足を伸ばした
perhaps she could get him out of the water
もしかしたら、彼女は彼を水から引き上げることができるかもしれない
But all their efforts were too late!
しかし、彼らの努力はすべて遅すぎました!
The monster had overtaken Pinocchio
怪物はピノキオを追い越した
he drew in a big breath of air and water
彼は大きな息と水を吸い込んだ
and he sucked in the poor puppet
そして彼は哀れな人形を吸い込みました
like he would have sucked a hen's egg
まるで鶏の卵を吸うように
and the Dog-Fish swallowed him whole
そして犬の魚は彼を丸ごと飲み込みました

Pinocchio tumbled through his teeth
ピノキオは歯を食いしばった
and he tumbled down the Dog-Fish's throat
そして彼は犬の魚の喉を転がり落ちました
and finally he landed heavily in his stomach
そしてついに彼は胃に重く着地しました
he remained unconscious for a quarter of an hour
彼は15分半の間、意識を失ったままだった
but eventually he came to himself again
しかし、やがて彼は再び我に返った
he could not in the least imagine in what world he was
自分がどんな世界にいるのか、少しも想像できなかった
All around him there was nothing but darkness
彼の周りは暗闇ばかりだった
it was as if he had fallen into a pot of ink
それはまるで彼がインクの壺に落ちたかのようでした
He listened, but he could hear no noise
彼は耳を澄ましましたが、物音は聞こえませんでした
occasionally great gusts of wind blew in his face
時折、大きな突風が彼の顔に吹かれました
first he could not understand from where it came from

最初、彼はそれがどこから来たのか理解できませんでした
but at last he discovered the source
しかし、ついに彼はその源を発見しました
it came out of the monster's lungs
それは怪物の肺から出てきた
there is one thing you must know about the Dog-Fish
ドッグフィッシュについて知っておくべきことが1つあります
the Dog-Fish suffered very much from asthma
ドッグフィッシュは喘息にとても苦しんでいました
when he breathed it was exactly like the north wind
彼が息をすると、それはまさに北風のようでした
Pinocchio at first tried to keep up his courage
ピノキオは最初、勇気を保とうとしました
but the reality of the situation slowly dawned on him
しかし、状況の現実は徐々に彼に明らかになっていきました
he was really shut up in the body of this sea-monster
彼は本当にこの海の怪物の体に閉じ込められていた
and he began to cry and scream and sob
そして彼は泣き、叫び、すすり泣き始めました
"Help! help! Oh, how unfortunate I am!"
「助けて!ヘルプ!ああ、なんて残念なの!」
"Will nobody come to save me?"
「誰も私を救いに来ないの?」
from the dark there came a voice
暗闇から声が聞こえてきた
the voice sounded like a guitar out of tune
その声は、ギターの調子が狂っているように聞こえた
"Who do you think could save you, unhappy wretch?"
「誰が君を救うと思う、不幸な哀れな者め」
Pinocchio froze with terror at the voice
ピノキオはその声に恐怖で凍りついた
"Who is speaking?" asked Pinocchio, finally
「誰が話しているの?」ピノキオがようやく尋ねた

"It is I! I am a poor Tunny Fish"
「私です!私はかわいそうなタニーフィッシュです」
"I was swallowed by the Dog-Fish along with you"
「君と一緒に犬の魚に飲み込まれた」
"And what fish are you?"
「それで、お前は何の魚だ?」
"I have nothing in common with fish"
「魚と共通点がない」
"I am a puppet," added Pinocchio
「私は人形です」とピノキオは付け加えました
"Then why did you let yourself be swallowed?"
「じゃあ、なんで自分を飲み込んだの?」
"I didn't let myself be swallowed"
「自分を飲み込まなかった」
"it was the monster that swallowed me!"
「私を飲み込んだのは怪物だった!」
"And now, what are we to do here in the dark?"
「さて、暗闇の中で私たちは何をすればいいのでしょう?」
"there's not much we can do but to resign ourselves"
「私たちにできることは、自分自身を諦めるしかない」
"and now we wait until the Dog-Fish has digested us"
「そして今、私たちは犬の魚が私たちを消化するまで待ちます」
"But I do not want to be digested!" howled Pinocchio
「でも、私は消化されたくありません!」ピノキオは吠えました
and he began to cry again
そして彼は再び泣き始めました
"Neither do I want to be digested," added the Tunny Fish
「私も消化されたくありません」とタニーフィッシュは付け加えました
"but I am enough of a philosopher to console myself"
「しかし、私は自分自身を慰めるのに十分な哲学者です」

"when one is born a Tunny Fish life can be made sense of"
「1つが生まれたとき、タニーフィッシュの人生は意味をなすことができる」
"it is more dignified to die in the water than in oil"
「油の中で死ぬよりも水で死ぬ方が尊厳がある」
"That is all nonsense!" cried Pinocchio
「そんなの馬鹿げている!」ピノキオは叫んだ
"It is my opinion," replied the Tunny Fish
「それが私の意見だ」とタニーフィッシュは答えました
"and opinions ought to be respected"
「そして、意見は尊重されるべきです」
"that is what the political Tunny Fish say"
「それが政治的なタニーフィッシュが言っていることだ」
"To sum it all up, I want to get away from here"
「要するに、ここから逃げたいんだ」
"I do want to escape."
「逃げたいんだ」
"Escape, if you are able!"
「逃げられるなら!」
"Is this Dog-Fish who has swallowed us very big?"
「この犬の魚は、私たちをとても大きく飲み込んでいるの?」
"Big? My boy, you can only imagine"
「大きい?私の息子、あなたは想像することしかできません」
"his body is two miles long without counting his tail"
「彼の体は尻尾を数えずに2マイルの長さです」
they held this conversation in the dark for some time
彼らはしばらくの間、暗闇の中でこの会話を続けました
eventually Pinocchio's eyes adjusted to the darkness
やがてピノキオの目は暗闇に順応した
Pinocchio thought that he saw a light a long way off
ピノキオは、はるか遠くに光が見えると思った
"What is that little light I see in the distance?"

「遠くに見える小さな光は何だろう?」
"It is most likely some companion in misfortune"
「それはおそらく不幸な仲間です」
"he, like us, is waiting to be digested"
「彼も私たちと同じように、消化されるのを待っています」
"I will go and find him"
「彼を探しに行く」
"perhaps it is an old fish that knows his way around"
「もしかしたら、それは彼の道を知っている古い魚かもしれません」
"I hope it may be so, with all my heart, dear puppet"
「そうであることを願っています、心から、親愛なる人形」
"Good-bye, Tunny Fish" - "Good-bye, puppet"
"Good-bye, Tunny Fish" - "Good-bye, puppet"
(さようなら、人形)
"and I wish a good fortune to you"
「そして、あなたに幸運を祈ります」
"Where shall we meet again?"
「またどこで会おうか?」
"Who can see such things in the future?"
「将来、誰がそんなものを見ることができるのだろう?」
"It is better not even to think of it!"
「考えない方がいい!」

A Happy Surprise for Pinocchio
ピノキオのうれしいサプライズ

Pinocchio said farewell to his friend the Tunny Fish
ピノキオは友人のタニーフィッシュに別れを告げました
and he began to grope his way through the Dog-Fish
そして彼は手探りでドッグフィッシュの中を進み始めました
he took small steps in the direction of the light
彼は光の方向に小さな一歩を踏み出しました
the small light shining dimly at a great distance
遠くでぼんやりと輝く小さな光
the farther he advanced the brighter became the light
彼が遠くに進めば進むほど、光は明るくなりました
and he walked and walked until at last he reached it
そして、彼は歩いて歩いて、ついにそこにたどり着きました
and when he reached the light, what did he find?
そして、彼が光にたどり着いたとき、彼は何を見つけたのでしょうか?
I will let you have a thousand and one guesses
私はあなたに千と一の推測をさせます
what he found was a little table all prepared
彼が見つけたのは、すべてが準備された小さなテーブルでした
on the table was a lighted candle in a green bottle
テーブルの上には、緑の瓶に入った火のついたキャンドルが置かれていました
and seated at the table was a little old man
そしてテーブルに座っていたのは小さな老人でした
the little old man was eating some live fish
小さな老人は生きた魚を食べていました
and the little live fish were very much alive
そして、小さな生きた魚はとても生き生きとしていました

some of the little fish even jumped out of his mouth
彼の口から飛び出してきた小さな魚もいました
at this sight Pinocchio was filled with happiness
その光景にピノキオは幸せでいっぱいになりました
he became almost delirious with unexpected joy
彼は予想外の喜びでほとんど錯乱状態になりました
He wanted to laugh and cry at the same time
彼は笑いながら泣きたかった
he wanted to say a thousand things at once
彼は一度に何千ものことを言いたかったのです
but all he managed were a few confused words
しかし、彼がなんとかできたのは、混乱した言葉だけだった
At last he succeeded in uttering a cry of joy
ついに彼は喜びの叫び声をあげることに成功しました
and he threw his arm around the little old man
そして彼は小さな老人に腕を回しました
"Oh, my dear papa!" he shouted with joy
「ああ、私の愛するパパ!」彼は喜びで叫びました
"I have found you at last!" cried Pinocchio
「やっと見つけた!」ピノキオは叫んだ
"I will never never never never leave you again"
「私は決して、決して、二度とあなたから離れない」
the little old man couldn't believe it either
小さな老人も信じられませんでした
"are my eyes telling the truth?" he said
「私の目は真実を語っているのか?」と彼は言った
and he rubbed his eyes to make sure
そして彼は目をこすって確認した
"then you are really my dear Pinocchio?"
「じゃあ、あなたは本当に私の親愛なるピノキオなの?」
"Yes, yes, I am Pinocchio, I really am!"
「はい、はい、私はピノキオです、本当にそうです!」
"And you have forgiven me, have you not?"
「そして、あなたは私を許したのではないのですか?」

"Oh, my dear papa, how good you are!"
「ああ、親愛なるパパ、君はなんていいんだ!」
"And to think how bad I've been to you"
「そして、私があなたにどれだけひどいことをしてきたか考えてみてください」
"but if you only knew what I've gone through"
「でも、私が経験したことを君が知っていればいいだけなら」
"all the misfortunes I've had poured on me"
「私が私に注いだすべての不幸」
"and all the other things that have befallen me!"
「そして、私に降りかかった他のすべてのこと!」
"oh think back to the day you sold your jacket"
「ああ、ジャケットを売った日のことを思い出して」
"oh you must have been terribly cold"
「ああ、ひどく寒かったんだろう」
"but you did it to buy me a spelling book"
「でも、君は僕にスペリングの本を買うためにやったんだね」
"so that I could study like the other boys"
「他の男の子と同じように勉強できるように」
"but instead I escaped to see the puppet show"
「でも、その代わりに人形劇を見るために逃げてしまった」
"and the showman wanted to put me on the fire"
「そして、ショーマンは私を火にかけたかった」
"so that I could roast his mutton for him"
「彼のために羊肉を焼くために」
"but then the same showman gave me five gold pieces"
「でも、その時、同じ芸能人が金貨を5枚くれたんだ」
"he wanted me to give you the gold"
「彼は私に金をくれて欲しかった」
"but then I met the Fox and the Cat"
「でも、それからキツネと猫に出会った」
"and they took me to the inn of The Red Craw-Fish"
「そして、彼らは私を赤いザリガニの宿に連れて行って

くれました」
"and at the inn they ate like hungry wolves"
「そして宿屋では、彼らは空腹のオオカミのように食べました」
"and I left by myself in the middle of the night"
「そして、私は真夜中に一人で出発しました」
"and I encountered assassins who ran after me"
「そして、私を追いかけてきた暗殺者に遭遇した」
"and I ran away from the assassins"
「そして私は暗殺者から逃げた」
"but the assassins followed me just as fast"
「でも、暗殺者たちは同じくらい速く私を追いかけてきた」
"and I ran away from them as fast as I could"
「そして、私はできるだけ早く彼らから逃げました」
"but they always followed me however fast I ran"
「でも、どんなに速く走っても、彼らはいつも私についてきました」
"and I kept running to get away from them"
「そして、私は彼らから逃げるために走り続けました」
"but eventually they caught me after all"
「でも、結局、彼らは私を捕まえた」
"and they hung me to a branch of a Big Oak"
「そして、彼らは私をビッグオークの枝に吊るしました」
"but then there was the beautiful Child with blue hair"
「でも、青い髪の美しい子がいたんだ」
"she sent a little carriage to fetch me"
「彼女は私を迎えに小さな馬車を送った」
"and the doctors all had a good look at me"
「そして、医者たちは皆、私をよく見ていました」
"and they immediately made the same diagnosis"
「そして、彼らはすぐに同じ診断を下しました」
"If he is not dead, it is a proof that he is still alive"
「彼が死んでいないなら、それは彼がまだ生きている証拠です」

"and then by chance I told a lie"
「そして、たまたま嘘をついた」
"and my nose began to grow and grow and grow"
「そして、私の鼻はどんどん大きくなり始めました」
"and soon I could no longer get through the door"
「そしてすぐにドアを通り抜けることができなくなりました」
"so I went again with the Fox and the Cat"
「だからまたキツネと猫と一緒に行った」
"and together we buried the four gold pieces"
「そして、私たちは一緒に4つの金貨を埋めました」
"because one piece of gold I had spent at the inn"
「だって、宿で使った金一枚だから」
"and the Parrot began to laugh at me"
「そしてオウムは私を笑い始めました」
"and there were not two thousand pieces of gold"
「そして、金貨は二千枚もなかった」
"there were no pieces of gold at all anymore"
「もう金貨は全くなかった」
"so I went to the judge of the town to tell him"
「だから、町の裁判官のところに行って伝えたんだ」
"he said I had been robbed, and put me in prison"
「彼は私が強盗に遭ったと言い、私を刑務所に入れた」
"while escaping I saw a beautiful bunch of grapes"
「逃げている間に、美しいブドウの房を見ました」
"but in the field I was caught in a trap"
「でも、野原では罠にかかった」
"and the peasant had every right to catch me"
「そして、農民には私を捕まえる権利があった」
"he put a dog-collar round my neck"
「彼は私の首に犬の首輪をつけた」
"and he made me the guard dog of the poultry-yard"
「そして彼は私を養鶏場の番犬にした」
"but he acknowledged my innocence and let me go"
「しかし、彼は私の無実を認め、私を行かせてくれました」

"and the Serpent with the smoking tail began to laugh"
「そして、煙の尾を持つ蛇は笑い始めました」
"but the Serpent laughed until he broke a blood-vessel"
「しかし、蛇は血管を壊すまで笑った」
"and so I returned to the house of the beautiful Child"
「そして、私は美しい子供の家に戻りました」
"but then the beautiful Child was dead"
「でも、その美しい子は死んでしまった」
"and the Pigeon could see that I was crying"
「そして鳩は私が泣いているのを見ることができました」
"and the Pigeon said, 'I have seen your father'"
「そして鳩は言った。『お前の父さんに会ったよ』」
'he was building a little boat to search of you'
「彼は君を探すために小さなボートを作っていた」
"and I said to him, 'Oh! if I also had wings,'"
「そして私は彼に言いました。『ああ!もし私にも翼があったら』と」
"and he said to me, 'Do you want to see your father?'"
「そして彼は私に言った、『お父さんに会いたいか?』と」
"and I said, 'Without doubt I would like to see him!'"
「そして私は言いました、『間違いなく彼に会いたいです!』」
"'but who will take me to him?' I asked"
「でも、誰が私を彼のところに連れて行くの?」とお願いしました」
"and he said to me, 'I will take you,'"
「そして彼は私に言った、『お前を連れて行く』」
"and I said to him, 'How will you take me?'"
「そして私は彼に言いました。『どうやって私を連れて行くのですか?』」
"and he said to me, 'Get on my back,'"
「そして彼は私に言った、『私の背中に乗れ』と」
"and so we flew through all that night"

「そして、私たちはその夜をずっと飛んだ」
"and then in the morning there were all the fishermen"
「そして朝になると、漁師たちはみんな集まっていました」
"and the fishermen were looking out to sea"
「そして、漁師たちは海を眺めていました」
"and one said to me, 'There is a poor man in a boat'"
「そして、一人が私に言った、『舟に貧しい男がいる』」
"he is on the point of being drowned"
「彼は溺れそうになっている」
"and I recognized you at once, even at that distance
「そして、その距離でもすぐに君に気づいた」
"because my heart told me that it was you"
「だって、心が君だって教えてくれたから」
"and I made signs so that you would return to land"
「そして、あなたが陸に戻るように標識を作りました」
"I also recognized you," said Geppetto
「君にも見覚えがあったよ」とゼペットは言った
"and I would willingly have returned to the shore"
「そして、私は喜んで岸に戻ったでしょう」
"but what was I to do so far out at sea?"
「でも、こんなに遠く離れた海で何をすればいいんだ?」
"The sea was tremendously angry that day"
「あの日、海はものすごい怒撲をしていた」
"and a great wave came over and upset my boat"
「そして、大きな波が来て、私のボートをひっくり返しました」
"Then I saw the horrible Dog-Fish"
「それから、恐ろしい犬の魚を見た」
"and the horrible Dog-Fish saw me too"
「そして、恐ろしい犬の魚も私を見ました」
"and so the horrible Dog-Fish came to me"
「そして、恐ろしい犬の魚が私のところに来た」
"and he put out his tongue and swallowed me"

"そして彼は舌を出して私を飲み込んだ"
「そして彼は舌を出して私を飲み込んだ」
"as if I had been a little apple tart"
「まるで小さなリンゴのタルトだったかのように」
"And how long have you been shut up here?"
「それで、君はいつからここに閉じ込められていたの?」
"that day must have been nearly two years ago"
「あの日は2年近く前だったはずだ」
"two years, my dear Pinocchio," he said
「2年だよ、親愛なるピノキオ」彼は言った
"those two years seemed like two centuries!"
「その2年間は2世紀のように思えました!」
"And how have you managed to live?"
「それで、どうやって生きていけばいいの?」
"And where did you get the candle?"
「それで、ろうそくはどこで手に入れたの?」
"And from where are the matches for the candle?
「それで、ろうそくのマッチはどこから来るの?」
"Stop, and I will tell you everything"
「やめて、全部話してあげる」
"I was not the only one at sea that day"
「あの日、海にいたのは私だけではなかった」
"the storm had also upset a merchant vessel"
「嵐は商船も動揺させた」
"the sailors of the vessel were all saved"
「船の船員は全員助かった」
"but the cargo of the vessel sunk to the bottom"
「しかし、船の貨物は底に沈んでしまった」
"the Dog-Fish had an excellent appetite that day"
「その日、ドッグフィッシュは食欲が旺盛だった」
"after swallowing me he swallowed the vessel"
「私を飲み込んだ後、彼は容器を飲み込んだ」
"How did he swallow the entire vessel?"
「彼はどうやって船全体を飲み込んだのですか?」
"He swallowed the whole boat in one mouthful"

「彼は一口でボート全体を飲み込んだ」
"the only thing that he spat out was the mast"
「彼が吐き出したのはマストだけだった」
"it had stuck between his teeth like a fish-bone"
「それは魚の骨のように彼の歯の間に突き刺さっていた」
"Fortunately for me, the vessel was fully laden"
「幸いなことに、船は満杯でした」
"there were preserved meats in tins, biscuit"
「缶詰、ビスケットに保存された肉がありました」
"and there were bottles of wine and dried raisins"
「そして、ワインのボトルとドライレーズンがありました」
"and I had cheese and coffee and sugar"
「そして、チーズとコーヒーと砂糖を食べました」
"and with the candles were boxes of matches"
「そして、ろうそくと一緒にマッチの箱がありました」
"With this I have been able to live for two years"
「これで2年間生きることができた」
"But I have arrived at the end of my resources"
「しかし、私は自分の資源の終わりにたどり着きました」
"there is nothing left in the larder"
「食料貯蔵庫には何も残っていません」
"and this candle is the last that remains"
「そして、このろうそくは最後に残る」
"And after that what will we do?"
「それで、その後はどうするの?」
"oh my dear boy, Pinocchio," he cried
「ああ、親愛なる息子、ピノキオ」彼は叫んだ
"After that we shall both remain in the dark"
「その後、私たちは両方とも暗闇の中に留まるでしょう」
"Then, dear little papa there is no time to lose"
「じゃあ、親愛なる小さなパパ、一刻の猶予もないよ」
"We must think of a way of escaping"

"what way of escaping can we think of?"
「脱出方法を考えなければならない」
「どんな逃げ方が考えられるの?」
"We must escape through the mouth of the Dog-Fish"
「ドッグフィッシュの口から逃げなければならない」
"we must throw ourselves into the sea and swim away"
「海に身を投げて泳ぎ去らなければならない」
"You talk well, my dear Pinocchio"
「よくしゃべるね、親愛なるピノキオ」
"but I don't know how to swim"
「でも、泳ぎ方がわからない」
"What does that matter?" replied Pinocchio
「それがどうしたの?」ピノキオは答えた
"I am a good swimmer," he suggested
「僕は泳ぎが上手だよ」と彼は提案した
"you can get on my shoulders"
「君は僕の肩に乗れる」
"and I will carry you safely to shore"
「そして、私があなたを無事に岸まで運びます」
"All illusions, my boy!" replied Geppetto
「全部の幻想だよ、坊や!」とゼペットは答えた
and he shook his head with a melancholy smile
そして彼は憂鬱な笑みを浮かべて首を振った
"my dear Pinocchio, you are scarcely a yard high"
「親愛なるピノキオ、あなたはまだ1ヤードも高くありません」
"how could you swim with me on your shoulders?"
「どうして私を肩に乗せて泳げるんだ?」
"Try it and you will see!" replied Pinocchio
「やってみればわかるよ!」ピノキオは答えた
Without another word Pinocchio took the candle
ピノキオは何も言わずに、ろうそくを取りました
"Follow me, and don't be afraid"
「私についてきて、恐れることはありません」
and they walked for some time through the Dog-Fish
そして、彼らはしばらくの間、ドッグフィッシュの中を

歩きました
they walked all the way through the stomach
彼らは胃の中をずっと歩きました
and they were where the Dog-Fish's throat began
そして、彼らは犬の魚の喉が始まった場所でした
and here they thought they should better stop
そしてここで彼らはやめた方がいいと思った
and they thought about the best moment for escaping
そして、彼らは逃げるのに最適な瞬間について考えました
Now, I must tell you that the Dog-Fish was very old
さて、ドッグフィッシュは非常に古いと言わなければなりません
and he suffered from asthma and heart palpitations
そして彼は喘息と動悸に苦しんでいました
so he was obliged to sleep with his mouth open
だから彼は口を開けたまま眠らざるを得なかった
and through his mouth they could see the starry sky
そして彼の口を通して、彼らは星空を見ることができました
and the sea was lit up by beautiful moonlight
そして、海は美しい月明かりに照らされていました
Pinocchio carefully and quietly turned to his father
ピノキオは慎重に静かに父親に向き直った
"This is the moment to escape," he whispered to him
「今こそ逃げる時だ」と彼は彼にささやいた
"the Dog-Fish is sleeping like a dormouse"
「犬の魚はヤマネのように眠っている」
"the sea is calm, and it is as light as day"
「海は穏やかで、昼のように軽い」
"follow me, dear papa," he told him
「ついてきて、親愛なるパパ」と彼は言った
"and in a short time we shall be in safety"
「そして、すぐに私たちは安全になるでしょう」
they climbed up the throat of the sea-monster
彼らは海の怪物の喉を登った

- 335 -

and soon they reached his immense mouth
そしてすぐに彼らは彼の巨大な口に到達しました
so they began to walk on tiptoe down his tongue
それで、彼らは彼の舌をつま先立ちで歩き始めました
they were about to make the final leap
彼らは最後の飛躍を遂げようとしていました
the puppet turned around to his father
人形は父親の方を振り返った
"Get on my shoulders, dear Papa," he whispered
「私の肩に乗れ、親愛なるパパ」彼はささやいた
"and put your arms tightly around my neck"
「そして、私の首にしっかりと腕を回して」
"I will take care of the rest," he promised
「あとは私が面倒を見るよ」と彼は約束した
soon Geppetto was firmly settled on his son's shoulders
すぐにジェペットは息子の肩にしっかりと落ち着きました
Pinocchio took a moment to build up courage
ピノキオは勇気を振り絞るのに少し時間をかけました
and then he threw himself into the water
そして、彼は水に身を投げました
and began to swim away from the Dog-Fish
そして犬の魚から離れて泳ぎ始めました
The sea was as smooth as oil
海は油のように滑らかでした
the moon shone brilliantly in the sky
空には月がきらめく輝いていました
and the Dog-Fish was in deep sleep
そしてドッグフィッシュは深い眠りに落ちていました
even cannons wouldn't have awoken him
大砲でさえ彼を目覚めさせることはできなかったでしょう

Pinocchio at last Ceases to be a Puppet and Becomes a Boy
ピノキオはついに人形であることをやめ、少年になります

Pinocchio was swimming quickly towards the shore
ピノキオは岸に向かって素早く泳いでいました
Geppetto had his legs on his son's shoulders
ゼペットは息子の肩に足を乗せていました
but Pinocchio discovered his father was trembling
しかし、ピノキオは父が震えていることに気づきました
he was shivering from cold as if in a fever
彼はまるで熱にかかったかのように寒さに震えていました
but cold was not the only cause of his trembling
しかし、彼の震えの原因は寒さだけではなかった
Pinocchio thought the cause of the trembling was fear
ピノキオは、震えの原因は恐怖だと思った
and the Puppet tried to comfort his father
そして人形は父親を慰めようとしました
"Courage, papa! See how well I can swim?"
「勇気を出して、パパ!どれだけ上手に泳げるか見てみて?」
"In a few minutes we shall be safely on shore"
「数分で安全に岸に着くよ」
but his father had a higher vantage point
しかし、彼の父はより高い視点を持っていました
"But where is this blessed shore?"
「でも、この祝福された海岸はどこにあるの?」
and he became even more frightened
そして彼はさらに怖くなりました
and he screwed up his eyes like a tailor
そして彼は仕立て屋のように目をつぶった
when they thread string through a needle
彼らが針に糸を通すとき
"I have been looking in every direction"

「私はあらゆる方向を見てきました」
"and I see nothing but the sky and the sea"
「そして、空と海以外は何も見えない」
"But I see the shore as well," said the puppet
「でも、岸辺も見えるよ」と人形は言いました
"You must know that I am like a cat"
「私が猫のようだって知ってるでしょ」
"I see better by night than by day"
「昼間よりも夜の方がよく見える」
Poor Pinocchio was making a pretence
かわいそうなピノキオはふりをしていた
he was trying to show optimism
彼は楽観主義を示そうとしていた
but in reality he was beginning to feel discouraged
しかし、実際には彼は落胆し始めていました
his strength was failing him rapidly
彼の体力は急速に衰えていた
and he was gasping and panting for breath
そして彼は息を切らし、喘いでいました
He could not swim much further anymore
彼はもうこれ以上泳ぐことができませんでした
and the shore was still far off
そして、海岸はまだ遠いところにあった
He swam until he had no breath left
彼は息がなくなるまで泳ぎ続けました
and then he turned his head to Geppetto
そして、彼は頭をゼペットに向けました
"Papa, help me, I am dying!" he said
「パパ、助けて、俺は死にそうだ!」と彼は言った
The father and son were on the point of drowning
父と息子は溺れそうになりました
but they heard a voice like an out of tune guitar
しかし、彼らは調子の狂ったギターのような声を聞いた
"Who is it that is dying?" said the voice
「死んでいるのは誰だ?」と声が言った
"It is I, and my poor father!"

"私です、そして私のかわいそうな父です!」
"I know that voice! You are Pinocchio!"
「あの声知ってる!お前はピノキオだ!」
"Precisely; and you?" asked Pinocchio
「その通りです。そしてあなたは?」とピノキオは尋ねた
"I am the Tunny Fish," said his prison companion
「俺はタニーフィッシュだ」と刑務所の仲間が言った
"we met in the body of the Dog-Fish"
「私たちは犬の魚の体で出会った」
"And how did you manage to escape?"
「それで、どうやって逃げることができたの?」
"I followed your example"
「私はあなたの例に倣いました」
"You showed me the road"
「道を見せてくれた」
"and I escaped after you"
「そして、私はあなたの後を逃げた」
"Tunny Fish, you have arrived at the right moment!"
「タニーフィッシュ、君はちょうどいいタイミングで来た!」
"I implore you to help us or we are dead"
「助けてください、さもないと私たちは死んでしまいます」
"I will help you willingly with all my heart"
「心から喜んでお手伝いします」
"You must, both of you, take hold of my tail"
「お前たち二人とも、俺の尻尾を掴んで」
"leave it to me to guide you
「君の案内は僕に任せておいてね
"I will take you both on shore in four minutes"
「お前たち二人を4分後に岸に連れて行く」
I don't need to tell you how happy they were
彼らがどれほど幸せだったかは言うまでもありません
Geppetto and Pinocchio accepted the offer at once

ゼペットとピノキオはすぐにオファーを受け入れました
but grabbing the tail was not the most comfortable
しかし、尻尾をつかむのは最も快適ではありませんでした
so they got on the Tunny Fish's back
それで彼らはタニーフィッシュの背中に乗りました

The Tunny Fish did indeed take only four minutes
タニーフィッシュは確かにわずか4分しかかかりませんでした
Pinocchio was the first to jump onto the land
ピノキオは最初に陸に飛び降りました
that way he could help his father off the fish
そうすれば、彼は父親を魚から追い払うことができる
He then turned to his friend the Tunny Fish
それから彼は友人のタニーフィッシュに目を向けました
"My friend, you have saved my papa's life"

「友よ、君がパパの命を救ってくれた」
Pinocchio's voice was full of deep emotions
ピノキオの声は深い感情に満ちていました
"I can find no words with which to thank you properly"
「きちんとお礼を言う言葉が見つからない」
"Permit me at least to give you a kiss"
「せめてキスだけさせて」
"it is a sign of my eternal gratitude!"
「それは私の永遠の感謝のしるしです!」
The Tunny put his head out of the water
タニーは頭を水から出しました
and Pinocchio knelt on the edge of the shore
そしてピノキオは岸辺にひざまずきました
and he kissed him tenderly on the mouth
そして彼は彼の口に優しくキスをしました
The Tunny Fish was not used to such warm affection
タニーフィッシュは、そのような温かい愛情に慣れていませんでした
he felt both very touched, but also ashamed
彼は非常に感動したと同時に、恥ずかしさも感じました
because he had started crying like a small child
彼が小さな子供のように泣き始めたからです
and he plunged back into the water and disappeared
そして彼は再び水に飛び込み、姿を消しました
By this time the day had dawned
この時までに、その日は明けていました
Geppetto had scarcely breath to stand
ゼペットは息を切らして立つのがやっとだった
"Lean on my arm, dear papa, and let us go"
「私の腕に寄りかかって、親愛なるパパ、そして私たちを行かせてください」
"We will walk very slowly, like the ants"
「私たちはアリのようにとてもゆっくりと歩きます」
"and when we are tired we can rest by the wayside"
「そして、疲れているときは道端で休むことができます」

"And where shall we go?" asked Geppetto
「それで、どこへ行こうか?」とゼペットは尋ねた

"let us search for some house or cottage"
「どこかの家やコテージを探そう」

"there they will give us some charity"
「そこで彼らは私たちに慈善をくれるでしょう」

"perhaps we will receive a mouthful of bread"
「もしかしたら、一口のパンがもらえるかもしれない」

"and a little straw to serve as a bed"
「そしてベッドとして役立つ小さなストロー」

Pinocchio and his father hadn't walked very far
ピノキオと彼の父はそれほど遠くまで歩いていませんでした

they had seen two villainous-looking individuals
彼らは悪役のような人物を二人見たのだ

the Cat and the Fox were at the road begging
猫とキツネは道で物乞いをしていました

but they were scarcely recognizable
しかし、彼らはほとんど認識できませんでした
the Cat had feigned blindness all her life
猫は一生盲目を装っていた
and now she became blind in reality
そして今、彼女は現実に盲目になりました
and a similar fate must have met the Fox
そして、同じような運命がフォックスに出会ったに違いない
his fur had gotten old and mangy
彼の毛皮は古くなり、しゃがんでいました
one of his sides was paralyzed
彼の片方の脇腹が麻痺していた
and he had not even his tail left
そして、彼は尻尾さえ残っていませんでした
he had fallen in the most squalid of misery
彼は最も不潔な惨めさに落ちてしまった
and one fine day he was obliged to sell his tail
そしてある晴れた日、彼は尻尾を売らざるを得ませんでした
a travelling peddler bought his beautiful tail
旅の行商人が彼の美しい尻尾を買いました
and now his tail was used for chasing away flies
そして今、彼の尻尾はハエを追い払うために使われました
"Oh, Pinocchio!" cried the Fox
「ああ、ピノキオ!」とキツネは叫びました
"give a little in charity to two poor, infirm people"
「貧しく、虚弱な二人の人々に少しだけ慈善を捧げてください」
"Infirm people," repeated the Cat
「虚弱な人だよ」と猫は繰り返しました
"Be gone, impostors!" answered the puppet
「行け、詐欺師ども!」人形は答えました
"You fooled me once with your tricks"
「君は一度、君のトリックで僕を騙した」

"but you will never catch me again"
「でも、君はもう二度と僕を捕まえられないよ」
"this time you must believe us, Pinocchio"
「今度は信じてくれ、ピノキオ」
"we are now poor and unfortunate indeed!"
「私たちは今、貧しく、本当に不幸です!」
"If you are poor, you deserve it"
「貧しいなら、それに値する」
and Pinocchio asked them to recollect a proverb
そしてピノキオは彼らにことわざを思い出すように頼みました
"Stolen money never fructifies"
「盗まれたお金は決して砕けない」
"Be gone, impostors!" he told them
「行け、詐欺師ども!」彼は彼らに言った
And Pinocchio and Geppetto went their way in peace
そして、ピノキオとゼペットは平和に自分たちの道を進みました
soon they had gone another hundred yards
すぐに彼らはさらに100ヤード進んだ
they saw a path going into a field
彼らは畑に入る道を見ました
and in the field they saw a nice little hut
そして野原で彼らは素敵な小さな小屋を見ました
the hut was made from tiles and straw and bricks
小屋はタイルとわらとレンガで作られていました
"That hut must be inhabited by someone"
「あの小屋は誰かが住んでいるに違いない」
"Let us go and knock at the door"
「さあ、ドアをノックしましょう」
so they went and knocked at the door
それで彼らは行ってドアをノックしました
from in the hut came a little voice
小屋の中から小さな声が聞こえてきた
"who is there?" asked the little voice
「そこにいるのは誰だ?」と小さな声が尋ねた

Pinocchio answered to the little voice
ピノキオは小さな声に答えた
"We are a poor father and son"
「私たちは貧しい父と息子です」
"we are without bread and without a roof"
「私たちにはパンがなく、屋根もない」
the same little voice spoke again:
同じ小さな声が再び話しかけた。
"Turn the key and the door will open"
「キーを回すとドアが開きます」
Pinocchio turned the key and the door opened
ピノキオが鍵を回すと、ドアが開きました
They went in and looked around
彼らは中に入って周りを見回しました
they looked here, there, and everywhere
彼らはここ、あそこ、そしてどこでも見ました
but they could see no one in the hut
しかし、小屋の中には誰も見えませんでした
Pinocchio was much surprised the hut was empty
ピノキオは小屋が空っぽであることにとても驚きました
"Oh! where is the master of the house?"
「ああ!家の主人はどこにいますか?」
"Here I am, up here!" said the little voice
「ここにいる、ここにいる!」小さな声が言った
The father and son looked up to the ceiling
父と息子は天井を見上げました
and on a beam they saw the talking little Cricket
そして梁の上には、しゃべる小さなコオロギが見えました
"Oh, my dear little Cricket!" said Pinocchio
「ああ、愛する小さなクリケット!」ピノキオは言った
and Pinocchio bowed politely to the little Cricket
そしてピノキオは小さなコオロギに丁寧にお辞儀をしました
"Ah! now you call me your dear little Cricket"
「あぁ!今、あなたは私をあなたの愛する小さなクリケ

ットと呼んでいます」

"But do you remember when we first met?"
「でも、初めて会ったときのことを覚えてる?」

"you wanted me gone from your house"
「君は僕を家から出してほしかったんだ」

"and you threw the handle of a hammer at me"
「そして、あなたは私にハンマーの柄を投げつけました」

"You are right, little Cricket! Chase me away also!"
「君の言う通りだよ、小さなクリケット!私も追い払ってください!」

"Throw the handle of a hammer at me"
「ハンマーの柄を私に投げて」

"but please, have pity on my poor papa"
「でも、どうか、可哀想なパパを憐れんでください」

"I will have pity on both father and son"
「父も息子も憐れむ」

"but I wish to remind you of my ill treatment"
「でも、私の虐待を思い出していただきたいんです」

"the ill treatment I received from you"
「君から受けた虐待」

"but there's a lesson I want you to learn"
「でも、君に学んでほしい教訓があるんだ」

"life in this world is not always easy"
「この世での生活は必ずしも簡単ではない」

"when possible, we must be courteous to everyone"
「可能な限り、誰に対しても礼儀正しくしなければならない」

"only so can we expect to receive courtesy"
「そうしてこそ、私たちは礼儀を受けることを期待できる」

"because we never know when we might be in need"
「いつ必要になるかわからないから」

"You are right, little Cricket, you are right"
「君の言う通りだよ、小さなクリケット、君の言う通りだよ」

"and I will bear in mind the lesson you have taught me"
「そして、あなたが私に教えてくれた教訓を心に留めておきます」
"But tell me how you managed to buy this beautiful hut"
「でも、どうやってこの美しい小屋を買ったのか教えて」
"This hut was given to me yesterday"
「この小屋は昨日くれたものだよ」
"the owner of the hut was a goat"
「小屋の持ち主はヤギだった」
"and she had wool of a beautiful blue colour"
「そして、彼女は美しい青色のウールを持っていました」
Pinocchio grew lively and curious at this news
ピノキオはこのニュースに元気になり、好奇心旺盛になりました
"And where has the goat gone?" asked Pinocchio
「それで、ヤギはどこに行ったの?」ピノキオは尋ねた
"I do not know where she has gone"
「彼女がどこに行ったのかわからない」
"And when will the goat come back?" asked Pinocchio
「それで、ヤギはいつ戻ってくるの?」ピノキオは尋ねた
"oh she will never come back, I'm afraid"
「ああ、彼女は二度と戻ってこない、怖い」
"she went away yesterday in great grief"
「彼女は昨日、大きな悲しみの中で亡くなりました」
"her bleating seemed to want to say something"
「彼女の鳴き声は何かを言いたがっているように見えた」
"Poor Pinocchio! I shall never see him again"
「かわいそうなピノキオ!もう二度と彼に会うことはないでしょう」
"by now the Dog-Fish must have devoured him!"
「今頃は犬の魚が彼をむさぼり食っているに違いない!

"Did the goat really say that?"
「ヤギは本当にそう言ったの?」
"Then it was she, the blue goat"
「じゃあ、あの子、青いヤギだった」
"It was my dear little Fairy," exclaimed Pinocchio
「それは私の愛する小さな妖精でした」とピノキオは叫びました
and he cried and sobbed bitter tears
そして彼は泣き、苦い涙を流しました
When he had cried for some time he dried his eyes
しばらく泣いていたとき、彼は目を乾かしました
and he prepared a comfortable bed of straw for Geppetto
そして彼はゼペットのために快適な藁のベッドを用意しました
Then he asked the Cricket for more help
それから彼はクリケットにもっと助けを求めました
"Tell me, little Cricket, please"
「教えて、小さなクリケット、お願い」
"where can I find a tumbler of milk"
「ミルクのタンブラーはどこにありますか」
"my poor papa has not eaten all day"
「かわいそうなパパは一日中食べていない」
"Three fields from here there lives a gardener"
「ここから3つの畑がある、そこには庭師が住んでいる」
"the gardener is called Giangio"
「庭師はジャンジオと呼ばれています」
"and in his garden he also has cows"
「そして彼の庭には牛も飼っています」
"he will let you have the milk you want"
「彼はあなたが望むミルクをあなたに飲ませるでしょう」
Pinocchio ran all the way to Giangio's house
ピノキオはジャンジオの家まで走った
and the gardener asked him:

庭師は彼に尋ねました。
"How much milk do you want?"
「ミルクはどれくらい欲しいの?」
"I want a tumblerful," answered Pinocchio
「タンブラーが欲しい」とピノキオは答えた
"A tumbler of milk costs five cents"
「牛乳のタンブラーは5セントです」
"Begin by giving me the five cents"
「まずは5セントをくれ」
"I have not even one cent," replied Pinocchio
「私は1セントも持っていません」とピノキオは答えました
and he was grieved from being so penniless
そして、彼は無一文であることに悲しみました
"That is bad, puppet," answered the gardener
「それはまずい、人形」と庭師は答えました
"If you have not one cent, I have not a drop of milk"
「君が1セントも持っていなければ、僕は一滴のミルクも持っていない」
"I must have patience!" said Pinocchio
「我慢しなきゃ!」とピノキオは言った
and he turned to go again
そして彼は再び行こうと振り返った
"Wait a little," said Giangio
「ちょっと待って」とジャンジオは言った
"We can come to an arrangement together"
「一緒に取り決めに行こう」
"Will you undertake to turn the pumping machine?"
「ポンプ機を回すのを引き受けてくれませんか?」
"What is the pumping machine?"
「ポンプマシンって何?」
"It is a kind of wooden screw"
「木のネジの一種です」
"it serves to draw up the water from the cistern"
「貯水槽から水を汲み上げる役割を果たします」

"and then it waters the vegetables"
「そして、野菜に水をやる」
"I can try to turn the pumping machine"
「ポンピングマシンを回してみられる」
"great, I need a hundred buckets of water"
「すごい、バケツ100杯の水が必要だ」
"and for the work you'll get a tumbler of milk"
「そして、仕事には牛乳のタンブラーがもらえます」
"we have an agreement," confirmed Pinocchio
「私たちは合意を得ています」とピノキオは確認しました
Giangio then led Pinocchio to the kitchen garden
その後、ジャンジオはピノキオを家庭菜園に連れて行きました
and he taught him how to turn the pumping machine
そして、彼は彼にポンプ機の回し方を教えました
Pinocchio immediately began to work
ピノキオはすぐに働き始めました
but a hundred buckets of water was a lot of work
しかし、100バケツの水は大変な作業でした
the perspiration was pouring from his head
彼の頭から汗が流れ出ていました
Never before had he undergone such fatigue
彼がこれほどの疲労を経験したことは一度もありませんでした
the gardener came to see Pinocchio's progress
庭師はピノキオの進歩を見に来ました
"my little donkey used to do this work"
「私の小さなロバがこの仕事をしていた」
"but the poor animal is dying"
「でも、かわいそうな動物は死にかけている」
"Will you take me to see him?" said Pinocchio
「彼に会いに連れて行ってくれませんか?」とピノキオは言った
"sure, please come to see my little donkey"
「いいよ、僕の小さなロバに会いに来てね」

Pinocchio went into the stable
ピノキオは厩舎に入った
and he saw a beautiful little donkey
そして、彼は美しい小さなロバを見ました
but the donkey was stretched out on the straw
しかし、ロバは藁の上で伸びていました
he was worn out from hunger and overwork
彼は飢えと過労で疲れ果てていました
Pinocchio was much troubled by what he saw
ピノキオは彼が見たものに大いに困惑しました
"I am sure I know this little donkey!"
「きっとこの小さなロバを知っているよ!」
"His face is not new to me"
「彼の顔は私にとって新しいものではありません」
and Pinocchio came closer to the little Donkey
そしてピノキオは小さなロバに近づいてきました
and he spoke to him in asinine language:
そして彼は無邪気な言葉で彼に話しかけた。
"Who are you?" asked Pinocchio
「あなたは誰ですか?」ピノキオは尋ねました
the little donkey opened his dying eyes
小さなロバは彼の死にゆく目を開けました
and he answered in broken words in the same language:
そして、彼は同じ言語で片言で答えた。
"I... am... Candle-wick"
「私は...キャンドルウィック」
And, having again closed his eyes, he died
そして、再び目を閉じて、彼は死んだ
"Oh, poor Candle-wick!" said Pinocchio
「ああ、かわいそうなキャンドルウィック!」とピノキオは言いました
and he took a handful of straw
そして彼は一握りの藁を取りました
and he dried a tear rolling down his face
そして、彼は頬を伝う涙を拭いた
the gardener had seen Pinocchio cry

庭師はピノキオが泣くのを見たことがあった
"Do you grieve for a dead donkey?"
「死んだロバを嘆くの?」
"it was not even your donkey"
「それはあなたのロバでさえありませんでした」
"imagine how I must feel"
「私がどう感じるか想像してみて」
Pinocchio tried to explain his grief
ピノキオは彼の悲しみを説明しようとしました
"I must tell you, he was my friend!"
「言わなきゃだめだ、彼は僕の友達だったんだ!」
"Your friend?" wondered the gardener
「あなたの友達?」庭師は不思議に思いました
"yes, one of my school-fellows!"
「そうだ、僕の学校の仲間の一人だよ!」
"How?" shouted Giangio, laughing loudly
「どうやって?」とジャンジオは大声で笑いながら叫んだ
"Did you have donkeys for school-fellows?"
「学校の仲間にロバを持っていたの?」
"I can imagine the wonderful school you went to!"
「君が通っていた素晴らしい学校が想像できるよ!」
The puppet felt mortified at these words
人形はこれらの言葉に悔しい思いをしました
but Pinocchio did not answer the gardener
しかし、ピノキオは庭師に答えませんでした
he took his warm tumbler of milk
彼は温かいミルクのタンブラーを手に取りました
and he returned back to the hut
そして彼は小屋に戻りました
for more than five months he got up at daybreak
5ヶ月以上もの間、彼は夜明けに起きた
every morning he turned the pumping machine
彼は毎朝、ポンプ機を回しました
and each day he earned a tumbler of milk

そして毎日、彼は牛乳のタンブラーを稼ぎました
the milk was of great benefit to his father
ミルクは彼の父にとって非常に有益でした
because his father was in a bad state of health
彼の父が健康状態が悪かったからです
but Pinocchio was now satisfied with working
しかし、ピノキオは今や仕事に満足していました
during the daytime he still had time
昼間はまだ時間があった
so he learned to make baskets of rushes
それで彼はイグサのバスケットを作ることを学びました
and he sold the baskets in the market
そして、彼は市場でバスケットを売りました
and the money covered all their expenses
そして、そのお金は彼らのすべての費用をカバーしました
he also constructed an elegant little wheel-chair
彼はまた、エレガントな小さな車椅子を作りました
and he took his father out in the wheel-chair
そして彼は父親を車椅子に乗せて外に出しました
and his father got to breathe fresh air
そして彼の父は新鮮な空気を吸うことができました
Pinocchio was a hard working boy
ピノキオは勤勉な少年でした
and he was ingenious at finding work
そして、彼は仕事を見つけるのに巧妙でした
he not only succeeded in helping his father
彼は父を助けることに成功しただけではありません
but he also managed to save five dollars
しかし、彼はまた5ドルを節約することにも成功しました
One morning he said to his father:
ある朝、彼は父親に言いました。
"I am going to the neighbouring market"
「近所の市場に行くよ」
"I will buy myself a new jacket"

「新しいジャケットを自分で買う」
"and I will buy a cap and pair of shoes"
「そして、帽子と靴を買うよ」
and Pinocchio was in jolly spirits
そしてピノキオは陽気でした
"when I return you'll think I'm a gentleman"
「私が戻ったら、君は僕を紳士だと思うだろう」
And he began to run merrily and happily along
そして、彼は陽気に、楽しそうに走り始めました
All at once he heard himself called by name
突然、彼は自分の名前を呼ばれるのを聞いた
he turned around and what did he see?
彼は振り返り、何を見たのでしょうか?
he saw a Snail crawling out from the hedge
彼はカタツムリが生け垣から這い出てくるのを見ました
"Do you not know me?" asked the Snail
「お前は俺を知らないのか?」とカタツムリは尋ねました
"I'm sure I know you," thought Pinocchio
「きっと君のことを知っているよ」とピノキオは思った
"and yet I don't know from where I know you"
「それでも、どこからあなたを知っているのかわからない」
"Do you not remember the Snail?"
「カタツムリを覚えていないの?」
"the Snail who was a lady's-maid"
「女中だったカタツムリ」
"a maid to the Fairy with blue hair"
「青い髪の妖精のメイド」
"Do you not remember when you knocked on the door?"
「ドアをノックしたのがいつだったか覚えてないの?」
"and I came downstairs to let you in"
「そして、君を中に入れるために階下に降りてきたんだ」
"and you had your foot caught in the door"
「そして、ドアに足が引っかかっていた」

"I remember it all," shouted Pinocchio
「全部覚えてるよ」とピノキオは叫んだ
"Tell me quickly, my beautiful little Snail"
「早く教えて、私の美しい小さなカタツムリ」
"where have you left my good Fairy?"
「私の良い妖精をどこに置き去りにしたの?」
"What is she doing?"
「彼女は何をしているの?」
"Has she forgiven me?"
「彼女は私を許してくれたの?」
"Does she still remember me?"
「彼女はまだ私のことを覚えているの?」
"Does she still wish me well?"
「彼女はまだ私の幸せを願っているの?」
"Is she far from here?"
「彼女はここから遠いの?」
"Can I go and see her?"
「彼女に会いに行ってもいいですか?」
these were a lot of questions for a snail
これらはカタツムリにとって多くの質問でした
but she replied in her usual phlegmatic manner
しかし、彼女はいつもの気まぐれな態度で答えた
"My dear Pinocchio," said the snail
「親愛なるピノキオ」とカタツムリは言いました
"the poor Fairy is lying in bed at the hospital!"
「かわいそうな妖精が病院のベッドに横たわっています!」
"At the hospital?" cried Pinocchio
「病院で?」ピノキオは叫んだ
"It is only too true," confirmed the snail
「それはあまりにも真実です」とカタツムリは確認しました
"she has been overtaken by a thousand misfortunes"
「彼女は千の不幸に襲われました」
"she has fallen seriously ill"

「彼女は重病にかかってしまった」
"she has not even enough to buy herself a mouthful of bread"
「彼女は自分で一口のパンを買うのに十分でさえありません」
"Is it really so?" worried Pinocchio
「本当にそうなのか?」ピノキオは心配した
"Oh, what sorrow you have given me!"
「ああ、あなたは私に何という悲しみを与えたのでしょう!」
"Oh, poor Fairy! Poor Fairy! Poor Fairy!"
「ああ、かわいそうな妖精!かわいそうな妖精!かわいそうな妖精!」
"If I had a million I would run and carry it to her"
「もし100万ドルあったら、走って彼女のところに持って行くだろう」
"but I have only five dollars"
「でも、僕は5ドルしか持ってない」
"I was going to buy a new jacket"
「新しいジャケットを買うつもりだった」
"Take my coins, beautiful Snail"
「私のコインを取って、美しいカタツムリ」
"and carry the coins at once to my good Fairy"
「そして、すぐにコインを私の良い妖精に運んでください」
"And your new jacket?" asked the snail
「それで、新しいジャケットは?」とカタツムリは尋ねました
"What matters my new jacket?"
「新しいジャケットはどうしたの?」
"I would sell even these rags to help her"
「彼女を助けるために、このぼろきれさえ売る」
"Go, Snail, and be quick"
「さあ、カタツムリ、そして早く」
"return to this place, in two days"

「この場所に戻る、2日後」
"I hope I can then give you some more money"
「じゃあ、もう少しお金をあげられるといいな」
"Up to now I worked to help my papa"
「今まではパパを助けるために働いていた」
"from today I will work five hours more"
「今日からあと5時間働く」
"so that I can also help my good mamma"
「私も良いママを助けることができるように」
"Good-bye, Snail," he said
「さようなら、カタツムリ」と彼は言った
"I shall expect you in two days"
「二日後にお待ちしております」
at this point the snail did something unusual
この時点で、カタツムリは何か変わったことをしました
she didn't move at her usual pace
彼女はいつものペースで動かなかった
she ran like a lizard across hot stones
彼女は熱い石の上をトカゲのように走りました
That evening Pinocchio sat up till midnight
その夜、ピノキオは真夜中まで起きていました
and he made not eight baskets of rushes
そして、彼はイグサの8つのバスケットを作らなかった
but be made sixteen baskets of rushes that night
しかし、その夜は16個の瓰にイグサを作った
Then he went to bed and fell asleep
それから彼はベッドに入り、眠りに落ちました
And whilst he slept he thought of the Fairy
そして眠っている間、彼は妖精のことを考えました
he saw the Fairy, smiling and beautiful
彼は微笑んで美しい妖精を見ました
and he dreamt she gave him a kiss
そして彼は彼女が彼にキスをした夢を見ました
"Well done, Pinocchio!" said the fairy
「よくやった、ピノキオ!」と妖精は言いました
"I will forgive you for all that is past"

「過去の全てを許してあげる」
"To reward you for your good heart"
「あなたの善良な心に報いるために」
"there are boys who minister tenderly to their parents"
「親に優しく仕える男の子がいる」
"they assist them in their misery and infirmities"
「彼らは彼らの悲惨さと弱さを助けます」
"such boys are deserving of great praise and affection"
「そのような少年たちは、大きな賞賛と愛情を受けるに値する」
"even if they cannot be cited as examples of obedience"
「たとえ彼らが服従の例として挙げられなくても」
"even if their good behaviour is not always obvious"
「たとえ彼らの良い行動が必ずしも明白でなくても」
"Try and do better in the future and you will be happy"
「将来、もっとうまくやろうと努力すれば、きっと幸せになれる」
At this moment his dream ended
この瞬間、彼の夢は終わりました
and Pinocchio opened his eyes and awoke
そしてピノキオは目を開けて目を覚ました
you should have been there for what happened next
次に起こったことのために、あなたはそこにいるべきだった
Pinocchio discovered that he was no longer a wooden puppet
ピノキオは、自分がもはや木製の人形ではないことを発見しました
but he had become a real boy instead
しかし、彼はそれどころか本物の少年になっていた
a real boy just like all other boys
他の男の子と同じように、本物の男の子です
Pinocchio glanced around the room
ピノキオは部屋を見回した
but the straw walls of the hut had disappeared
しかし、小屋の藁の壁は消えていました

now he was in a pretty little room
今、彼はきれいな小さな部屋にいました
Pinocchio jumped out of bed
ピノキオはベッドから飛び降りた
in the wardrobe he found a new suit of clothes
ワードローブで彼は新しい服を見つけました
and there was a new cap and pair of boots
そして、新しい帽子とブーツがありました
and his new clothes fitted him beautifully
そして彼の新しい服は彼に美しくフィットしました
he naturally put his hands in his pocket
彼は自然にポケットに手を入れた
and he pulled out a little ivory purse
そして彼は小さな象牙の財布を取り出した
on on the purse were written these words:
財布には次の言葉が書かれていました。
"From the Fairy with blue hair"
「青い髪の妖精から」
"I return the five dollars to my dear Pinocchio"
「5ドルを愛するピノキオに返します」
"and I thank him for his good heart"
「そして、彼の善良な心に感謝します」
He opened the purse to look inside
彼は財布を開けて中を覗きました
but there were not five dollars in the purse
しかし、財布には5ドルも入っていませんでした
instead there were fifty shining pieces of gold
代わりに、50枚の輝く金貨がありました
the coins had come fresh from the minting press
硬貨は鋳造プレスから新鮮なものでした
he then went and looked at himself in the mirror
それから彼は行って、鏡に映った自分を見た
and he thought he was someone else
そして彼は自分が他の誰かだと思った
because he no longer saw his usual reflection
なぜなら、彼はもはやいつもの姿を見ていなかったから

だ
he no longer saw a wooden puppet in the mirror
彼はもはや鏡に木製の人形を見ませんでした
he was greeted instead by a different image
彼は代わりに別のイメージで迎えられました
the image of a bright, intelligent boy
明るく知的な少年のイメージ
he had chestnut hair and blue eyes
彼は栗色の髪と青い目をしていました
and he looked as happy as can be
そして、彼はこの上なく幸せそうに見えた
as if it were the Easter holidays
まるでイースター休暇のように
Pinocchio felt quite bewildered by it all
ピノキオは、そのすべてにかなり戸惑った
he could not tell if he was really awake
彼は本当に起きているのかどうかわからなかった
maybe he was dreaming with his eyes open
もしかしたら、目を開けたまま夢を見ていたのかもしれない
"Where can my papa be?" he exclaimed suddenly
「パパはどこにいるの?」と彼は突然叫びました
and he went into the next room
そして彼は隣の部屋に入った
there he found old Geppetto quite well
そこで彼は古いゼペットをかなり見つけました
he was lively, and in good humour
彼は生き生きとしていて、ユーモアにあふれていました
just as he had been formerly
彼が以前そうであったように
He had already resumed his trade of wood-carving
彼はすでに木彫りの仕事を再開していました
and he was designing a beautiful picture frame
そして、彼は美しい額縁をデザインしていました
there were leaves flowers and the heads of animals
葉っぱや花、動物の頭がありました

"Satisfy my curiosity, dear papa," said Pinocchio
「私の好奇心を満たしてください、親愛なるパパ」とピノキオは言いました
and he threw his arms around his neck
そして彼は腕を首に回した
and he covered him with kisses
そして彼は彼にキスをしました
"how can this sudden change be accounted for?"
「この突然の変化をどう説明できるのでしょうか?」
"it comes from all your good doing," answered Geppetto
「それは君の善行から来ているんだ」とゼペットは答えた
"how could it come from my good doing?"
「どうして私の善行から来るのだろう?」
"something happens when naughty boys turn over a new leaf"
「いたずらっ子が新しい葉をめくると何かが起こる」
"they bring contentment and happiness to their families"
「彼らは家族に満足と幸せをもたらします」
"And where has the old wooden Pinocchio hidden himself?"
「それで、古い木製のピノキオはどこに隠れたの?」
"There he is," answered Geppetto
「そこにいるよ」とゼペットは答えた
and he pointed to a big puppet leaning against a chair
そして、椅子にもたれかかっている大きな人形を指差しました
the Puppet had its head on one side
人形は頭を片側に持っていました
its arms were dangling at its sides
その腕は脇にぶら下がっていました
and its legs were crossed and bent
そして、その足は交差して曲がっていました
it was really a miracle that it remained standing
立ったままだったのは本当に奇跡でした
Pinocchio turned and looked at it
ピノキオは振り返ってそれを見た

and he proclaimed with great complacency:
そして彼は大いに満足げに宣言した。
"How ridiculous I was when I was a puppet!"
「人形だったとき、私はなんてばかげていたのでしょう!」
"And how glad I am that I have become a well-behaved little boy!"
「そして、行儀の良い小さな男の子になったなんて、なんてうれしいんでしょう!」